EUROPEAN SECURITY AND INTERNATIONAL INSTITUTIONS AFTER THE COLD WAR

European Security and International Institutions after the Cold War

Edited by

Marco Carnovale

St. Martin's Press

First published in Great Britain 1995 by
MACMILLAN PRESS LTD
Houndmills, Basingstoke, Hampshire RG21 2XS
and London
Companies and representatives
throughout the world

A catalogue record for this book is available
from the British Library.

ISBN 0–333–63210–9

10   9   8   7   6   5   4   3   2   1
04   03   02   01   00   99   98   97   96   95

Printed and bound in Great Britain by
Antony Rowe Ltd
Chippenham, Wiltshire

First published in the United States of America 1995 by
Scholarly and Reference Division,
ST. MARTIN'S PRESS, INC.,
175 Fifth Avenue,
New York, N.Y. 10010

ISBN 0–312–12488–0

Library of Congress Cataloging-in-Publication Data
European security and international institutions after the Cold War /
edited by Marco Carnovale.
p. cm.
Includes index.
ISBN 0–312–12488–0
1. National security—Europe. 2. World politics—1989–
I. Carnovale, Marco.
UA646.E9238   1995
355'.03304—dc20
                                                      94–34879
                                                         CIP

to all those few who know how to change their opinions

Contents

Notes on the Contributors

Ronal Asmus is a Senior Analyst in the International Policy Department of the Rand Corporation, Santa Monica, California.

Marco Carnovale is an Officer in the Political Affairs Division at NATO, Brussels. Until June 1994, and for the duration of this book project, he was Head of Eastern European Studies at the Istituto Affari Internazionali in Rome, Italy.

Maurizio Cremasco is a Scientific Advisor at the the Istituto Affari Internazionali in Rome, Italy.

Nur Bilge Criss is an associate at the Department of International Relations of Bilkent University, Ankara, Turkey.

Giuseppe Cucchi is a Major General in the Italian Army, and Director of the Military Center for Steategic Studies (CeMiSS) in Rome, Italy.

Marta Dassù is Director of the Centro Studi sulla Politica Internazionale (CeSPI) in Rome, Italy.

Marco De Andreis is a Researcher at the Centro Studi sulla Politica Internazionale (CeSPI) in Rome, Italy.

Alexander Honcharenko is Counsellor on Political Military Affairs at the Embassy of Ukraine in Brussels. Until December 1992, he was the Head of the International Security Department at the Institute for World Economy and International Relations, of the Ukrainian Academy of Sciences, Kiev, Ukraine.

Karl-Heinz Kamp is a Researcher at the Konrad Adenauer Stiftung, Sank Augustin, Germany.

Aleksandr Konovalov is a Researcher at the Institute for the United States and Canada in Moscow, Russia.

Reihardt Rummel is a Senior Analyst at the Stiftung Wissenschaft und Politik in Ebenhausen, germany.

Jamie Shea is Deputy Director of Information and Spokesman of the North Atlantic Treaty Organization, Brussels, Belgium.

Dmitri Trenin is a Researcher at the Institute of Europe, Moscow, Russia. Until 1993, he was a Colonel in the Russian Army.

Preface

This book is the product of a collective international research project of the Istituto Affari Internazionali (IAI) of Rome, Italy. The project, which I directed as Senior Research Fellow at the Institute, was conducted between March 1993 and March 1994. It represents an additional step in the long series of studies that the IAI has dedicated, since its foundation, to the questions of international integration and interdependence.

Within this framework, the main aim of this book is to stimulate the on-going debate on the future of security in Europe. That this debate should be vigorously pursued is demonstrated by the deterioration of international and domestic conflicts since the revolutions of 1989 in Eastern Europe. That it needs intellectual stimulus is made evident by the lack of attention that it is currently receiving in the political debate in most major Western countries. Post-Cold War Europe is too preoccupied with internal and economic problems and tends to take too much for granted as far as international stability (a precondition for domestic prosperity) is concerned.

The first part of this book analyzes two theoretical issues and some case studies. In the first chapter, I look at the relation between vital and national interests: two definitions which are often used interchangeably but which, in the 1990s, denote different sets of issues requiring different solutions. In chapter two, Giuseppe Cucchi analyzes the related question of national sovereignty and international institutions. These first two chapters provide two alternative but complementary approaches to the central question of what states can and should delegate to international institutions, and how.

Chapter three, by Maurizio Cremasco, provides an exhaustive case study of how international institutions, and the member states that operate them, fared in what has been the most serious post-Cold War crisis in Europe so far: the collapse of the Yugoslav Federation.

Chapter four, by Dmitri Trenin, looks at another simmering source of war: conflicts among the former republics of the Soviet Union, and the role of Russia in them. While not as central to

European security as the Yugoslav war, conflicts in the former USSR pose fundamental questions on the role and political motivation of international institutions in the new Europe which emerged after the disintegration of the Soviet Union.

In chapter five, Karl Heinz Kamp looks at an emerging issue in European security debates: after the end of the paramount preoccupation with the Central front, Europeans (and their North American allies) must look at threats to their security which arise from areas other than that of the old East-West confrontation. However, they are not yet ready to draw the necessary conclusions in terms of policy implications or to make the necessary instruments available.

In Part Two of the book, all the issues outlined above are addressed by several authors who analyze the national debate in their respective countries. Not all countries are represented here: in some cases, scholars declined to participate in the project; in other cases, it was a matter of space constraints. The national debates discussed here are essential to the resolution of the questions left open by the chapters in Part One: international institutions can only operate as long and as far as their sovereign member states will let them. A general theme which emerges in most of the chapters in Part Two is that, while international institutions are regarded as essential to European security, states are still reluctant to delegate sufficient powers to them.

For the future, it remains to be seen whether the governments of the major sovereign states will conclude that the new security challenges are best addressed on a multilateral basis, often through a multidimensional approach, and therefore provide the appropriate institutions with adequate means to meet them; or whether they will drift toward a disorderly multipolarity within which each pursues more narrowly defined interests on an individual basis.

Many people have been instrumental to the success of this project, but I would like to thank a few in particular. Mr. Nicola de Santis, Liaison Officer, Italy, at the NATO Office of Information and Press provided encouragement from the very beginning of this initiative. His office supported both a conference, in Rome, in December 1993, at which preliminary versions of all chapters were discussed, and the publication of this volume. Special gratitude goes also to the US Mission to NATO, and in particular to Mr. Robert Bemis, who helped secure a generous grant for the project.

On behalf of the IAI, I would also like to thank all international participants to the Rome conference, who contributed their expertise to the enrichment of the papers presented on that occasion. The Italian Armed Forces Center for Higher Defense Studies (CASD) and particularly its then president, Gen. Franco Angioni, kindly agreed to host us at their premises. Katia Marchesi of the IAI secretariat ensured that the conference and related logistics ran as smoothly as possible and generously provided her assistance in following the project up through its completion.

Finally, my thanks go to Susanna Barbatbun for helping to clarify the language of the manuscripts.

As is customary, all authors of this book are personally responsible for the content of their respective chapters; nothing in their work is to be attributed to any of the organizations to which they belong, to me, to IAI, to the NATO Office of Information and Press or to the US Mission to NATO.

Rome, July 1994   Marco Carnovale

1 Vital and National Security Interests After the End of the Cold War

Marco Carnovale

Since the end of the Cold War, a contradiction has developed in the way security problems are approached in Europe: on the one hand, there is a generalized tendency toward multilateral solutions to vital European security problems; on the other, a renewed nationalist trend has emerged in the foreign policy focus as many states on both sides of the former Iron Curtain. But this contradiction is only apparent and can be resolved if security in Europe is redefined such that vital security interests are no longer national interests, and national security interests are no longer vital. Furthermore, West European and American security interests are more intertwined in the new geopolitical scenario that emerged from the dissolution of the Eastern bloc than they had been, and the former socialist countries increasingly share there interests as well.

Security Institutions in Europe after the Cold War

Since the Cold War began to fade into history, a wide international consensus has developed on the need for the establishment of an institutionalized international system of cooperative security. In Europe, this has been particularly true among Western states and the Soviet Union—and later also among the states emerging from its dissolution. Soviet President Mikhail Gorbachev began talking about the desirability of building a 'Common European House' rather early on in his tenure, and one of the most common phrases at the twilight of the Cold War was the need for a common security 'architecture'.

More recently, Central and Eastern European (C&EE) states have been in the forefront of initiatives to overhaul the European institutional structure. To a significant extent, and despite excruciating subsequent disappointments, this broad consensus on principles has shaped the foreign policies of major international actors. Consequently, it has also influenced the thinking on and the development of the diplomatic and military instruments which are intended to serve those policies.

The need for a profound restructuring of international security institutions has come forcefully to the fore since the 1989 democratic upheaval in Eastern Europe and the subsequent collapse of the Eastern bloc, which marked the end of the Cold War. These epochal changes highlighted the increasing inadequacy of existing institutions, which had been created to cope with what have now become non-issues: the United Nations (UN) to manage the post-World War II global geopolitical reorganization; the North Atlantic Treaty Organization (NATO) to deal with the Soviet threat; the Western European Union (WEU) to forestall the danger of a resurgent Germany and to consolidate a special relationship between France and the UK; and the Conference on Security and Cooperation in Europe (CSCE) to mitigate various aspects of a conflictual East-West relationship. Also the role of the European Community (EC), initially concerned only with the integration of member states, has evolved to the point where the nascent foreign and security policy of the European Union (EU) that was inaugurated with the entry into force of the Maastricht Treaty on 1 November 1993 now includes a greater opening toward security issues outside of the Union itself.

The urgency for stronger international security institutions has been further emphasized by the disappointing realization that the end of the Cold War did not make Europe 'whole and free'. Rather, it produced a new array of conflicts. As of late 1993, several new post-Cold War wars have either broken out or seem about to explode. In many parts of Eastern Europe, the end of communism has been accompanied not by the flourishing of democracy but mainly by the virulent revival of old, long-repressed cleavages. As several old Cold War problems have been solved (mainly in the field of arms control and confidence-building) new problems have developed, in economic cooperation, sub-regional arms control, human rights, ethnic disputes, border disputes, etc.

International institutions have been widely seen as the most appropriate instruments for dealing with these new problems. In the West, the reasoning has been that the peaceful management of post-

Cold War transition from confrontation to cooperation would not have been possible without multilateral arrangements and the momentous break-up of the Soviet bloc. Post-Soviet and East European states themselves, emerging from the isolation of Soviet times, have been eager to join whatever forum the West has been willing to accept them in. Existing institutions have been earmarked for additional responsibilities and expanded membership, and new institutions, such as the North Atlantic Cooperation Council (NACC) have been created *ad hoc*.

Since the end of the Cold War, international security institutions have already evolved; the UN has been increasingly active in various parts of the world, so far with mixed results; the CSCE has considerably increased in membership thus becoming truly pan-European; the EU and the WEU have been given increased responsibilities, at least on paper; in NATO, the debate among member states over the adaptation of the organization's missions to changing circumstances is still on-going. The thorny issue of expanded membership is still on the table, if somewhat more muted, after the Summit of January 1994.[1] In some cases, old European institutions are even being considered as models for new ones in other parts of the world (e.g. the CSCE, which is sometimes envisaged as a model for the proposed creation of a Conference for Security and Cooperation in Asia).

An additional argument in favor of the multilateralization of security policies is that as contemporary problems become intrinsically multidimensional they require a multilateral approach. The more security is defined in economic, political and social terms, beyond purely military considerations, the more individual states are likely not to be prepared to address the complex solutions single-handedly.[2]

A final reason to push toward multilateralization in Europe is the sad realization that nationalism (whether it is real or, as is often the case, it is built-up spuriously around 'imagined communities'[3] instead of real nations) is likely to be associated with war. Such nationalism may be a cause or a consequence of war. Most often, and most dangerously, it is used by political *élites* as a catalyst for the channeling of military and other resources toward the achievement of war aims.[4]

The Re-nationalization of Security Policies

Paradoxically, while security institutions have gained increasing appeal and face more challenging tasks ahead, the end of the Cold War has also ushered in a trend toward reinforced national outlooks in the foreign and security policies of most major countries, both from the West and from what used to be the Eastern bloc. This trend has been caused by several factors, which vary from country to country, though there are some common denominators. The main question which applies to all countries involved in European security affairs (broadly speaking, members of the CSCE) is: What do states and nations expect of international security institutions? The following paragraphs will aim to create a sort of 'map' of political forces which are for or against additional security roles for international institutions. It will seek both to analyze how they might be intertwined and to assess their relative strengths and weaknesses. The analysis will cover the major countries from Western Europe, the United States, the Commonwealth of Independent States, and Eastern Europe.

In the United States,[5] a strong bipartisan support has developed for continued American involvement in world security affairs through international institutions. At the same time, certain tendencies toward unilateralism and isolationism may be observed as well. Some have argued for a unilateral US role as the world's only superpower, able to persuade or compel all others to follow a policy of political democracy, free-market economy, and respect for the rule of law and human rights.[6] In European affairs, the US has placed a strong emphasis on the UN and NATO, has been largely skeptical of the CSCE, and has displayed a thinly veiled opposition to a greater EU role in security issues; however, it has generally supported a stronger role for the WEU.

In most of Western Europe, prevailing political forces are still at least nominally in favor of an increasingly multilateral approach to security policies, but there is a lesser degree of consensus than before. Germany is a special case, and is addressed separately below. In the UK, a continued adherence to the Atlantic Alliance clashes with the British reluctance to contribute to the creation of a supranational European pillar within it. In France, a continued propensity toward national solutions contradicts a renewed interest in coordination with the US and NATO. In Italy, there is a continued consensus on the necessity of a NATO and European Union framework of reference, as well as a yet undefined and uneasy mix of nationalist ambitions in the Balkans and the Mediterranean.

More or less everywhere in the Western world, there is a diffuse if somewhat rudimentarily articulated feeling that the disappearance of the Soviet enemy means there is no longer any need for common security arrangements, much less for commitment to a common defense. Because the common Soviet threat no longer exists, the reasoning goes, national priorities among the Allies now prevail over collective ones, and they just happen to diverge, thus requiring unilateral ways and means to address them.

There is abundant evidence of this in recent history—e.g. in the different perceptions among the major Western sates toward the crises in Yugoslavia, Somalia, Eastern Europe and the former USSR. In addition, domestic security problems, such as the survival of a viable national defense industry, are becoming more pressing, and politicians must tackle them on a national basis. Therefore, the proponents of this line of reasoning argue there is now a need to reorient Western security postures toward a revaluation of national instruments to be used for national purposes.

This sentiment becomes manifest in two ways: some argue for a straightforward renationalization of foreign policy in general, and of defense posture and procurement plans in particular. Defense budget cuts also contribute to impairing collaborative procurement programs—though the laws of the economies of scale should suggest otherwise—as each state tries to save a proportionally greater slice of a shrinking pie for its national industry.

Others in Western Europe and in the US argue that collective defense arrangements must enlarge their membership or risk becoming out-of-date. According to this view, Eastern Europe is no longer a potential enemy, but a security cooperation partner to be integrated as soon as possible in Western security institutions. In some cases, however, this second view might be used by the advocates of the first to provoke a dilution of the effectiveness of international institutions in security affairs: the British advocacy of a quick EU expansion to the C&EE countries comes to mind.

For Germany, the issue is complicated by the fact that the process of renationalization of its foreign and security policy is part of the process of its recent re-acquisition of full national sovereign rights. Both processes have catalyzed a marked degree of national reassertion.[7] German predominance in the EU has become more manifest, not only in the economic and monetary field, but also in foreign policy. The finest example of this was the diplomatic recognition of the independence of Slovenia and Croatia, which the EU adopted under strong German pressure—something which would have been unimaginable before reunification.

In 1992, the decision was taken to send troops out of German territory (for the first time since World War II) when they were earmarked to contribute to the UN operation *Restore Hope* in Somalia (albeit in a non-combat role). Whether Germany's new activism will be an expression of renewed nationalism or a contribution to collective, multinational and institutionalized Western security policies remains to be seen. An important test-case will be the way Germany handles its increasingly assertive request for permanent membership (and right of veto) in the UN Security Council.

Much of the same that was said above with respect to Germany applies, *mutatis mutandis*, to C&EE and non-Russian former Soviet states. Germany had to accept limited sovereignty and mandatory military integration with the United States for forty years because it had been defeated in World War II. Eastern Europeans see the renationalization of their foreign and security policies as an instrument of emancipation from the forced integration they were subjected to under the Soviet Union's hegemonic influence.

The post-Soviet Russian government has been at the forefront of the efforts by former communist states to gain an increasing role, if not outright cooptation, into Western multilateral security institutions. In this effort, it has been supported by a majority of opinion makers and security specialists in the country.[8] At the same time, again as a result of the rebirth of the Russian nation after the collapse of the USSR, there is an on-going renationalization of Russian foreign and security policy. Moreover, nationalism in foreign policy is perceived by many in Moscow as a means to maintain world-power status without being forced to compete with the US according to Western rules. More recently, nationalism in security policy has been a tool in the hands of conservatives and would-be restorers of autocracy, who have argued that both the Gorbachev and the Yeltsin leaderships have been selling the country out to the West.

Economic failures, the lack of decisive Western aid, and recent disagreements over the role of some international institutions in world crises (most notably in the ex-Yugoslavia) have dangerously reinforced this trend. Whether and how Russia will contribute to the institutionalized and multilateral management of European security in the future will depend to a large extent on the outcome of this domestic political struggle. In short, this struggles resembles the historical juxtaposition between *Westernizers* and *Slavophiles*, which has shaped so much Russian history since Peter the Great. Successful reforms, coupled with effective Western aid, will likely produce a victory for the *Westernizers*, and this will result in a more internationally cooperative and multilaterally-oriented Russia. On the contrary, ineffective or half-hearted reforms, and/or insufficient or ineffecient aid will make a victory of some combination of *Slavophile* forces easier, and would likely produce a more inward-looking and nationalist attitude.

Much as in Eastern Europe, nationalism in foreign and security affairs has been an instrument of nation-building in many non-Russian ex-Soviet republics. The Central Asian republics have shown a propensity to retain close ties to Moscow. The newly independent Caucasian and European states initially displayed greater national assertiveness, but were later forced to revise their position and they, too, are again rebulding security connections with Russia. The viability of these national choices remains to be seen, however, and it is hoped that national identities will develop in an institutionally cooperative context rather than through the assertion of mutually incompatible national claims. The challenge for the West (and for those Western states, like Turkey, which have the greatest influence in that region) is to assess what, if anything, can be done to channel national debates in some of the major non-Russian ex-Soviet states toward the exploitation of the best opportunities for a cooperative rather than a conflictual approach to multilateralism.

Thus, the end of the blocs in Europe has not brought about, a romantic cultural renaissance of pre-Yalta European nations as some naïvely hoped after the revolutions of 1989. Rather, it has resulted in the revamping of national perspectives that might lead to a network of incompatible and therefore conflictual claims. In some cases, this is the myopic resurgence of narrow-minded political chauvinism, often masqueraded behind the old spiritual and moral values which for centuries pitted Europeans against Europeans in a tragic sequence of negative-sum wargames.

National and Vital Security Interests in Europe

Like most political paradigms (both domestic and international) the concept of 'national interest' has changed since the Cold War. This is especially true in security affairs. Despite the rather bleak picture presented in the preceding paragraphs, there do exist genuine national interests which are perfectly compatible with a cooperative multinational approach to security. These may be economic interests (e.g. milk or steel production capacity; or agricultural import quotas in the EU). They may be related to the environment (e.g. the regulation of international transit rights for cargo, or control of pollutants that are not usually very respectful of national borders).

National interests may also be political, as country A may jostle for political advantage *vis-à-vis* country B by establishing special bilateral ties with country C, (e.g. to push its export products, to obtain special access to C's economic resources or technologies or to foster the rights of its affiliated ethnic community in country C). Finally, there may even be military-related national security interests, as might be the case in future contingencies similar to the Falklands war, the US-Libyan clashes of 1981 and 1986, and the US intervention in Grenada or Panama. But the national interests involved in this type of operations can hardly be described as vital.

The interests described in the preceding paragraphs are definable and defensible at the national level, but they are not vital. In light of this contradictory trend to look at security problems from an international perspective while nationalist pressures build, it seems appropriate to refer no longer to 'national' security interests, but, rather, to 'vital' security interests in the contemporary European landscape.[9]

The most fundamental vital interest for post Cold War European states remains the protection of the physical safety and territorial integrity of nation states against the danger of attack from resurgent, residual or wholly new military threats—including internal threats from within existing states. While the Soviet threat is gone, a variety of actual or potential military threats still exists. Newly independent Russia seeks to become a security partner today, and in some circumstances it has proved that it is able to be one, but it is far from certain that this will be true in the future. While the danger of post-Soviet proliferation is usually exaggerated in the press, other nuclear powers might emerge from the ashes of the USSR. The proliferation of weapons of mass destruction is a distinct possibility around Europe's southern periphery. Any of these developments could threaten the vital security interests of European states. As for threats from within existing states, the example of Yugoslavia speaks for itself: while not likely to be replicated in the same scale, it might not be the last European state to break-up violently, and the repercussions might yet be felt outside of Yugoslavia itself.

The second vital interest is to maintain a minimum standard of living and economic development. This implies, among other things, the preservation of a free market economy, unimpeded access both to sources of raw materials and to foreign markets, and freedom of navigation over the high seas. Recent events in the Gulf have demonstrated (if there had been any doubt) that the defense of this vital interest can not quite be taken for granted even after the end of the Soviet threat to NATO sea-lines of communication.[10]

The final, and most important, vital interest lies in the protection of the Western way of life. Despite all its shortcomings, is increasingly accepted as a pan-European model. This translates into the preservation of a pluralist democracy, which in turn means freedom of movement for people and information (and hence open borders) but also support for the social order of civil society (and hence regulation of migration flows).

Other formulations could be devised, but the above are by and large what the general consensus within the Western civilization has come to define as 'vital interests'. But these are not synonymous with 'national' interests; none is nationally definable or defensible, by any state, but especially not by European medium powers. The following paragraphs will discuss why this is true now even more than during the Cold War.

When two blocs divided Europe, Western nations had to join up forces to counter the Soviet Union. The possibility always existed, however, that one or more could try to strike a deal with Moscow, in extreme circumstances, for example in order to avoid the escalation of nuclear war on its territory. This possibility applied to the Allies on both sides of the Atlantic: the US at times feared that the Europeans might rather be 'red than dead'; the Europeans feared that the US would fight a limited war in Europe but not challenge the Soviets to the point of a reciprocal nuclear exchange. Such fears were based on rational calculations of national interests which took into account the probable behavior of concerned parties, *bona fide* allies as they might have been. Today, sources of resurgent, residual or new threats (nuclear, conventional, or anything in between, as they might come) are unlikely to be as amenable to the same rational thinking as was the centralized and monolithic Soviet state; hence, it is unlikely that the freedom of 'opting out' would still be available to any party in a future continental crisis.

A discussion of increasing international economic interdependence is beyond the scope of this chapter; suffice it to say that the end of the Cold War has opened far greater opportunities for international economic exchanges and therefore for growth. As recent vicissitudes in the Gulf have demonstrated, however, free access to raw materials must sometimes be guaranteed by collective efforts, including by means of armed force. On a different plane, the GATT negotiations demonstrate how, *mutatis mutandis*, an equal degree of collective political commitment is necessary to ensure free access to markets, the other essential ingredient of world economic growth and prosperity.

As for the third of the vital interests considered here, during the Cold War, it was possible, indeed obligatory, to protect democracy in the West while avoiding any determined effort to promote it in the East. Today, without the Iron Curtain, consolidating democracy in the East is increasingly becoming a pre-condition for maintaining it in the West. Indeed, as European borders are wide open to flows of people and information, it would be utopian to think that a privileged island of prosperity and freedom can be maintained only in selected parts of the continent. Again, multilateral effort are indispensable, for it is unthinkable that any single state, however influential, could pursue such an ambitious goal single-handedly.

The foregoing does not suggest that national interests no longer exist in Europe today; nor does it lead to a prescription of exclusively multilateral solutions. There are interests that can and should be defined at the national level, just as there are other interests that can be defined at the regional, provincial or municipal level. In fact, it is not a coincidence that this time of increasing nationalism is also a time of increasing demand for regional and local autonomy throughout Europe, both East and West.

What is sometimes referred to as the rebirth of 'nationalism' in reality is often tribalism, parochialism or fanaticism decorated with a patina of religious fervor. In post-Cold War Europe, the nation-state is in some cases as much in crisis than international alliances and organizations, if not more so. More Europeans are rediscovering the value of local autonomy than are revamping that of national independence. The recent support build-up garnered by Flemish separatists and Northern Italian secessionists are the latest additions to what seemed to be the isolated exceptions of Northern Ireland and the Basque Country. The nineties are more likely to go down in history as a decade of threats to nationhood than as a decade of nation-building.

Multilateralization vs. Renationalization of Security

The preceding section has argued that national approaches are not adequate for the defense of post-Cold War vital interests, both in Western Europe and in what used to be its political antagonist. Therefore, there is a need for a renewed multinational effort directed toward the solution of the new challenges to those interests, especially when it comes to security and defense. The major challenge in contemporary European security, then, is not whether, but how to make international security most effective to address current risks (which are more likely and more controversial than those of the Cold War) before they degenerate or escalate to uncontrollable levels of violence.[11]

Assuming that the future harbors the need for a multinational approach, the question arises as to how to pursue it. Two basic avenues are possible: the first is that of *ad hoc* coalitions, in which, states reserve the right to act on a case-by-case basis.[12] The advantage of this type of multilateral action is that it is easier to achieve, as it does not demand any renunciation of national sovereignty by those states which agree to take part in it.

An approach of this kind was adopted in the multilateral response to the Gulf crisis of 1990-1991. It might suffice in extreme circumstances, such as those which are most threatening, least controversial but also least likely (e.g. the Gulf). But the international community (or even just the Western community) will not enjoy the luxury of operating under such clear-cut circumstances very often. It is more likely that most future security threats will be less extreme, and therefore more controversial. In these cases, improvisation might be risky, and there is a greater need to develop a set of pre-arranged criteria, rules, and standard operating procedures; in other words, there is a need for an institutionalized approach.

One example in which an improvised decision-making process has failed tragically is the crisis in Yugoslavia. The perceived security threat has been considered (rightly or wrongly) as less than an extreme danger by the US and by Western Europeans (but also by most C&EE countries). Institutions have not been empowered with either the political and legal mandate or the necessary instruments to intervene effectively. *Ad hoc* collective arrangements have turned out to be half-hearted and failed.[13] States have preferred a largely national approach, and the result has been a nearly complete failure.[14] Some states (as well as journalists and scholars) have unfairly blamed various institutions for this failure. There is certainly much that needs to be done at the UN, in NATO and most of all in the EU/WEU to make those organizations better fit to deal with future challenges. But the main responsibility for international institutional failure rests with the governments of member states which, unlike in the Iraq/Kuwait case, did not put the instruments of those institutions in a position to act effectively.

Conclusions

International security institutions are indispensable for an adequate approach to the post-Cold War security problems of Europe. One does not need to be an 'idealist of the post-Cold War mend-the-world school'[15] to realize that no single state can address, let alone begin to resolve, the complex intricacies of resurgent nationalistic cleavages, civil struggles and potential conflagrations across borders. This emerges with sobering clarity from most of the chapters presented in this volume. Nevertheless, because of the new strength gained by old pre-Cold War (rather than new post-Cold War) thinking, multilateralism is still all too often seen as an unaffordable luxury.[16] But it is *Realpolitik*, not idealism, which calls for a wider and more structured pattern of international cooperation in order to best serve the vital interests of European democracies (both old and new).[17] It would be naïve idealism to presume that those interests can be served through the romantic restoration of the nation-state to its pre-Cold War prerogatives, cultural, political or moral as they may be.

To pursue this multilateral approach, all countries of Europe (but the principal responsibility inevitably falls upon Western Europe) need to both deepen and widen international security cooperation. In this, Europe does not have to start from scratch; much was done during the Cold War which can still be utilized if it is properly built upon. NATO is the obvious place to start to maintain a collective security and collective defense apparatus, the first of the three vital interests considered in this study. The WEU has been revived after the end of Cold War, and there is no question that, in time, it might work as the future European pillar of the transatlantic alliance if the political will is there to make that happen. The member states of these two organizations (together, but not individually) clearly possess the necessary military, technological and economic resources to face the new risks of the post-Cold War world in which Central and Eastern Europe in no longer an enemy but an increasingly effective security partner.

As of mid-1994, however, partnership with the former Eastern adversaries is still fragile. Collective security bridges to Eastern Europe are being built, among others through the NACC and the WEU's Forum for Consultation, but success is not guaranteed. It is not enough to pile economic, military, and technological resources, to organize conferences and sign agreements. There is a much deeper need to build up political coherence among states and peoples which have long been suspicious of and estranged from one another. This will take time, but there is no reason to think that the successful construction of a collective security system in Western Europe in the 1950s and 1960s could not be replicated, in the late 1990s and beyond, across the whole continent.

The second vital interest has been defined here as the maintenance of unimpeded access to raw materials and the fostering of market economy. Here, too, there are useful precedents that make good examples: the energy sharing schemes of both the International Energy Agency (IEA) and the EU have proven largely successful. The European system of pipelines guarantees that energy security is a preeminently international end, which will require international means to achieve and maintain. They could be further improved to guarantee access to primary sources and provide a safety net in case of emergency.

Here, too, there is a need to expand the multilateral approach to Eastern Europe. Again, there is some degree of similarity to what was done in Western Europe in the 1960s, 1970s and 1980s, when the democracies, threatened by rising prices and the two oil crises, effectively overcame their narrowly defined national interests in order to foster the common good.

The strengthening of democracy, the on-going gradual opening of frontiers to movement of goods, people, and ideas strengthen democracy, the third vital interest considered in this paper is concerned. The CSCE and the Council of Europe have contributed to achieve this, and their further strengthening will be useful to accomplish more. But their action, particularly in the case of the CSCE, will need the backing of adequate military force by other institutions if necessary.

Unlike during the Cold War, when the West had to close its eyes to human rights violations because of overriding security concerns, ignoring violations of those human rights today can be a determinant to political instability. During Cold War, stability was a synonym for preservation of the *status quo*; today, on the contrary, stability can only be maintained through a careful management of change, and there is a change toward increased democracy; change must be actively assisted.

Implications for the Atlantic Alliance

The broad conclusion that emerges from this analysis for North American and European vital interests (as defined in this chapter) is that they are even more inseparable after than they were during the Cold War. It is becoming increasingly evident, as argued in several chapters in this volume, that Europe is less than fully prepared to act alone if the US does not lead. It is also evident that the US is not ready to act alone (whether because it can not afford do so—politically or militarily—or because domestic politics will not allow it) if Europe does not contribute significantly. If the US can not face post-Cold War security challenges unilaterally, it would be preposterous to think that others can.

Therefore, in the context of the debate over a new European security identity, a true post-Cold War 'Europeanist' is an Atlanticist. Because Western Europe is still far from reaching the point where strategic independence from its Atlantic partners is a viable option, an alleged supporter of a European security policy or defense identity who advocates that it be distinct from a North American one is more likely to be a nationalist in disguise.

In recent cases where real post-Cold War security challenges had to be met (e.g. the Iraqi aggression in Kuwait, simmering threats of nuclear and missile proliferation, the break-up of the USSR and Yugoslavia) one lesson has emerged clearly: when the US has become involved, the Europeans have acted; when the US has been recalcitrant, Europeans have hesitated. This will likely be a pattern for the rest of the 1990s and beyond.

Yet, to call for a continued Euro-Atlantic security partnership is not to advocate its immutability. It has changed in the past, and, after the revolutions of 1989-1991, it must change again. While the US inexorably reorients much of its political and economic attention toward the Pacific, Europeans must take up a greater share of both burden and responsibility for the handling of Atlantic security. This means Europeans must expand their security horizon, not contract it as they have gradually been doing since World War II. If Europeans continue to retreat and narrow their security focus to national interests, they will not be able to protect their vital interests.[18]

To assume greater responsibilities in a wider security horizon, Europeans have no choice but to act together, selecting and reinforcing the appropriate institutional military and political instruments as needed. For most Western Europeans, this increased role of international institutions has the additional function of keeping the US involved in European security affairs. In addition, some institutions continue to be the venue for Western Europeans to integrate their own foreign and security policies and postures, implement burden-sharing, build coalitions on an *ad hoc* basis, and exchange information.

The US, of course, can protect its vital security interests on a national basis to a somewhat greater extent than Europeans can, but not much more; it also requires multilateral political legitimation and allied military cooperation for the protection of its interests, in

Europe and elsewhere. In the past, the US has sometimes been less than forthright about its position *vis-à-vis* the formation of a European identity in foreign and security policy.[19] It might be helpful if this ambiguity were soon resolved in favor of an unequivocal recognition that increased European commitments (political, economic, and military) will earn additional European responsibilities in the transatlantic decision-making process on security affairs.

In sum, there is an urgent need for what has been referred to as a 'new partnership'[20] between the US and Europe (initially Western Europe). This is necessary to keep the transatlantic alliance strong in these rapidly changing times, and it is therefore also a pre-condition for a fruitful expansion of this historically successful partnership eastward. Only a strong and renewed Western alliance will be able to satisfy the quest for collective security (and perhaps, later, collective defense) that is coming from its earstwhile adversaries in C&EE and in the former Soviet Union.

Notes

1. See the chapter by Jamie Shea in this volume.

2. Hassner, Pierre: 'Beyond Nationalism and Internationalism', *Survival*, Vol. 35, No.2, Summer 1993.

3. Kitromilides, Paschalis M.: '«Imagined Communities» and the Origin of the National Question in the Balkans', in Blinkhorn, Martin and Thanos Veremis (Eds.): *Modern Greece: Nationalism and Nationality* (Athens: ELIAMEP, 1990).

4. Posen, Barry S.: 'Nationalism, the Mass Army and Military Power', *International Security*, Vol. 18, No.2, Fall 1993.

5. See also the chapter by Ronald Asmus in this volume.

6. This was the thesis of the 'Defense Planning Guidance', a document leaked from the Pentagon in early 1992, but never officially issued by the US government.

7. For a more detailed exposition of the issue considered here, see the chapter by Reinhardt Rummel in this book.

8. See the chapter by Aleksandr Konovalov in this book.

9. For a discussion of this issue, see Zelikow, Philip: 'The New Concert of Europe', *Survival*, Vol. 34 , No.2, Summer 1992. For a slightly different set of definitions, see also Cucchi, Giuseppe: 'Gli Interessi Vitali che l'Italia Protegge', *Relazioni Internazionali*, June 1993.

10. For an extensive discussion on maritime security after the Cold War, see the special issue of *The International Spectator*, Vol. XXXVIII, No. 4, 1993.

11. For an in-depth discussion of these aspects, see Mahnke, Dieter: *Parameters of European Security, Chaillot Paper No. 10* (Paris: Institute for Security Studies of the Western European Union, 1993).

12. Jean, Carlo: 'Ripensare la Sicurezza nell'Età dei Mazionalismi', *Limes*, No.1-2, 1993.

13. See the chapter by Maurizio Cremasco in this volume.

14. Burg, Steven L.: 'Why Yugoslavia Fell Apart', *Current History*, Vol. 92, No. 577, November 1993, pp. 362-363.

15. *The Economist*, 2 October 1993, p. 13.

16. International Institute for Strategic Studies: 'Perspectives', *Strategic Survey 1992-1993* (London: Brassey's, 1993), p.14.

17. Smith, Tony: 'Making the World Safe for Democracy', *The Washington Quarterly*, Vol. 16, No.4, Autumn 1993.

18. Zelikow, Philip: 'The New Concert of Europe', *Survival*, Vol. 34, No. 2, Summer 1992.

19. Murray, Christopher W.: 'View from the United States: Common Foreign and Security Policy as a Centerpiece of U.S. Interest in European Political Union', in Rummel, Reinhardt (Ed.): *Toward Political Union* (Boulder, CO: Westview Press, 1992).

20. Steinberg, James B.: 'The Case for a New Partnership', in Gantz, Nanette C. and John Roper (Eds.): *Towards a New Partnership* (Paris: Institute for Security Studies of the Western European Union, 1993). For a detailed proposition on how to re-structure allied military and political relations, see Brenner, Michael: 'Multilateralism and European Security', *Survival*, Vol.35, No.2, Summer 1993.

PART ONE:

The International Context

2 International Security Institutions and National Sovereignty After the Cold War

Giuseppe Cucchi

A study of the future role of international security institutions in the relationship between security and sovereignty requires an examination of doctrine. The 'new' question of the feasibility and desirability of attributing sovereign rights of states to international organizations is connected with 'old' issues long addressed by jurists and theorists of international relations.[1] The link between sovereignty and security dates back to the Peace of Westphalia of 1648, which gave the international society their present structural features. It is because of these features that we speak of an international 'society' as opposed to an international 'community'.

Two universal institutions (the Papacy and the Holy Roman Empire) averted the anarchy and conflicts of international society: the former through ethical and political universalism; the latter through the global verticalization of sovereign power. The strengthening of the modern state was set in motion, and with it the national and international implications of sovereignty.

At the internal level, sovereign power is that which prevails over all other agencies that govern the citizens of a given state; at an international level, it consists in the series of rights through which the state, while pursuing its aims, can ensure its political independence and territorial integrity.[2] This dual nature of sovereignty is connected with the two major issues that the modern state must tackle to assert its autonomy: cohesion and exclusion. Ensuring the institutional and social cohesion of a community in a given territory and subject to common laws implies the exclusion of those who not belong to it. The entire system is organized around the friend/foe dichotomy.

As the level of cohesion of a political system increases, with its dysfunctions and vulnerability, the exclusion of anyone who rejects the state's ambitious goals becomes increasingly imperative. For example, the viability of a multi-racial and multi-cultural society requires the preservation of freedom and equality, and thus implies a considerable degree of complexity and on-going adjustments, with the consequent vulnerability of institutional mechanisms. Hence, the state is bound to feel the need to endow itself with an efficient military instrument, capable of dissuading other actors from threatening its system. The democratization of states does not automatically give rise to a cooperative attitude among the states, unless the threat of a common, external enemy arises. This should be understood by those who believe, through a mixture of enthusiasm and superficiality, that the process of reform and democratization of Eastern Europe implies the simplification of the international security scenarios.

The principle of equality among international sovereign states is justified by the existence of a great number of formally equal states without an institutional apparatus above them. This is a fundamental and objective principle of the international society. As such, it is also enshrined in the statute of the organization with the highest universalist aims, the United Nations (UN). Article 2 of Charter states that the UN is based on the principle of sovereign equality of its members, and acknowledges that each state enjoys all the attributes of sovereignty, specifically the right to protect its political independence and territorial integrity.

This formal equality of states, however, is made moot by the substantial diversification of their real powers. Perhaps one of the greatest challenges facing individual members of the system of international relations is preventing the conflict between formal equality and real power imbalances, which would lead to long-term and severe dysfunctions of the system.

In the past three centuries, two different approaches have been taken to prevent such conflict. The first, is balance of power, explicitly sanctioned for the first time by the Treaty of Utrecht of 13 July 1713. As an expedient for the creation of a political and diplomatic system, this approach is risky, and must never be taken for granted. Furthermore, it presupposes both the application of Clausewitz's theories on the subordination of war to politics, and the obligation to frame a set of military rules on the logic of politics.[3]

The second approach is multilateralism and the assignment of some of the sovereign rights of states to international organizations with autonomous organs and interests that are different (and presumably nobler) than the mere sum of those of their individual member states. This approach has been taken since World War II,[4] until the events of 1989-91 put its underlying principles into question.

The protection of the physiological interaction between the formal equality and the real differences between states makes it necessary to give them different weights in international organizations. The most obvious instance of this is the veto right granted to the five permanent members of the UN Security Council. A more recent example can also be found in the Treaty of Maastricht, which gives each member of the European Union (EU) a different voting weight. Thus, institutional mechanisms ensure the predominance of state power within supranational bodies. It is impossible to separate the feasibility from the desirability of assigning sovereign prerogatives of states to international organizations.

Thus, it is clear how both the world's greatest international organization and the supranational community based on the long-term aim of the federation of Europe both tend to curb their aims and modes of action with a good dose of realism. One can therefore conclude that the expedients through which they moderate the prerogatives of international organizations are actually a physiological aspect of the interaction between equality of status and difference of power, not a pathological one. In other words, given that the interaction between state and supranational bodies is governed by principle actual power, either institutional mechanisms ensure the predominance of the former over the latter, or this predominance will be secured by the balance of power, no longer hampered by a common decision-making mechanism.

Hence, a first important conclusion can be drawn: it is impossible to separate the feasibility from the desirability of assigning sovereign prerogatives of states to international organizations. It must not be forgotten that the UN Charter itself is compelled to acknowledge the existence of this. Attempting to separate these two aspects amounts to tackling the issue from the wrong perspective: the handing over of the sovereign rights of a state is feasible only to the extent to which it is realistic. Otherwise, it is quite useless to wonder whether or not it is desirable, as it would 'simply' be foreign to the logic of the international system.

The Relative Spheres of Action of States and International Institutions

On the basis of the above assumptions, the interaction and possible dysfunctions of the spheres of action of states and those of international security organizations may be addressed. The latter is a species of the 'international organizations' genus which is distinguished from the others in that it has a greater tendency to assume a role that is somewhat different from the one it has been assigned.

In order to do so, it is first necessary to deal with a misunderstanding which is perhaps 'the' key issue that has confronted anyone concerned with international relations since the end of bipolarism,[5] and which might be instrumental to a clear understanding of what can reasonably be expected of the strategic horizons of the next few years. Many believed that the end of the antagonistic confrontation between the two blocs may, or even must, pave the way for an efficient revival of the mechanisms of collective security. It has been widely suggested that, rather than a misunderstanding, this is a working hypothesis that has been confirmed in Iraq though tragically proven wrong in Bosnia. The following will demonstrate that this is not in fact a realistic hypothesis.

On the whole, the notion of collective security is a rather recent one, dating only from 1919. Furthermore, this notion did not originate from natural mechanisms of international relations among states; rather it was conceived by an individual.[6] Woodrow Wilson's principle 'all for one and one for all', is the cornerstone of collective security. It followed from the conclusion that the rise of two opposite blocs, following the crises in Morocco and the Balkans at the beginning of the century, had led to World War I. Hence, the notion of collective security rests on the assumption that a system of checks and balances eventually acts as an intrinsic factor of destabilization of the strategic theater to which it is applied.

But this assumption is plagued by a fundamental flaw, as demonstrated by the immediate antecedents of the first World War; by the attempts to apply the principle of collective security between the two world wars; and, lastly, by the geostrategic characteristics of the Cold War. The analysis of each of these three periods leads to important considerations which remove the false appeal of collective security and can be applied to the assessment of the present state of affairs.

A detailed study of the crisis of July 1914 reveals that the mechanisms which led to the war were the fruits of a perverse string of coincidences caused by dysfunctions in the system of perceptions among the parties involved. But this system had worked properly up to the first decade of the twentieth century, and had not therefore been doomed to failure from the start. Europe, with its political and diplomatic balance between the various nation-states, had certainly been a continent 'at risk', but not one intrinsically, automatically and unavoidably doomed to self-destruction.[7]

After the World War I, the attempt to put the mechanisms of collective security into practice on a geographically limited but geographically crucial scale (the Locarno Treaty, which applied the logic of the Geneva Protocol to the situation in the Rhine) proved to be a very strong catalyst that precipitated the end of the European equilibrium built at Versailles. When the Europe of nations met the Europe of collective security a tremendous short-circuit was produced. Wilson's principles did not work, and the attempt to unite the international logic with the supranational one only made future crises unpredictable first, and harsher later.[8]

The situation after 1945 will be dealt with in a subsequent section of this article in order to emphasize what appears be the 'fundamental flaw' of the concept of collective security: putting the principle 'all for one and one for all' into practice requires the existence of mechanisms for the transfer of sovereignty that would have to be filtered through the system of weighted votes; in the case of international security organizations, this transfer concerns the protection of the two essential attributes of sovereignty itself, that is to say, political independence and territorial integrity.[9]

In the initial stage of this transfer of sovereignty, any restriction of state sovereignty is decided exclusively by a given state. Because of the anarchical nature of international society, the external sovereignty of a state will only be limited to the extent desired by the state itself, if at all. The transfer or restriction of the sovereignty of a state also entails a voluntary renunciation of a series of rights. But because the state has a monopoly on force and must ensure the welfare of its citizens, this transfer can not exceed the limit of the people's consensus on the one hand, and the state's international credibility on the other.

This might suggest that as the system of international law is inspired by some sort of 'international moral' the decision to support supranational and cooperative multilateralism automatically wins the support of the domestic public. But this is a simplistic illusion; the fact is that states can afford neither to lose credibility before their citizens and electorates, nor to lose face in the international arena. This imperative will become increasingly strict as the visibility of political actions and the accountability of political leaders increase, as they do in mature democracies. Once again, the link between democracy and multilateralism, which seems so clear in theory, is far from evident in practice.

Hence, when an international organization set up through a statute (which is the result of an intergovernmental bargaining process), must function in the real world, the initial and voluntary decision to delegate a state's sovereignty cannot be allowed to damage the possibility of protecting its vital national interests. Were this allowed to occur, the state whose prerogatives are threatened would immediately back out.

National and Supranational Spheres of Action

Every international organization must address the fundamental problem of reconciling the sphere in which it autonomously elaborates the political aims that transcend the aims of its members, with the sphere in which the states exercise their rights. This involves four main elements: the decision-making mechanism; statutes; interest vs ideals; and leaders.

The decision-making mechanisms of an international organization can be taken as an accurate indicator of the extent of its real supra-national attributes, and thus of the scope of the dichotomy between the supranational aims enshrined in the statute and the pragmatic compromises required. What is remarkable is that any attempt at reconciling the two spheres by means of decision-making mechanisms is inevitably doomed to fail; one must prevail over the other.

The problem of adjustment in codified regulations, which is so typical of international law, appears to be particularly strong in the case of the statutes of international organizations. Charters tend to freeze the balance of power that was prevalent at the founding of an organization. Thereafter, it is inevitable that each state develops along different paths, according to different logic and mechanisms which might not always be compatible with those chosen by the supra-national organization of which its is a member. The process of reconciliation that occurs in the negotiating stage of the Charter is encouraged by the intergovernmental scope of the entire process. The success of the subsequent interaction between the multilateral organization and the intergovernmental dimension cannot, however, be taken for granted.

It could be objected that these statements are borne of an unspoken and questionable hypothesis, namely that the states are only spurred by 'interests', not by 'ideals'. This is indeed the case. However, it is far from a groundless hypothesis, for the simple reason that it is wrong to tackle the issue from the stand-point of the contrast between 'interests' and 'ideals'. When ideals forge a country's way of life, they become a constituent part of its interests. Hence, each state has its own way of achieving even those ideals it may share with other states. In this manner, each one preserves its national identity, and the state is therefore encouraged to protect and assert it while interacting with others.

Lastly, although international organizations may exercise some power of coercion, Their actions depend on the individuals in leadership positions. The UN of the 1990s is not the UN of the 1970s.[10] This is not just because the world has changed in the meantime, but also because Boutros Ghali differs from Waldheim. The contradictions of the European Union can be said to be, in part, the contradictions of Jacques Delors himself; the principle of subsidiarity is the also the making of Eurocrats. Just as at a national level the degree of imperfection that statespersons inevitably transmit to the abstract juridical purity of the institutions, statespersons make the already delicate relationship between states and international organizations even more complex. The difference between the two cases is that, while at an internal level the cohesion of the state is guaranteed by a core of common values, in an international context this only occurs in exceptional and limited instances.

The theory that it is impossible to reconcile the contrast between multilateralism and individual interests is sadly confirmed by the significant examples of the European Union, the Western

European Union (WEU), and the Conference on Security and Cooperation in Europe (CSCE).

The EU has been plagued mainly by two problems. The first is the antagonism between the Commission, which is made up of individuals and gives impetus to the entire integration process, and the Council, which is made up of states, is intergovernmental, and is the greatest expression of traditional diplomacy. The second problem is the contradiction of a Europe torn between federalism and national identity. This contradiction became apparent in four fundamental instances:

 (i) the challenge of De Gaulle, which was solved through the EU's mechanisms thanks to the Luxembourg compromise, which amounted to a marked political decline of federal aspirations;

 (ii) the principle of subsidiarity, which is characterized by a fundamental ambiguity as to which of the two authorities, the federal or the federated one, is to be considered marginal;

 (iii) the issue of the treaty-making power, which has been *de facto* avoided thanks to the expedient of mixed agreements;

 (iv) the Common Foreign and Security Policy (not yet operational in the Yugoslav crisis), which will only find a solution, if ever, at a purely intergovernmental level.[11]

The WEU has a burdensome mandate that presupposes the existence of a political union, which, by definition, it cannot create alone. Therefore, if EU (not yet a functioning union) and the WEU were to be merged, a dangerous paralysis would surely ensue. Given that the WEU treaty expires in 1998, this merger might take place in the course of the revision of the Maastricht treaty, due to begin in 1996.

The CSCE, despite its fundamental political role in the evolution of the confrontation between the two blocs between 1973 and 1990 was no more than a consultative organ based on consensus. The institutionalization set in motion by the 1990 'Paris process' has led to an increase in the number of decision-making bodies. Given the over-sized nature of this agency (53 'European' member states which do not form a geographical entity, let alone a geopolitical one), this increase has turned its decision-making into a cumbersome process, through expedients such as the rule of consensus minus one, or the procedure of silence, which barely hide the uncertainties on the very identity of the CSCE.[12]

These uncertainties are exacerbated by an additional factor. In

July 1992, at Helsinki, the CSCE decided to rethink the foundations of the security system inherited from the Cold War, and update its instruments for conflict prevention and crisis management. Faced by the explosion of ethnic and nationalistic tensions and rivalries, the main idea of 'Helsinki 2' was to establish a permanent tie between the first (security) and the third (human rights) baskets of 'Helsinki 1'. The confidence-building system was therefore still considered valid in preventing a further widening of conflicts. The systematic monitoring of the obligations related to human rights was thought to be the most effective system of prevention, especially with respect to internal strife. But the CSCE overlooked the fact that respect of human rights is the result, not the cause, of a stable and reliable security framework.

The conclusions drawn so far on the transfer of the states' sovereign rights to international organizations seem rather dismal. It could be said that, notwithstanding the contradictions and imperfections of the time, the Cold War years appeared to be the 'golden age of multilateralism'. This was the age of experiments within the European Community, stalemate in the UN, a low level of institutionalization in the CSCE. This period is marked by two elements of considerable importance: the restricted behavior of geostrategic entities, and the ensuing phenomenon of the erosion of national sovereignty.

The mechanism of nuclear deterrence was managed by the two superpowers, which, it should be noted, spoke the same language (Russia in its Marxist period was the most 'Western' Russia ever). It constrained the freedom of action of the two superpowers within the framework established by the logic of the balance of terror, which made unpredictable developments virtually impossible. The sovereignty of lesser participants in this game was similarly restricted by the imperative to conform to the logic of the bipolar balance. Naturally, the same limitations also applied to the failed effort of non-alignment. This restricted freedom of action and the consequent limits imposed on national sovereignty seemed to be a prerequisite for any form of collective security. In fact, the bipolar balance turned out to be an effective instrument of collective security, at least in Europe.

Thus, a paradox is evident: since the antagonism between the blocs has disappeared, collective security might only be able to function if the conditions of stability ensured by this antagonism

were restored; however, if this stability were to return in a multipolar and renationalized situation, multilateralism would become at
once both feasible and unnecessary, since the traditional instruments
of diplomacy would ensure a stabilization factor capable of
preventing conflicts.

Restricted freedom of action and limited sovereignty were in
fact the result of the balance of terror based on a bipolar system:
when the latter vanished, the notion of sovereignty recovered its full
nineteenth-century meaning. The limits imposed on the sovereignty
of states are once again based upon free will, and will actually be
determined by the potentially conflictual encounter of national
interests, without provoking an institutional paralysis.

Options for the Future

The above is compounded by the current notion of 'security', which
now concerns not just the military sphere, but is extended to other
domains, including the economy. Geopolitical issues are now
flanked by geoeconomic ones, which at times even become
indistinguishable from them.[13] This leaves four possible paths of
developments for the future.

This is, for the most part, what has been unsuccessfully
attempted over the past few years. These attempts failed because
states did not agree on a homogeneous way to intervene in the
various conflicts; inter-ethnic strife cannot be solved through the
involvement of external parties; the parties involved have tried to
take a 'free ride'; and control mechanisms have been unreliable.

Available instruments are inadequate because they are not
'bold' enough to dare to bring down the barrier of domestic
jurisdiction.

The 'predominant partner' of international peacekeeping and
peace-enforcing coalitions and the attempt to assert the principle
'main contribution only with main control', both lie on the blurred
borderline between the return of power politics and the forced
extension of collective security criteria to a reality which rejects
them, and at the same time, acts as an indicator of the danger of
denying the domestic jurisdiction. The Cold War, however, has left
us an inheritance consisting in well tested instruments—first and
foremost NATO—which, if politically reinvented, could enable us

to avoid the risk of another 'Europe *à la* Bismarck'.

This is perhaps the only viable alternative. Such multilateralism would not be founded on the transfer of sovereignty; it would be based on the creation of multilateral instruments of intervention whose application, preferably to crisis prevention rather than to crisis management, might work as a permanent clearing house for national conflicts, without aiming at its impossible institutionalization. But even this option would be far from a panacea, especially since the outline of this proposal is very unclear, just as the attempts at understanding what is presently occurring throughout the world are unclear.

What must be emphasized is that it is no longer possible to seek shelter in placid declarations on multilateral diplomacy, collective security and the cooperation of states. These had some sense, or were made to seem sensible, only as long as the nuclear threat paralyzed the entire system of international relations. The time has now come to face the responsibility of deciding what must be done and doing it.

Notes

1. An excellent survey of the main theoretical problems of international relations can be found in Bonanate, Luigi e Santoro, Carlo Maria: *Teoria e Analisi delle Relazioni Internazionali*, (Bologna: Il Mulino, 1990).

2. Ferrari Bravo, Luigi: *Lezioni di Diritto Internazionale*, (Napoli: Editoriale Scientifica, 1992), pp. 19-22.

3. Jean, Carlo: *Studi Strategici*, (Franco Angeli: Milan, 1990).

4. Casadio, Franco: *Il Sistema delle Relazioni Internazionali*, (Padova: Cedam-SIOI, 1991).

5. The entire range of issues related to the 'new world disorder' is dealt with in Lelluche, Pierre: *Le Nuveau Monde*, (Paris: Grasset, 1992) and in Cavallari, Alberto: *L'Atlante del Disordine*, (Milano: Garzanti, 1994).

6. A comprehensive discussion of the origins of the League of Nations can be found in Renouvin, Pierre: *Le Crisi del XX Secolo,* (Firenze: Vallecchi, 1961); Duroselle, Jean Baptiste: *Histoire Diplomatique de 1919 à Nos Jours,* (Paris: Dalloz, 1993); and in Di Nolfo, Ennio: *Storia delle Relazioni Internazionali, 1918-1992,* (Bari: Laterza, 1994).

7. For a discussion of the origins of World War I, see Duroselle, Jean Baptiste: *L'Età Contemporanea,* (Torino: UTET, 1969); and Droz, Jacques: *Les Causes de la Première Guerre Mondiale,* (Paris: Editions du Seuil, 1973).

8. D'Amoja, Fulvio: *Declino e Prima Crisi dell'Europa di Versailles,* (Milano: Giuffrè, 1967).

9. Conforti, Benedetto: *Diritto Internazionale,* (Napoli: Editoriale Scientifica, 1992), pp.3-9.

10. Prospects for the future of the US are analyzed in VV.AA.: *Le Nazioni Unite del 2000,* (Bari: Laterza, 1991).

11. The main aspects of the Community decision-making process can be found in Ballarino, Antonio: *Lineamenti di Diritto Comunitario,* (Padova: Cedam, 1993, 4th Edition) which also has an extensive bibliography; and in Pineau, Christian: *Le Grand Pari,* (Paris: Fayard, 1991).

12. Ronzitti, Natalino e Barberini, Giovanni: *La Nuova Europa della CSCE,* (Milano: Franco Angeli, 1994).

13. See Luttwak, Edward: *Strategia,* (Milano: Rizzoli, 1989).

Other sources which have been drawn upon for this chapter include:

Ferrari Bravo, Luigi: *Lezioni di diritto internazionale* (Napoli: Editoriale Scientifica), 1992.

Ferrari Bravo, Luigi: *Lezioni di diritto comunitario* (Napoli: Editoriale Scientifica), 1993.

Jean, Carlo: *Studi strategici* (Milano, Franco Angeli, 1990).

Jean, Carlo: *Morte e riscoperta dello Stato Nazione*, (Milano: Franco Angeli, 1991).

Lellouche, Pierre: *Le nouveau monde* (Paris: Grasset, 1992).

Rizzo, Aldo: *Guerra e Pace nel Duemila* (Roma-Bari: Laterza, 1987).

Romano, Sergio (et al.): *Crisi del bipolarismo: vuoti di potere e possibili conseguenze* (Roma: Rivista Militare, 1994).

3 Successes and Failures of International Institutions in the Post-Yugoslav Crisis

Maurizio Cremasco

Until 1989, the maintenance of security and stability in Europe was mainly seen as the result of the effective functioning of three different institutional structures: the North Atlantic Treaty Organization (NATO), the Warsaw Pact and the Conference on Security and Cooperation in Europe (CSCE). NATO and the Warsaw Pact provided a fairly balanced defense posture and a military stalemate under the nuclear umbrella of the two superpowers. The CSCE offered a larger number of countries a frame of reference for security, no matter how uncertain its true capabilities.

In the last five years, the strategic landscape has drastically changed. For a brief period, European security appeared assured by the emergence of a 'new world order', and multinational istitutions (some to be revised and some strengthened) were seen as building blocks that would eventually form a single construction. It was fashionable to discuss 'European security architectures' and 'concentric circles of security'. Another institution, the North Atlantic Cooperation Council (NACC), an offspring of NATO, was created to address the security concerns of the former members of the Warsaw Pact. In approving the Maastricht treaty, the European Union (EU) inserted its quest for a European security and defense identity into the overall picture and assigned new functions to the Western European Union (WEU).

However, the re-emergence of nationalistic sentiments and ethnic rivalries, the multiplication of trouble spots in the East, and the Yugoslav crisis rapidly dashed the hopes of a long period of international stability. In the Gulf crisis, international institutions mainly supported the strong leadership role played by the United States. The United Nations (UN) legitimated the actions of the anti-Saddam coalition, while NATO offered its well-tested logistics and support system. But without the leadership of the United States there would have been no coalition, no war against Iraq and no victory. By contrast, in the Yugoslav crisis, no international or European organization, or single country led the way to a solution, though they were all involved in it at different stages and to different degrees.

In light of the above, how have international institutions reacted to and performed in the course of the Yugoslav crisis? What are their main accomplishments and most evident failures? To what extent have these failures been the result of institutional shortcomings? To what extent can they be attributed to other factors? How well, and when, have different institutions co-operated? Has there been competition, a duplication of efforts or overlapping of responsibilities among them? What lessons may be learned for the future?

The Conference on Security and Cooperation in Europe

In June 1991, when the last act of the Yugoslav drama began to unfold, the CSCE was ill-prepared to play its institutional role. For the first time, it had to confront a crisis involving one of its members. As an internal crisis, it was particularly difficult to manage because of the fine line separating the international search for a diplomatic solution from interference in the internal affairs of a sovereign state. The task was made more difficult by an explosive mix of ethnic and nationalistic forces, economic failure, social unrest and political de-legitimation of the communist regime. Moreover, because of the consensus required for adopting resolutions, it was easy for Yugoslavia, prior to its suspension (for three months on 8 July 1992 and indefinitely on 7 August), to veto any CSCE action it considered against its interests. In the early phases, the CSCE task was complicated by the opposition of the Soviet Union to its peacekeeping role. Finally, CSCE mechanisms created to deal with events like the Yugoslav crisis (the emergency mechanism,[1] the Moscow mechanism,[2] the Conflict Prevention Center (CPC)[3] and the High Commissioner on National Minorities[4]) were either still too new[5] to be able to work effectively or created too late, when the crisis was unmanageable through their diplomatic instruments.

The CSCE Ministerial Council, meeting in Berlin on 20 June

1991, was only able to express concern about the crisis and support 'for the democratic development, unity and territorial integrity of Yugoslavia'. When Austria notified its concern about 'unusual military activity' close to its borders, and triggered a meeting of the CPC, and the first emergency meeting of the CSCE Council (in Prague on 3-5 July 1991), agreement was reached on only two points: to appeal the parties to halt the conflict and to send a mission of 'good offices' and an EC-arranged observer mission to monitor the cease-fire.[6]

From July 1991, the CSCE adopted a low-profile policy toward the Yugoslav crisis, leaving the EC to confront the situation and carry the whole burden of the diplomatic efforts. Yet, it was not inactive. It provided a forum in which regional countries, in particular those bordering Yugoslavia, channeled their concerns and discussed crisis management measures. It gave the EC a place to present its actions. The Committee of Senior Officials (CSO) legitimized the EC involvement by its explicit support. In August 1991, the CSCE persuaded Yugoslavia to accept an enlargement of the EC monitor mission to include observers from Canada, Czechoslovakia, Poland and Sweden. In December 1991, it launched a fact-finding mission on human rights, which visited all the Yugoslav republics and the province of Kosovo. In August 1992, it decided to establish long-term missions in Kosovo, Sandjak and Vojvodina.[7] Finally, it conducted sanctions assistance missions (SAM) in coordination with the EC and 'spill-over' missions in Macedonia to prevent the enlargement of the conflict to that Republic.

However, it can be argued that the CSCE's impact on the crisis was minimal. It was difficult to reach an agreement among 52 members, some of them with close historical ties to Yugoslavia.[8] When Belgrade vetoed a CSCE peace conference, the latter was forced out of a direct management role. Finally, the fact that all missions had to be approved by Yugoslavia represented a strong limiting factor.

The European Community (Union)

The EC (which became the European Union, EU, on 1 November 1993) was ill-prepared to confront the crisis. It did not seriously address the Yugoslav situation before the Croatian and Slovenian declarations of independence on 25 June 1991. From that moment, and until the summer of 1992, the EC was on the forefront of crisis management and tried all its mediation skills. It mediated an agreement to defuse the situation in Slovenia (Brioni, 7 July 1991); it organized a peace conference (The Hague, 7 September 1991); it offered a comprehensive plan for the reconstitution of Yugoslavia (18 October 1991) and it sent observer teams to monitor the cease-fires which were brokered by the EC mediator, Lord Carrington, between Serbia and Croatia. Serbia's rejection of the EC plan refocused attention on the UN, which had begun its involvement by appointing former US Secretary of State Cyrus Vance as its special envoy on 8 October.

The EC had already appealed to the UN in August 1991, and this was seen as the symbol of Europe's failure in the management of the crisis.[9] In early November, Serbia caught everybody by surprise by asking the Security Council to send a UN peacekeeping force to Yugoslavia. By mid-November, Croatia also asked for UN intervention and by the end of the month Cyrus Vance announced that an agreement had been reached between President Tudjman, President Milosevic, and the federal Minister of Defense, General Kadijevic, for a cease-fire (the fourteenth, soon violated like all others) and the acceptance of a 'blue helmet' contingent as an interposition force. From that moment, the role played by the EC, excluding the issue of diplomatic recognition, was limited to finding a political settlement through the continuation of the peace conference, while the UN efforts concentrated on peacekeeping. The Hague conference was reconvened on 9 December, after a break of more than a month. But little was expected of the talks, and the EC officials themselves described the new session as a stock-taking exercise.[10]

In April 1992, the war spilled over to Bosnia-Hercegovina. Sporadic clashes in August 1991, intensified immediately after the referendum in which 63.4% of Bosnia-Hercegovina's electorate voted overwhelmingly (99.43%) for secession.[11] By summer 1992 the fighting assumed the features of a blatant war of Serbian aggression against the new republic. By May 1992, the conference had become a sterile diplomatic exercise.[12] In June, a new attempt to revive the peace process failed, prompting Lord Carrington to declare that the results 'had been disheartening'.[13] In July, the same outcome emerged from talks held in London, where a new cease-fire (the 39th) was signed, and almost immediately violated. In August, the EC's attempt to revive the negotiations was boycotted by the Presidents of Serbia and Montenegro. Finally, on the eve of the EC/UN London conference on Yugoslavia on 26 August, Carrington resigned in frustration. By August 1992, the EC role had become somewhat marginal, subordinated to that of the UN.

The peace conference was a honest effort to gather the major actors of the crisis around a negotiating table and to broker a solution through a flurry of diplomatic activity conducted by the President of the EC Council and Lord Carrington, the chairman of the conference. As Michael Brenner has noted, 'they stressed their mandate to the limit in pressing the Yugoslav combatants with a mix of persuasion, cajolery and threat'.[14] The conference-convened, suspended, reconvened several times—was a failure. Insisting on the conference as the only instrument of EC policy, when it was clear that it was leading nowhere, was bound to tarnish the EC image, send wrong signals about the commitments made in Maastricht, and eliminated any further prospect of playing a significant role in shaping the new security arrangements in a post-Cold War Europe. There was little sense for the EC to persist in a brokerage role without being willing and able to make timely use of all potential political, economic and military levers.

As for military force, there were many good reasons for the WEU and the EC to avoid deploying ground troops in a highly volatile and risky military situation with the mission of not just keeping, but enforcing peace. Yet the EC's unwillingness to apply a limited amount of military force to support its formal admonitions and threats eventually had adverse effects on its overall diplomatic effort. It also revealed an EC incapable of managing the first real crisis on its door-steps in post-Cold War Europe.

This does not necessarily mean that the EC should have sent a ground troop contingent to Yugoslavia. It means that more thinking should have been given to the selective use of air and sea power. The initial phase of the crisis, at the end of 1991, at the time of the siege and shelling of Dubrovnik, which the EC considered 'an illegal act clearly aimed at the seizure of an indisputably Croatian city',[15] was the right moment to use military force as an instrument of political pressure.

The air and naval forces of major European states would have been capable of performing the three tasks needed to send a strong signal mainly to Belgrade, but also to Zagreb. These tasks were: (i) keeping the federal aircraft on the ground—by offensive combat air patrol (CAP) missions conducted in Yugoslav air space and possibly counterair missions against selected airbases; (ii) maintaining sea control of the Adriatic; (iii) implementing interdiction with surgical strikes of the main assets of Serbian superiority, i.e. tanks and heavy artillery, together with their vulnerable logistics tail.[16] The possibility of US air and naval forces participating in the operations would have represented a powerful support and would have given an even stronger signal. This course of action—militarily minimal, high-tech, low-casualty, internationally mandated and wrapped in a peace plan[17]—could have achieved three goals: (i) to reduce the military capabilities of the federal armed forces; (ii) to alter Serbian calculations of costs and benefits of EC peace proposals; (iii) to indicate the EC's willingness of going beyond words, thus strengthening its crisis-management effort.

Obviously, the potential political and military risks and repercussions of such an operation were not to be underestimated; each phase should have been planned considering all the possible contingencies and flawlessly executed. Even such a military intervention would probably not have solved the situation immediately. It was unlikely, though possible, that the punishment inflicted on the aggressors would have stopped the fighting. Moreover, the EC might have been forced to contemplate even harsher actions, such as the bombing of key strategic assets in Serbia itself, thus opening a totally new phase of the conflict. However, the intervention would have dispelled allusions to a European double standard, the image of an EC as a bystander, and the impression that it still intended its security in a very narrow sense—three elements which were bound to have long-lasting consequences. But a different EC would have been needed, even for a limited military option: more politically mature, less internally divided and more determined about its international role.

The EC was late and divided even on the use of the economic leverage at its disposal and nothing significant was done over the first four critical months of the crisis. Only by November 1991 did the EC decide to adopt restrictive economic measures,[18] later

applied solely to Serbia and Montenegro,[19] though insufficient to
be an instrument of pressure capable of opening new diplomatic
prospects.[20]

Throughout 1992, the Community gave the impression of being
very reluctant to isolate or punish Serbia. Even a French plan
presented at the EC meeting in Portugal in May seemed out of
touch with the situation in Bosnia.[21] By late May, the sanctions
proposed by the EC Commission were still seen as a draft to be
thoroughly discussed. The EC still maintained to the principles of
'progressive sanctions', hoping they would change Serbia's
behaviour.[22] On 27 May, the EC Permanent Representatives
decided on a two-stage sanctions package, with an oil embargo
delayed until the second stage.[23] Since these measures were taken
just three days after the Lisbon summit, where the Europeans were
criticized by US Secretary of State James Baker for acting too
slowly, there were speculations that the EC had acted more as a
result of US diplomatic pressures than of its own convictions. The
sanctions were officially approved by the EC Council on 1 June,
and expanded to cover the oil embargo, which had been included
in the package approved by the UN Security Council on 30 May
with Resolution 757.

On 17 August 1992 the EC, while stressing the need to tighten
the trade embargo against the new Yugoslav federation, agreed to
postpone any decision on how to reach that goal: another example
of the slow pace of European diplomacy, bordering on political
impotence. Only at the end of April 1993, did the EC again discuss
economic sanctions. (Germany was isolated among the Twelve in
a more intransigent position) and decided on a plan to enforce the
new measures adopted by the UN Security Council with Resolution
820.

The divisions among the Twelve determined the slow pace of
EC diplomacy and its ineffectiveness. The EC tried to prove its
cohesion by avoiding the tougher problems, but divisions emerged
on the following issues:

• recognition of the republics of the former Yugoslavia (first
Slovenia and Croatia, then Macedonia);

• imposition of economic sanctions, with diverging views about
their nature and the mode and timing of their application;

• application of measures to tighten the trade embargo, with
Greece being charged with tolerating its violations;

• proposal for an international conference on Yugoslavia advanced by France and initially rejected by Britain;

• resettlement of the refugees, with Germany asking for help because it felt it was shouldering an unfair burden;[24]

• protection of relief convoys, with differences about the troops needed and the possibility to use force;

• deployment of interposition force and an armed intervention which might go beyond military support for humanitarian aid;

• command, control and communication arrangements for NATO and WEU naval and air forces enforcing the embargo and the 'no-fly' zone;

• the possibility of using NATO air power to defend the 'safe areas' designated by the UN Security Council;

• the US proposal of ending the arms embargo for Bosnian government forces.

Finally, the prospect of a common foreign and security policy (CFSP) was badly damaged when, on 22 May 1993, France, Spain and the United Kingdom agreed with Russia and the United States on a 'Joint Action Statement', a plan to stop the war in Bosnia. This decision was taken without any previous consultation within the EC framework.[25]

These contradictions in the EC position weakened its credibility and its role as a true peacemaker. On the one hand, the EC repeatedly stated its eagerness to play a role in crisis management, in close coordination with the CSCE and the UN; on the other hand, there was a clear dicothomy between official declarations and concrete actions.[26] In early June 1993, EC foreign ministers meeting in Luxembourg stressed that the Vance-Owen plan remained a building block of EC policy. In less than two weeks, the EC had to face the agreement between Serbia and Croatia on the partition of Bosnia into three ethnic states, which practically killed the Vance-Owen plan. During the Council meeting in Copenhagen on 21-22 June, EC ministers expressed their support for the efforts conducted by the mediators 'on the principles of the London Conference, as referred to in the Vance-Owen plan'. The diplomatic wording was a clear signal that the EC was willing to forgo the plan, accepting the situation on the ground after the military operations and ethnic cleansing.[27] The dichotomy emerged more clearly when the EC agreed to accept the UN request for more troops, a commitment restated at the G-7 summit in Tokio. By the end of August, however, France was the only EC member that had committed 800 more soldiers to the UN force.

It would be easy to say—but it would not be fair—that Europe has done all it could to stop the civil war in Yugoslavia. And it would be easy to say—but it would not be fair—that Europe has done very little, or nothing at all. Europe was deeply divided and always late in acting, even on those measures which did not involve direct military intervention. Having failed to intervene in the earliest phase of the crisis, when perhaps there was a chance for positive results, the European countries did not find the way to do so later. A show of force when it still would have had political and military meaning, and would have been operationally easier, might have stopped the war and prevented it from expanding to Bosnia. As the crisis progressed, the possibilities of low-cost interventions decreased, and the European capacity to shape a Common Foreign and Security Policy became weaker.

Europe adopted the best of bad alternatives (endless diplomatic effort, support for humanitarian aid, tightened sanctions) hoping that a negotiated settlement would eventually emerge. Unfortunately, this was not the case and the EC was not capable of playing an effective role. True, no other country or international organization did, either, but Yugoslavia is on Europe's doorstep and after so much talk about Europe finally becoming an actor in the international scene, its performance did not meet expectations.

The United Nations

In the first months of the crisis the UN adopted a policy of maintaining a low profile. It was considered an internal affair of Yugoslavia, thus outside UN responsibility—a position shared by the United States.[28] The UN decided to become involved in October 1991, gradually assuming the main role in the management of the crisis, co-sponsoring the London and Geneva peace conferences with the EC.

On 23 November 1991, in the first show of direct UN involvement, the UN envoy, Cyrus Vance, negotiated a ceasefire and offered a plan for the deployment of UN troops. The plan was eventually accepted by Croatia and Serbia in January 1992, opening the way for sending some 12,000-13,000 peacekeepers to Croatia.

The deployment was endorsed by the Security Council on 14 February with Resolution 743, which established the principles and the rules for the United Nations Protection Force (UNPROFOR), but the full deployment was authorized almost one month later (Resolution 749) and the 'Blue Helmets' assumed operational responsibilities in Sector East on 15 May and in Sector West on 20 June.[29]

Although Bosnia-Hercegovina's president, Alija Izetbegovic, insisted on a UN preventive deployment in its republic, Vance did not follow up on his request. UN Secretary General Boutros-Ghali stated in his report to the Security Council on 5 January 1992, that 'for the moment' there were no reasons to change the original concept of deploying only UN observers in Bosnia, and only in the regions bordering Croatia.[30] Thus, an opportunity was lost to try to prevent the violent breakdown that, was largely anticipated at the time.

In 1992, the UN added to its responsibility for the deployment of peacekeepers (in September the Security Council approved the expansion of the UNPROFOR by up to 6,000 troops) the full range of crisis management instruments. It co-sponsored, with the EC, first the London and then the Geneva peace conferences and adopted a series of crucial resolutions:

• the imposition of progressively stiffer economic sanctions and the decision on a tight embargo to be enforced in the Adriatic Sea and the Danube river;

• the establishment of a ban on military flights (the 'no-fly' zone) over Bosnia, to be enforced by NATO aircraft;

• the creation of a war crimes commission;

• the authorization to adopt 'all measures necessary' to ensure the delivery of humanitarian aid;

• the decision on preventive deployment in Macedonia of 700 UN troops and an additional 100 or so observers, police personnel and staff;

• the establishment of six 'safe areas' (Bihac, Goradze, Sarajevo, Srebrenica, Tuzla and Zepa) to be protected by the UNPROFOR, supported where needed by NATO fighter-bombers.

But not even this broad-ranging action policy of the UN stopped the war in Bosnia, while the diplomatic effort conducted in Geneva by Thorvald Stoltenberg (who had replaced Vance) in coordination with his EC collegue David Owen stalled because no solution was acceptable to all parties. Though the UN had assumed the conduct of the diplomatic and military game, the military role of the EC countries, providing the bulk of the UN troops, and the air and naval units enforcing UN resolutions, was still fundamental and was expected to become crucial for the enforcement of a peace agreement.

The Western European Union

On 18 November 1991, the same day Vukovar fell to the Serbs, the WEU Council committed naval forces to the establishment of a 'humanitarian corridor' across the Adriatic to protect Red Cross missions rescuing wounded, women and children from Dubrovnik. It was stressed that it was not a military action but only a humanitarian measure.[31] One could argue that the WEU action was not much given that negotiations with Croatia and Serbia were considered necessary to establish the modalities of that naval action. This, together with the fact that the assistance was 'offered', made the WEU decision appear anything but a bold attempt to impose a humanitarian act on a reluctant Serbia. The European attitude appears less appeasing, however, considering that the WEU threatened retaliation against the Yugoslav navy in case of interference with the humanitarian operations.[32]

On 19 June 1992, at the Council meeting in Petersberg, the WEU was directed to examine and recommend measures to help enforce the UN embargo against Serbia. On 26 June, in London, the WEU expressed its intention of studying the feasibility of deploying naval units in the Adriatic. Finally, on 10 July, in Helsinki, it announced that it would send naval and air forces to the Adriatic to monitor the UN embargo. On the same day, NATO took an identical initiative. The 'OTRANTO' operation was organized, coordinated and directed by Italy.[33] WEU warships were to patrol the Otranto Channel, while NATO forces would monitor the Southern Adriatic, opposite the Montenegro coast.

In this context, some considerations seem pertinent. First, it took more than one month after the UN imposed sanctions for the WEU to make its decision—too long if one considers the importance of the trade embargo as a diplomatic tool to pressure Serbia into serious negotiations. Furthermore, such an operation should have been studied and planned long before sanctions were even considered so that it would have been ready to implement at once.

Second, it was significant that for the first time NATO and WEU forces were able to operate in a single mission and in the same area (albeit divided into two main zones), but under two different command authorities. However, the double command setting can be appropriately adopted only in a peacetime environment. In case of war, it would be operationally unacceptable.[34]

Third, the limits imposed on the monitoring mission i.e. to determine whether cargo banned by the UN was still arriving in Montenegro and Serbia, relying only on interrogations of the cargo commanders via radio (without the authority to stop and search ships) were evidently inconsistent with the aim of true control. Thus, the operation ended by appearing not as a naval blockade, but just as a diplomatic gesture with little impact on potential embargo breaches.

Fourth, the eventual addition of a German destroyer to the NATO naval force and Maritime Air Patrol (MAP) aircraft to the WEU force constituted an important change in Germany's attitude toward the participation of its armed forces in military operations connected with peacekeeping operations outside NATO's area of responsibility. For the first time, Germany accepted that German troops could participate in peacekeeping missions under UN authority, even though constitutional and political problems had yet to be solved.

Finally, responding to a Security Council resolution calling for a naval blockade, NATO and the WEU decided to start stop-and-search naval operations in the Adriatic.[35] This time, however, the German destroyer *Hamburg* was ordered not to participate in the enforcement action.

On 5 April 1993, at a special meeting in Luxembourg, the WEU Council decided to strengthen the embargo on the Danube by a 'police and customs' operation in cooperation with Bulgaria, Hungary and Romania. It was stressed that the operation, which would have been of a 'non-military nature', would be based 'on a system of coordinated control areas upstream and downstream of the Serbian border', to check that transports toward Serbia did not contain goods banned by the sanctions.[36] To contribute to the patrolling operations of the riparian countries, the WEU provided 10 fast patrol boats and 250-300 men. France, Germany, Italy,

Luxembourg, Norway and Spain declared their readiness to participate. Italy, then president of the WEU, coordinated the action with the Danubian countries.[37]

Even though the WEU had agreed at Petersberg, in the summer of 1992, to make military forces available, it suffered from the same constraints as the EC. EC internal divisions were logically reflected in WEU policy, and the latter was initially unable to decide on an interposition force, and later on the use of military power. Moreover, the WEU was aware of the limitation of its military instrument, in particular in terms of command and control capabilities, high-tech weapons systems and logistics support.

The North Atlantic Treaty Organization

In the early phases of the crisis, NATO maintained a low profile. It exchanged views on the crisis in the Political and Military Committees, and endorsed EC efforts, explicitly at the Rome summit in November 1991. But gradually NATO was somewhat forced to expand its military involvement. This was not an easy process. Divisions within NATO resembled those within the EC and the WEU. Yet, the emergence of a pre-eminent NATO role was unmistakable and was facilitated by the UN recognition of NATO as the sole organization capable of providing the military force needed to support and enforce its resolutions.

By mid-December 1992, UN Secretary General Butros Ghali requested NATO to draw contigency plans for military actions in Bosnia, including the enforcement of the 'no-fly' zone approved by the Security Council in October.[38] Thus, by the end of 1992, NATO was engaged in feasibility studies of military intervention options mandated by the UN.[39] Even the EC and UN mediators Vance and Owen wanted NATO aircraft to enforce their peace plan.[40] NATO provided equipment and personnel from its Northern Army Group to UNPROFOR headquarters in Bosnia. On 10 July 1992 NATO decided to join the WEU naval force off the Yugoslavian coast, first in the screening of the maritime traffic, then in enforcing the embargo when the rules of engagement were changed. As previously said, NATO eventually assumed the operational control of the whole operation.

NATO AWACS flying over Hungarian territory and the

Adriatic have transmitted essential information to UN authorities
and have helped NATO fighters deployed to Italian airbases (since
12 April 1993) to enforce the 'no-fly' zone established by Resolutions 781 and 816. Meeting in Athens on 10 June, the NATO
Council decided to accept the UN request for air cover and air
support for the protection of both Bosnian 'safe areas' and the
UNPROFOR, as mandated by Resolution 836. NATO aircraft
deployment began on 13 July and by 22 July British, Dutch, French
and American fighter-bombers were combat ready, joining the
interceptors already operating over Bosnia in operation 'Deny
Flight'.[41]

At a special Council meeting in Brussels on 2 August NATO
decided 'to make immediate preparations for action if the strangulation of Sarajevo and other areas continues, ... including air strikes
against those responsible, Bosnian Serbs and others, in Bosnia-
Hercegovina'.[42] 'Operational Options for Air Strikes in Bosnia-
Hercegovina' were approved by the NATO Council on 9 August.
It declared to be prepared to act in coordination with the United
Nations, when, and if, the situation demanded.[43] Finally, NATO
agreed 'in principle' to assume responsibility for the execution of
a peace treaty in Bosnia, but only under an unambigous mandate,
with clear objectives and rules of engagement.[44]

Implications and Lessons of the Yugoslav Crisis

As we write, in the Spring of 1994, the civil war is still raging.
Thus, it is difficult, at this stage, to speak about the implications
and lessons of Yugoslavia's disintegration. They will depend on the
result of the crisis and on how the international community will
assess it. However, several major implications may already be
inferred. First, in post Cold War and post Communist Europe it is
again possible to use military force for the achievement of specific
foreign policy goals, including territorial gains, without precipitating
the intervention of any international organization or big power. In
fact, it can be argued that the end of the East-West political and
ideological struggle favors those developments.

Second, the EC has failed, so far, to shape a Common Foreign
and Security Policy (CFSP). The divisions among the Twelve
dimmed the hopes raised by the Maastricht Treaty. The EC failed

to seize this opportunity to show the world that Europe had finally become an important actor on the international scene, capable of successfully managing a dangerous crisis developing at its doorsteps.

Third, there have been sharp differences between Europeans and Americans. However, the enforcement of the 'no-fly' zone over Bosnia, and the decision to apply NATO air-power in the event of a Serbian strangulation of Sarajevo and other Bosnian safe areas, are two good examples that close cooperation among NATO allies is a *conditio sine qua non*. In fact, only the NATO threat to use military force, at different stages of the crisis had an impact albeit limited because it appeared evident that behind the threat there was a weak and uncertain political will.

Fourth, a major problems was the slow pace of the UN decision-making and crisis management process (even when an agreement was reached within the Security Council) and the time needed for the deployment of UN troops, even when there were countries willing to provide them.

Fifth, there is a need to reassess the meaning and the scope of UN 'peacekeeping' and, more generally, of the use of force for the maintenance of international stability and peace. Peacekeeping, which should be conducted only when peace is firmly established, should be clearly differentiated from peacemaking and peace-enforcing operations which are likely to provide the use of military force. This is particularly true when UN troops must provide humanitarian aid and at the same time protect the population. In 1994, in Bosnia, Blue Helmets only escort humanitarian convoys when the various ethnic bands let them through, even though a specific Security Council Resolution requires that humanitarian aid should be delivered using all the necessary means. Putting an end to the carnage is not part of their mission; in any case, their military capability would be insufficient to accomplish it. In turn, this reassessment of the need to use military force in UN operations is ultimately bound to shape the restructuring of the armed forces of major EC countries.

Sixth, the Yugoslav crisis demonstrated that it is difficult, but inevitable, that the institutions must work in an 'interlocking mode'. The UN and the CSCE provided the legitimating framework for NATO and the WEU. The WEU needed the support of NATO. Only the UN had the authority to send Blue Helmets. The UN-EC cooperation was important for political management, while NATO countries provided the bulk of the UN military force and the aircraft for the enforcement of the 'no-fly' zone, and the possible use of airpower in Bosnia.

Finally, the principle of non-interference in the internal affairs of a state should be limited when internal affairs become a threat to international or regional stability and security. In the Yugoslav case, the huge flow of refugees created by the war, the total disregard for human rights epitomized by the practice of 'ethnic cleansing', widespread destruction and human suffering, the possibility that the civil war might turn into a wider regional conflict are all elements which rightly call for international intervention and interference in internal affairs.

Conclusions

It may be true that the international community has been forced to create international institutions to try to resolve problems that nation states cannot resolve on their own. But international institutions work only if member states make them work. In other words, if there is no convergent or, better, common political will, no international institution will be capable of performing a concrete and significant crisis management role. Thus, even when operating in an 'interlocking' mode, the international institutions are only as effective as their ability to agree and act together. In fact, the impression is that, in the Yugoslav crisis, national interests have still played an important role in hampering the effectiveness of the international institutions, and that members actually used the institutional framework to check and constrain positions and policies of other members.

In July 1992, the CSCE agreed to become a formal 'regional arrangement' under Chapter VII, Article 52, of the UN Charter. Under this provision, the CSCE could call on NATO and the WEU, as well as on individual countries, to provide peacekeeping units for conflicts among its members. However, it has been clearly stated that peacekeeping operations will require the consent of all parties directly concerned. Moreover, the CSCE has limited its own role to the peaceful settlement of disputes, leaving the UN with the sole responsibility of enforcing peace. NATO (at the Council in Oslo, in

June 1992) stated that it is ready to support peacekeeping activities under the responsibility of the CSCE.[45] In its Petersberg declaration, the WEU stated that it is prepared to support, on a case-by-case basis and in accordance with its procedures, the effective implementation of conflict-prevention and crisis-management measures, including peacekeeping activities of the CSCE or the United Nations Security Council.[46] Finally, it appears that even NACC might be preparing for a peacekeeping role.[47]

One can argue that this proliferation of international bodies has limited operational significance and may complicate peacekeeping, peacemaking and peace-enforcing missions. As previously said, the commitments of the different international organizations to cooperate with the CSCE and the UN obviously depend on the capacity of member states to find the necessary common political will. The Yugoslav crisis has demonstrated how difficult it is to reach a consensus when the use of military force is the predominant issue. No matter how close the relationship among members, the final word is still that of national governments, even in the case of the post-Maastricht European Union. National governments must consider their domestic situations and the reluctance (if not outright opposition) of the public opinion to accept a military involvement which could entail human losses.

The more international organizations that provide military forces for a peacekeeping or peacemaking operation, the more complicated the problems of coordination. Thus, the feasibility of the concept of 'interlocking institutions' and its eventual mode of integration should be realistically measured in terms of operational pros and cons, i.e. in terms of true effectiveness in confronting a crisis situation.

In this context, the Yugoslav crisis has shown elements of cooperation and joint actions, as in the case of the CSCE-EC Sanctions Assistance Mission which coordinated and assisted national efforts; the CSCE-WEU cooperation in sanction enforcement operations on the Danube; and the NATO and UN cooperation. But elements of tension emerged as well, as in between the EC and the UN on the UN supervision of Serbian heavy guns.[48]

NATO's effort to demonstrate its viability in the post-Cold War era, and its capacity to adapt to a different strategic environment, have become evident as has the WEU struggle for a security identity and a military role. This has led to a simmering competition between the two organizations and the emergence of a preeminent NATO role.[49]

So far, international organizations, even when working in a cooperative mode, ended in total failure because they were unable to manage the crisis in its initial phases or to stop the war later. Considering the military situation in mid-1994, the military option no longer appears feasible. A direct intervention to roll back Serb gains would require a huge ground force that no country or international institution is willing to provide, and the use of politically unacceptable military means. The use of airpower only is unlikely to change the situation on the ground, even if an extensive air campaign is contemplated, with escalatory options which would eventually involve Serbian territory and large collateral damage. However, the threat to use airpower could be a useful complement to strong political pressures.

If the use of military force to obtain territorial gains is eventually rewarded in the Yugoslav case, European security will be weakened. The Serbian and Croatian examples might be followed by other countries or ethnic minorities throughout the continent. The ability of the European Union to operate effectively as a protagonist in the international arena will depend exclusively on its political credibility, economic power and military preparedness, and on its willingness to use them when needed. It would be regrettable if the example in confronting the Yugoslav crisis were repeated in the future. One of the most important issues today is how, and with what organization and with which instruments the international community should respond to crises such as those in Yugoslavia, Somalia, Cambodia, Mozambique and Rwanda/Burundi, in which humanitarian aspects, though preeminent, are only one part of the problem.

Notes

1. A mechanism for consultation and cooperation in emergencies was approved during the Berlin's CSCE Council of June 1991. Any CSCE State affected or threatened by a dispute may call a crisis meeting of the CSCE Council if supported by 12 other States. The Arms Control Reporter, idds, 7-91, p. 402.B.280.11.

2. The mechanism allows for the deployment of CSCE monitors and observers in countries that do not respect the commitments taken under the Helsinki Treaty concerning human rights. The mechanism was adopted in September 1991.

3. The creation of the Conflict Prevention Center was decided during the CSCE summit in November 1990. The Center is located in Vienna.

4. One of the main responsibilities of The High Commissioner on National Minorities is to alert the Committee of Senior Officials on tensions in multi-ethnic CSCE countries. It was created in July 1992, but became operational only 5 months later.

5. The emergency mechanism was approved on 20 June and applied for the first time, after less than two weeks, on 3 July with the emergency meeting of the CSCE Council. The CPC could not fully activate the Procedures for the Peaceful Settlement of Disputes because the foreseen Register of Mediators had not yet been established.

6. Yugoslavia only had to answer Austria's request within the framework of the CPC to fulfill its obligations, while the CSCE 'good offices' mission was rejected by Belgrade and never took place.

7. The mission was supposed to promote dialogue, collect information on all aspects relevant to human rights violations, establish contact points for solving problems and assist in providing information on legislation concerning protection of minorities, freedom of the press and democratic elections. See the decisions of the CSCE's CSO in *Review of International Affairs*, n. 1007-1008, 1.VIII-1.IX 1992, pp. 24-26.

8. At the end of the July 1992 summit, participants nearly failed to agree even on a bland statement condemning violence in Yugoslavia. See Fisher, Marc and Don Oberdofer: 'U.S. to Join Europeans in Patrol Off Yugoslavia', in *The International Herald Tribune (hereafter IHT)*, 11-12 July 1992, p. 4.

9. For the most representative interpretation of the EC decision as reported in the Italian press, see Venturini, Franco: 'I Dodici in Serie B', (The Twelve [Play] in Second Division League) *Corriere della Sera (hereafter CS)*, 7 August 1991, p. 1.

10. *IHT*, 10 December 1991, p. 2.

11. *Europe*, n. 5553, 26-27 August 1991, p. 4, *IHT*, 4 March 1992, p. 6.

12.. A diplomat close to the conference declared after the 12th session held in Brussels on May 6: 'It is stuck. It had stopped making headway'. IHT, 7 May 1992, p. 2. Lord Carrington himself depicted a bleak picture of the conference declaring that none of its goals had so far been attained. Pietro Sormani, 'Insabbiata a Bruxelles la conferenza di pace', CS, 7 May 1992, p. 11.

13. IHT, 26 June 1992, p. 2. Europe, n. 5761, 28-29 June 1992, p. 4.

14. Brenner, Michael: 'The EC in Yugoslavia: A Debut Performance', in *Strategic Studies*, January 1992, p.14.

15. See the EC declaration in *IHT*, 28 October 1991, p. 2. Dubrovnik is on the UNESCO World Heritage List (i.e. its monuments have been declared of 'universal value', and their safekeeping 'the responsibility of mankind').

16. This type of assessment has also been applied to the Bosnian case. In particular, see Zelikov, Philip: 'The New Concert of Europe', *Survival*, vol. 34, n. 2, IISS, London, Summer 1992, pp. 12-30. Beedham, Brian: 'Europe and America Could Interdict Serbia's Arms', *IHT*, 18 May 1992, p. 4, and Lewis, Antony: 'What Was That About a New World Order?', *ibidem*.

17. This definition is used in Rosenfeld, Stephen S.: 'Moving to Intervention In Yugoslavia', *The Washinton Post (hereafter WP)*, 22 May 1992, p.A39.

18. On the EC declaration on Yugoslavia, and the details of the restrictive economic measures, see *Europe*, n. 5606, 9 November 1991, p. 3; and n. 5607, 12-13 November 1991, p. 5. See also: Evans, Michael: 'EC Imposes Sanctions on Yugoslavia', in *The Times*, 9 November 1991, p. 20; Sormani, Pietro: 'I Dodici Puniscono la Jugoslavia' (The Twelve Punish Yugoslavia), CS, 9 November 1991, p. 3; Usborne, David: 'EC starts sanctions against Yugoslavia', *The Independent*, 9 November 1991, p. 12; Riding, Alan: 'EC Imposes Sanctions on Yugoslavia', in *IHT*, 9-10 November 1991, p. 1.

19. The decision to differentiate the Yugoslav republics on the basis of their readiness to cooperate for a diplomatic solution of the crisis was taken by the EC Council in Brussels on December 2, 1991. It was not an easy decision and there were conflicts among the Twelve, culminating with the abstention of Greece. *Europe*, n. 5621, 2-3 December 1991, p. 6.

20. In fact, the economic measures were limited to: the suspension of a 1980 trade and cooperation agreement; limits on imports of Yugoslavian textiles; elimination of Yugoslavia from the benefits under the General System of Preferences; and the exclusion from the PHARE program.

21.. The main points of the French plan were as follows: to get access to the results of Mr. Goulding's mission on Bosnia-Hercegovina; on the basis of those results, to send to Bosnia an observation and protection mission composed of several hundred lightly armed men provided by the EC and CSCE countries, within the UN framework and under the WEU operational coordination; to intensify the work of the ad-hoc conference on Bosnia; to render systematic the air bridge from Belgrade to Sarajevo for the delivery of humanitarian aid; to work in the next session of the conference for the reciprocal recognition of the independence of the republics of the former Yugoslavia. For more details, see Europe, n. 5722, 4-5 May 1992, pp. 6-7.

22. *Europe*, n. 5737, 25-26 May 1992, p. 4.

23. Riding, Alan: 'Europeans Impose a Partial Embargo on Belgrade Trade', in *The New York Times (hereafter NYT)*, 28 May 1992, A1.

24. Germany had taken 275,000 refugees, while Britain and France had taken around 1,100 each. See *The Economist*, 1 August 1992, p. 11; and *IHT*, 14 September 1992, p. 1.

25. Spain was consulted by the others because it was, at the time, a rotating member of the Security Council. The Washington agreement raised criticism among other EC and NATO partners. The Italian Minister of Defense, Fabio Fabbri stated: 'I expressed the Italian disappointment, shared by other countries, not on the substance of the agreement but on the method which was followed'. See Bonanni, Andrea: 'E l'Italia protesta: sul piano di pace non siamo stati consultati' (Italy Protests: We Were Not Consulted on the Peace Plan), in *CS*, 26 maggio 1993, p. 9. Criticism and concern was voice also by Denmark, Germany, the Netherlands and Turkey. The NATO Defense Planning Committee discussed, but did not approve, the plan for Bosnia, declaring that it was a UN responsibility to define any new initiative. See *Atlantic News*, n. 2528, 27 May 1993, p. 1.

26. On the mainly declaratory EC policy, see Pfaff, William: 'Europe's Futility in Bosnia Is an Ominous Symptom', in *IHT*, 13 May 1993, p. 4.

27. The reality that the EC never seriously addressed had become a 'fact of life'. 'We do not like it, but there is nothing we can do about it' in the word of EC mediator David Owen. Ovizio, Riccardo: 'In cantiere un compromesso sulla Bosnia' (A Compromise on Bosnia in the making), in *Corriere della Sera*, 22 June 1993, p. 12.

28. The US Ambassador to the UN, Thomas Pickering, declared that the UN had no role in Yugoslavia unless the EC and the CSCE efforts failed. *Washington Post*, 4 July 1991, p. 19.

29. Steinberg, James B.: *The Role of European Institutions in Security after the Cold War: Some Lessons from Yugoslavia*, Rand Note N-3445FF, May 1992, p. 18.

30. Wynaendts, Henry: 'L'Engranage. Chroniques Yougoslaves, Juillet 1991-Août 1992' (The Clockwork. Yugoslavian Chronicles), (Paris: Edition Denoël, 1993) p. 141.

31. *IHT*, 19 November 1991, p. 2.

32. This was revealed by the Danish Foreign Minister, Ugge Elleman-Jensen, in an interview published by *Politiken*. See *Europe*, n. 5650, 20-21 January 1991, p. 3.

33. The 'Otranto' operation became 'Maritime Guard' and then 'Sharp Guard' on 15 June 1993. *Nouvelles Atlantiques*, n. 2536, 18 June 1993, p. 1.

34. On the confusion possibly arising from this setting, see *The Economist*, 15 August 1992, p. 20. All WEU countries but France considered a single command preferable, but at the same time wanted to give the WEU the right 'political visibility'. The divergences on the command were solved at a joint meeting of the Atlantic Council and the WEU Council on 8 June 1993. The two fleets were put under the operational control of the Commander Allied Naval Forces Southern Europe, Italian Admiral Carlo Alberto Vandini, directly under Cincsouth. See *Europe*, n. 5996, 9 June 1993, 4.

35. Drozdiak, William: 'NATO Agrees to Impose Blockade of Serbia', *Washington Post*, 19 November 1992, p. A31.

36. See the text of the WEU 'Declaration on implementation of U.N. sanctions on the former Yugoslavia' in *Atlantic News*, n. 2514, 7 April 1993, pp. 1-2.

37. The force became operational only in June 1993. Negotiations with the Danubian countries were more complicated than expected. Moreover, the WEU had to wait for the CSCE meeting of 22 April to determine the framework of the mission. On the reservations and conditions posed by those countries, see *Atlantic News*, n. 2515, 9

April 1993, p. 2. On the result of the controls, *Europe*, n. 6015, 5-6 July 1993, p. 3.

38. See 'NATO Drafts Contingency Plans for UN Bosnia Intervention', *IHT*, 16 December 1992, p. 2.

39. The plans prepared by NATO on the enforcement of the 'no-fly' zone were submitted to the UN Secretary General on 14 January 1993. Frederick Bonnart, 'Bosnia: Limited Force Won't Help', IHT, 27 January 1993, p. 6.

40. The intended use was for enforcement of the 'no-fly' zone, or for strikes against those forces violating the peace-plan provisions. Lewis, Paul: 'Mediators Seek NATO Air Support In Bosnia', *IHT*, 8 February 1993, p. 2.

41. *Atlantic News*, n.2545, 23 July 1993, p. 1. The United States deployed 12 A-10, 18 F-18 and 10 support planes (among them, 4 AC-130). France deployed 8 Jaguar, the Netherlands 12 F-16s and the United Kingdon 12 Jaguar. By 16 July, UNPROFOR had established an Air Operation Control Center in Kiseljak as well as Tactical Air Control Parties. *Atlantic News*, n. 2544, 16 July 1993, p. 1.

42. The meeting, held at the request of the United States, lasted longer than expected. There were divisions among the Sixteen on the issue of air strikes and concerns about the connected risks. See the text of the statement of the Secretary General to the press in *Atlantic News*, n. 2547, 4 August 1993, p. 1.

43. It is interesting to note that the Council underlined that the air strikes foreseen by its 2 August declaration were limited to the support of humanitarian relief, and were not to be interpreted as a decision to intervene militarily in the conflict. In reality, the 2 August declaration clearly indicated the strangulation of Sarajevo and other Bosnian areas as a *casus* for air strikes.

44. On 29 September the NATO Council approved the preliminary operational concept developed by the military authority. But details had yet to be defined in particular on the subject of command and control arrangements and funding of the operations. The projected

size of the military force would be around 50,000 soldiers, about half provided by the United States.

45. Ministerial Meeting of the North Atlantic Council in Oslo, 4 June 1992, NATO Press Communiqué M-NAC-1(92)51.

46. WEU Council of Ministers, Bonn, 19 June 1992, Petersberg Declaration, Chapter 1, 'On the WEU and European Security', Para 2 and Chapter 2 'On Strengthening WEU's Operational Role'.

47. At the NACC meeting on 18 Decemebr 1992 a decision was taken to establish an Ad Hoc Group On Cooperation and Peace-keeping. The Group prepared a report which was presented to the NACC meeting in Athens on June 11, 1993. Text of the report in *Atlantic News*, n. 2536 (Annex), 18 June 1993.

48. Steinberg, James B.: *op.cit.*, p. 23-24.

49. Similarly to NACC, the WEU has established a 'WEU Forum of Consultation' to allow regular consultations between its members, the Baltic countries and the C&EE countries. For the competition between the two organizations in the Yugoslav case, let us recall: the decision of WEU and NATO to deploy naval forces in the Adriatic to enforce the embargo; the contingency planning conducted by the two organizations for the same mission to be performed under the same command and control arrangements; the offer to the UN for a level of troops which could be reached only with the participation of forces of NATO countries which were also members of the WEU. For more details, see Cremasco, Maurizio: Europe and the Yugoslav Crisis, unpublished paper, Istituto Affari Internazionali, DOCIAI9359, pp. 31-32.

4 International Institutions and Conflict Resolution in the Former Soviet Union

Dmitri Trenin

The end of the Cold War and the resolution of the Gulf War generated widespread enthusiasm over the potential role of the United Nations (UN), and also the Conference on Security and Cooperation in Europe (CSCE), in the construction of a 'New World Order' and a new 'security architecture' for Europe. It was generally felt at the time that the apparent passivity and inefficiency of those organizations in the preceding period had been the product of the East-West ideological confrontation and superpower rivalry. Freed from those shackles, the international institutions could now exercise their full potential as envisaged in their charters.

This thesis was soon put to the test. The successes of international mediators and peacekeepers (e.g. in El Salvador, Namibia and Cambodia) were followed, and quickly overshadowed by their perceived failures (notably, in Somalia and ex-Yugoslavia). In the eyes of many, the UN, the CSCE, the European Union (EU) and the North Atlantic Treaty Organization (NATO) have all become symbols of international impotence and, occasionally, even appeasement. Thus, initial enthusiasm has given way to much confusion and disappointment, and there are growing fears of renationalization of foreign and security policies in Europe.

Both the initial optimism and the current pessimism are misguided. While the former was clearly based on unrealistic expectations, the latter uses skewed assessment scales, letting the negatives easily outweigh whatever positive results international involvement may have scored. To expect international institutions, many of them products of World War II or the Cold War, to 'police' a transition to the ideals envisioned by their founders so many decades ago, is to take leave of the realm of the possible and indulge in pure idealism. It may take years for world politics to enter a new period of relative stability.

On the other hand, it would be wrong to believe that internationalism has failed, that the institutions which embody it are merely self-serving bureaucracies, and that national unilateralism is the only solution. This should be avoided also because the most salient feature of the new era is the extreme instability which challenges the cohesiveness of nations, the permanence of their borders and the long-established social, economic and ideological patterns of national life. The disintegration of the Soviet Union alone has released so much previously pent-up energy that it is likely to take at least two or three decades for a new system of relations to mature and to reorganize the vast geopolitical, geoeconomic and geostrategic space which for the last several hundred years has known only one form of organization: a continent-wide empire.

This chapter examines the roles of various international institutions in resolving conflicts in the former Soviet Union (FSU). It first assesses the changing perceptions of those institutions in Russia and in the newly independent states of the FSU; it analyzes the performance as compared to the potential of those institutions in preventing, managing and settling conflicts in the post-Soviet space. Special attention is given to the prospects of interaction between the relevant institutions and Russia as the major power in Central Eurasia. The chapter concludes with a discussion of problems and prospects for selected international institutions involved in conflict-resolution in the ex-USSR.

Changing Perceptions of International Institutions in the FSU

The dissolution of the Soviet Union was accompanied by the formation of a new international grouping, a Commonwealth of Independent States (CIS). From its inception in December 1991, however, the post-Soviet Commonwealth functioned more as a forum for occasional consultation among its heads of states than as an organization in its own right. Agreements within the CIS soon became famous for their virtually universal non-compliance. Thus, the CIS initially facilitated the further disassociation of the republics rather than their re-integration. The Russian Federation emerging from the dissolved Soviet Union initially adopted a world view which was influenced by much romanticism and wishful thinking.

Thus, it substantially downplayed the conflict potential resulting from the fall of communism and Soviet disintegration, while at the same time displaying unrealistic optimism as to Russia's immediate prospects.

In an attempt to minimize imperial liabilities and isolate itself from the 'hot spots' on its periphery, Russia withdrew its forces from Nagorny Karabakh (Spring 1992), effectively abandoned Central Asia to its fate, and chose to ignore the issue of the ethnic Russian minorities (25.3 million Russians live in former Soviet non-Russian republics, as compared to the Russian Federation's own population of about 148 million) whose status had changed virtually overnight from full-fledged citizens (of the state which had ceased to exist) to mere residents - with uncertain rights - of the emerging independent states. The Russian government hastily agreed on a hazy formula for the status of Soviet nuclear weapons and conventional forces. It embraced a concept of the Commonwealth of Independent States (CIS) without having made up its mind whether it wanted a mechanism for a smooth divorce or for a new cohabitation.

In contrast to these uncertainties, there was a very clear desire to 'rejoin the civilized (i.e. Western) world' to which Russia was linked through its Christian tradition, the undeniable 'Europeanness' of its culture and its ruling élite's renewed adherence to democratic anti-communist principles. As the successor state to the Soviet Union at the UN Security Council, the Russian Federation also inherited the Soviet fascination with universal principles, such as the defense of universal values and human rights, and the use of global mechanisms for their implementation. The UN was considered capable of satisfactorily resolving post-Soviet conflicts. By the same token, Moscow continued to place emphasis on the CSCE, which it wanted transformed into a smaller version of the United Nations, in which Russia would enjoy a relatively high status. One of the main interests of the new Russia was joining one organization which had been its prime adversary during the preceding decades—NATO. In a speech to the leaders of the Atlantic Alliance in December 1991, Yeltsin was not clear on whether Russia viewed NATO membership as short- or long-term goal.

Whereas Russia did not have to spend much time or effort to win international recognition through adherence to world and regional bodies, the new independent states, which had, at most, enjoyed only brief periods of rather ephemeral independence during the Civil War of 1918-1921, sought precisely that. Not unlike the Asian and African nations emerging from the process of European decolonization in the 1950s and the 1960s, they viewed admission to the UN and the CSCE as the ultimate recognition of their national statehood. In the long-standing Soviet tradition, their post-communist power élites were also looking to those international bodies as the 'new center' replacing Moscow as a court of appeal and an arbiter *par excellence.*

To some of the former Soviet republics (including Ukraine), suffering from the 'little brother syndrome' in their new—and not wholly conflict-free—relationship with Russia, seeking support from international organizations was a means of counterbalancing their powerful neighbor. Thus, Ukraine's national security was officially proclaimed an integral element of the international security system.[1] Also, in contrast to Russia, most of the new states, apparently weary of their previous role as military staging areas or strongholds of the former Soviet Union, have declared their intention to become neutral countries.[2] Appeals for joining NATO (in Ukraine, Georgia, etc.) were coming at that time mainly from opposition politicians who were mostly concerned about perceived or potential resurgence of Russian imperialism.

In 1991-92, the United Nations, was quick to recognize the Russian Federation as the successor to the USSR, and to admit the newly independent states as its full members; Russia, for its part, made no attempt to gain concessions from the new republics in exchange for granting its approval within the Security Council. The CSCE, after initial hesitation, and some German prodding, decided to extend invitations for membership to all former Soviet republics, thus expanding the notion of 'Europe' far beyond its generally recognized geographical or cultural boundaries. This was motivated by the CSCE's desire to involve the new states in the pan-European process, and create new means and incentives for upholding the principles of the 1990 Paris Charter.

The Atlantic Alliance, definitely both unable and unwilling to accept any new members, could not ignore the momentous change in the geostrategic landscape in Central and Eastern Europe. At the end of 1991, to offer its erstwhile adversaries some prospects, NATO proposed the establishment of a North Atlantic Cooperation

Council (NACC). The former Soviet republics perceived the NACC as a half-way house between the coveted full membership and the dreaded further exclusion.

During 1992 these perceptions were somewhat corrected or altered. Russian foreign policy began its difficult transition from the idealism of universal values to the reality of national interests. There was extensive discussion on this subject as part of a more fundamental debate on the future path for Russia, which was inextricably linked with the intensifying power struggle that culminated in the October 1993 showdown in Parliament.

As time went on and as the Yugoslav crisis continued, Russia joined those who had lost faith in the capabilities of the United Nations and the CSCE. A greater cause for concern was that some members of the Russian national security establishment started to perceive the policies of leading NATO countries vis-à-vis the crisis in the Balkans as one-sided and unjustly directed against the one country which had been Russia's traditional ally, i.e., Serbia. Fears were expressed that in a conflict within the former USSR, Western-led international institutions might side with anti-Russian forces.[3]

The other republics have also found reality to be very different from their original expectations. International recognition was granted, but funds and expertise necessary to establish a credible diplomatic presence abroad were not. International institutions started showing an interest in the problems of the former Soviet republics, but this interest was often considered to be superficial or intermittent. Complaints by Ukraine (and others) notwithstanding, world's attention continued to be almost exclusively focussed on Russia. Some of the new states reacted by looking for allies and sponsors among the more powerful countries with which they shared historical or cultural affinities: thus, the Baltic States were increasingly turning to Scandinavian countries, the Moldovans to Romania, and the Azeris to Turkey.

Another option probed during 1992-1993 was that of creating new regional security associations or alliances. Having internalized the CSCE principles in its foreign and security policy documents, Ukraine, for example, soon found out that those principles had no guarantees. Thus, in February 1993, Ukrainian President Leonid Kravchuk proposed the establishment of a security system in the Baltic-Black Sea area, including eleven Central and Eastern European nations positioned between Russia and Germany. A

'Baltic-Black Sea Community' is also promoted by the opposition Popular Front in Belarus. Central Asian states have issued declarations on their intention for regional organizations, either among themselves or with the participation of the neighboring Moslem nations. So far, however, none of these alternatives, has proven viable.

The year 1993 witnessed the chronic political crisis in Russia degenerate into an armed battle between the forces of the presidency and those of the parliament in the center of Moscow. This was followed by a strong showing of extreme nationalist and Communist forces in the first free parliamentary election. Even before this reemergence of the specter of Russian imperialism, Moscow's policies in what it called the 'near abroad' had become markedly more assertive. Peacemaking by Russian troops in some of the new states was perceived as the sign of change in the Kremlin's attitudes. Interpreting this as a sign of things to come, the Central-East European countries intensified their efforts to get access to NATO, complete with the Alliance security guarantees.

On the other hand, most of the former Soviet republics, pressed by the economic crisis which had been partially caused by the dislocation in the wake of the Soviet Union's breakup, started rediscovering the CIS. In January 1993, the Commonwealth Charter was signed. In May, the Collective Security Treaty, a dead letter for the previous 12 months, went into force. Belarus, which had previously abstained, joined in. Armed cross-border incursions into Tajikistan from Afghanistan have helped to rally the governments of Central Asian countries around Russia which at last succeeded in organizing a framework for a multinational peacemaking force in Tajikistan. Military developments in Transcaucasia have made the leaders of Azerbaijan and Georgia seek membership in the CIS, while the Moldovan president proposed to do the same for economic reasons. Toward the end of the year, the prospects for an economic union within the CIS definitely improved. Belarus merged its financial system with Russia's. Moscow's special role in the Commonwealth was recognized in the symbolic election of President Yeltsin as the first chairman of the grouping.

Thus, two years into their independence, the former Soviet republics had to revise their initial perception of international institutions. The UN is now regarded largely as a symbol of international recognition or status (for Russia), but hardly as a world policeman. The CSCE is respected for its principles and for its egalitarianism, which ironically makes those principles difficult to enforce. The Council of Europe, with the obligations it imposes matching its prestige, is a distant goal for many republics, with the exception of the Baltic States. NATO, although its membership is still out of reach for the surviving nations of the former Soviet Union, also remains popular from the Baltic to the Caucasus. In January 1994, Lithuania became the first former republic to request membership officially. In Ukraine, most of the political *élite* and 40.6 per cent of the population are in favor of joining the Alliance; however, 45.3 per cent of Ukrainians support the country's nuclear status, despite international pressure. Only 35.5 per cent of respondents are against maintaining nuclear weapons.[4] According to President Kravchuk, Ukraine 'has become a full member of the international community' and now needs to become 'an influential European power'.[5] A resurgence of Ukrainian nationalism, however, may be as detrimental to the security of the post-Soviet area as the revival of imperialist tendencies elsewhere.

International Institutions and Conflict Resolution in the FSU

The perceptions described above are largely conditioned by the *élite* and by the popular evaluation of the performance of those institutions. The Soviet Union is a cluster of many actual and potential conflicts. Many of them are of a distinct ethnic character. As devised by Stalin, the Union of Soviet Socialist Republics was composed of 54 national territories enjoying various degrees of nominal autonomy. Although in 35 of these entities no interethnic conflicts were reported, as of the time of this writing (mid-1994), sixty disputes have taken place since the Soviet Union began to be dismantled. Thirty-two of these disputes degenerated into violent confrontations, while eight of them can be described as ethnic wars.[6] The fatalities have increased from 800 in 1991 to at least 50,000 in 1992 in Tajikistan alone.[7] The Azeri-Armenian conflict has claimed 16,000 lives so far.[8] While even the combined total is substantially lower than the number of victims in Bosnia-Herzegovina, post-Soviet conflicts may have with consequences that are potentially far worse than those in the ex-Yugoslavia.

The following sections of this chapter assess the performance of international institutions in conflict prevention, crisis management and dispute resolution in the former USSR.

Conflict prevention

It is generally recognized by the international security institutions that internal disputes over ethnic minorities within certain countries constitute a greater threat to peace in Europe than interstate disputes. This prompted the CSCE, to establish the post of a high commissioner for national minorities in July 1992. The situation of ethnic Russians in the newly independent states of the former Soviet Union is perhaps the greatest source of conflict.

Potential conflict areas in the ex-Soviet Union urgently requiring preventive care include the Baltic States (Russian minority rights and Russian troop presence), Ukraine (internal cohesion, status of ethnic and religious minorities and the whole complex of Russo-Ukrainian disputes including nuclear weapons, the Black Sea Fleet, and the status of Crimea), and Central Asia with its extremely arbitrary boundaries and numerous territorial claims. In Kazakhstan this is aggravated by the problem of ethnic Russians and the Russo-Kazakh border. A case apart is the 'non-issue' of Kaliningrad, the former Königsberg, the only exclave in Europe, which could be vulnerable, or threatening, or both.

Predictably, it is the Baltic States which receive the most attention from the international institutions. Special commissions from the UN Center for Human Rights, a CSCE mission in Estonia and frequent visits to the area by the CSCE High Commissioner for National Minorities, intervention by the Council of Europe, and subtle diplomacy by the Nordic and EU countries have contributed to the continuation of the internal dialogue between the local Russian communities and the governments in Riga, Tallinn, and Vilnius. This did not always work out to everyone's satisfaction. Losing its nerve in mid-1993, Russia even voiced opposition to Estonia's admission into the Council of Europe, only to discover that it had no veto rights on the subject. Snubbed by the Council, Moscow's diplomacy became convinced of an 'anti-Russian lobby' at work in Strasbourg. But a potentially provocatory Estonian law on aliens was amended, in July 1993; ethnic Russians were allowed to participate in municipal elections and won a major share in the local government bodies. But the conflict is far from over.

On the other hand, NATO expressed concern over the lack of clarity on Russian military withdrawal from the Baltic States. The Russian military, worried about what they interpret as NATO's excessive interest in an area so close to Russia's nerve centers, has been trying to link the withdrawal of its troops from Estonia and Latvia to a satisfactory solution to the problem of Russian minorities in those two countries.

Unlike relations with of the Baltic States, Russo-Ukrainian relations are less susceptible to intervention by international institutions. The UN Security Council denunciation, in July 1993, of a Russian Supreme Soviet resolution on the Crimea/Sebastopol issue was made possible only because of the conscious decision by the Russian government to have its parliament internationally exposed as a war-monger. This seems to have been mainly symbolic; On the other hand, NATO's threat, in the fall of 1993, to freeze cooperation with Ukraine until it formally renounces all claims to nuclear weapons now on its territory and ratifies the NPT is a clear form of international pressure.

On the whole, Moscow's attempts at international condemnation of the 'irresponsible' Ukraine, and Kiev's efforts to seek Western security guarantees to keep 'Russian imperialism' at bay appear to offer very limited (and sometimes controversial) results. There seems to be no substitute for seeking compromise between the two largest former Soviet republics through serious dialogue.

Central Asia is as yet largely 'out of bounds' for international institutional involvement. This leaves room for major neighboring states (Russia, Iran, Turkey, Pakistan, India and China) to play an active role, but given the competition between them, they are not likely to contribute to conflict-prevention. As to Kaliningrad, it is probably considered by international institutions as too sensitive an issue to be approached directly.

Conflict management

Several conflicts in the FSU have degenerated into violent crises: Nagorny Karabakh, South Ossetia, Moldova, Abkhazia, Tajikistan, Western Georgia. For the first time, the United Nations and the CSCE had to deal with areas on the periphery of the FSU which had been relatively unknown to the outside world. Top international functionaries paid official visits there; fact-finding missions were sent to collect information and present reports; permanent monitoring stations were set up to keep track of new developments. The UN Security Council took up the cases of Karabakh and Abkhazia.

For example, when a cease-fire agreement was reached in Abkhazia, the UN and CSCE provided military observers to monitor it.[9] The CSCE started looking into the Karabakh conflict as early as 1990, when it was still an internal Soviet confrontation. Initially, its efforts were confined to providing humanitarian assistance to refugees and victims of artillery bombardments. In 1992, the CSCE started a negotiating process (the Minsk Conference) to settle the Karabakh dispute by peaceful means. While the good offices offered by the UN Secretary General in the summer of 1993 and the shuttle diplomacy of his personal representative failed to prevent a new eruption of violence in the Abkhazia conflict, the UN was instrumental in bringing Abkhazian and Georgian representatives together in Geneva for face-to-face talks later in the same year. Various international organizations, (including non-governmental ones) have been very active in providing humanitarian assistance, and particularly aid to the refugees of the various conflicts.

Post-conflict dispute resolution
With the acute phase of the crisis now over in some of the cases mentioned above, international organizations have been attempting to play a constructive role in dispute resolution. Thus, a special CSCE mission to Moldova was given the task to help formulate the status of the country's eastern region, monitor the human rights situation in Moldova and look into the problem of the withdrawal of Russia's 14th army from Transdnestria. International experts have also been asked to present their proposals for an eventual settlement in Abkhazia.

In an attempt to promote internal stability in the newly independent states, international organizations have been willing to send observers to monitor elections and referenda. Both Edward Shevardnadze's government in Georgia and Gaidar Aliev's presidency in Azerbaijan owe their legitimacy largely to the presence of international observers during elections there in 1993.

The performance of international organizations has not been

perceived in the same way by the new countries themselves. Azerbaijan and Georgia were disappointed over the slowness of the Security Council reaction with respect to offensive from Armenia and Abkhazia. In the latter case, there was bitter disappointment when only 22 of the planned 88 UN observers had arrived before the resumption of the Abkhazian offensive and were then unable to carry out their mission. (By the end of 1993, the number of UN observers had dwindled to 8). In other cases, the credibility of international organizations, such as the CSCE, was occasionally put into question (i.e. by Azerbaijan, which found CSCE actions in October 1993, at variance with the UN Security Council resolutions 822 and 853).

Some governments took action to influence international organizations, either directly, or indirectly through the more prominent member states of these organizations or world public opinion. The Azerbaijani foreign ministry adopted the practice of organizing guided tours to the war zones for the ambassadors of the five permanent members of the UN Security Council. The Georgian leader, while appealing to the international community, (especially the UN) for help, made maximum use of his personal contacts with his US and German counterparts.

Following the pattern of the national liberation movements of the 1960s and the 1970s, the self-proclaimed republics of Abkhazia, Karabakh and Transdnestria have been trying to use international organizations (primarily the UN and the CSCE) to win a measure of international recognition. Karabakh Armenians have been attempting to do this through the Minsk peace talks, while the Abkhazians have offered the UN a referendum on the sovereignty issue. Nevertheless, all these self-proclaimed entities have learned to rely more on their military prowess.

While all sides in the conflicts appealed to the world public for support, the media devoted comparatively little attention to the troubled spots in the former Soviet Union. The intensive media reporting which created high public awareness of other world crises (sometimes called the 'CNN factor) was singularly absent. Consequently, there has been virtually no public pressure in favor of international intervention in any of the former republics.

Based on their perceived records individual organizations clearly enjoy very different standing in the eyes of the *élites* in the post-Soviet countries. The United Nations has continued to be universally respected by Russia and the new states. For the former, currently in a period of weakness, an active UN is a guarantee against domination drives by other, more powerful states. Russia's permanent membership in the Security Council, a status symbol in itself, ensures that the world body will take no action against Russian interests.[10] For the other new republics, participation in the UN serves the purpose of nation-building. On a more practical level, the UN is not considered to be particularly effective in dealing with ongoing crises. Within the Ukrainian political *élite*, for instance, there is uneasiness over Russia's privileged position within the organization.

The CSCE, long a favorite with Soviet diplomacy as the preferred version of a pan-European security structure, has preserved its high standing with Moscow. Russia wants the CSCE to become a regional organization in its own right, a mini-UN, complete with a scaled-down version of a Security Council. Russian academics have been offering proposals for building up the CSCE to enable it deal with inter-ethnic strife in Europe.[11] Even so, some Russian diplomats have been voicing private complaints that Washington has been using the 'Minsk Conference' on Nagorny Karabakh to reduce the Russian role and influence in Transcaucasia and to make the United States into the arbiter among the various powers in the region.[12].

From the perspective of some other republics, the CSCE has become too large without improving its conflict-resolution mechanisms. More limited mutual security combinations of neighboring states are proposed as a complement and perhaps an alternative in Ukraine and in the Baltic. In Central Asia, interest in a reinvigorated CSCE is not self-evident. Kazakhstan and Uzbekistan, however, are making proposals for the creation of a regional security (sub)system or, alternatively, the establishment of closer bilateral links in the hope of bringing conflicts under some control.[13].

NATO has taken a very discreet public role in the affairs of the FSU countries, where developments are certainly of great interest to the Alliance. It appears that its policies largely depend on the assessment of the development of the political and socio-economic situation in Russia. One proposed step—an enlargement of NATO eastward to incorporate the Visegrad countries of East Central Europe—provoked a major controversy in the fall and winter of

1993-1994, involving the West, the Central Europeans and Russia.

While the proponents of NATO's expansion pointed to the deterrence value of that measure in view of Russia's potential imperialist inclinations (e.g. concerning Ukraine, which, incidentally, was to be left out), its opponents argued that the effect was likely to be the opposite: it would serve to strengthen the authoritarian, chauvinistic and aggressive forces within Russia. One probable result of a NATO enlargement which did not include Russia would be a powerful move to include Belarus and, above all, Ukraine, into a Moscow-led military alliance. This would recreate Europe's security divisions somewhat further to the east.

At its Brussels summit in January 1994, NATO adopted the US-proposed concept of a 'Partnership for Peace' (PFP). This invites NACC members and other CSCE countries to 'participate in political and military bodies at NATO Headquarters' in the hope that this cooperation will 'increase stability', and 'diminish threats to peace' throughout Europe. NATO would consult with any active participant which feels its territorial integrity, political independence, or security directly threatened. Specific areas of practical cooperation and expansion of liaison facilities have also been offered.[14] The governments of Russia, Ukraine and Belarus promptly welcomed the offer.

The Partnership for Peace is likely to involve strengthening the NACC. This Council, which started as a symbolic gesture, has established itself as a modest, but useful forum for political and strategic dialogue in the field of international security. It has a very practical approach to peace support operations,[15] and suggestions have been offered to transform the Council gradually into a new security association, surpassing and succeeding NATO. This appears to be Moscow's preference: at the NACC meeting in December 1993, the Russian foreign minister proposed institutionalizing political consultations and developing procedures leading 'almost to' mutual assistance commitments. The European Union and the Western European Union, by contrast, have taken a comparatively low profile in post-Soviet conflict resolution, which may be explained by their political and structural problems.

Despite initial hopes and renewed enthusiasm, the Commonwealth of Independent States so far has been unable to function as a conflict-resolution agency. Although both Armenia and Azerbaijan are now CIS members, this in itself has not brought the settlement of the Karabakh dispute any closer. Most political negotiations have taken place on a bilateral basis, and it took the CIS more than 20 months to mount its first peacekeeping operation (in Tajikistan), which remains largely a Russian affair.

Potential Capabilities of International Organizations

International organizations provide a range of capabilities which could be used to prevent, manage or resolve disputes in the FSU. In all cases, the institutions should remain credible guarantors of national independence and territorial integrity of the new states, and guardians of the rights of their citizens and minorities.

Conflict prevention
Global monitoring of human rights could provide the international community with an early warning system. There seems to be a good argument for expanding the activities of the Office of the High Commissioner for National Minorities and of the Conflict Prevention Center of the CSCE which, at present, have extremely limited capacities.

Other potential sources of conflict should not be ignored. Thus, the disastrous ecological situation in Central Asia and the issue of water rights in the region should be seriously addressed. The specialized UN agencies, and international economic organizations, which have considerable experience in this field, should be asked to address the former Soviet Union, a new area of potential disaster for the 1990s. A specialized international agency such as the IAEA is also capable of keeping a close watch on nuclear powerplants and chemical installations in the FSU. More should be done to preserve the intellectual potential of Russia's 'atomic cities'; otherwise, by the end of the decade, when these issues are expected to come to the fore with even greater urgency, Russia will not have enough experts to deal with them.

Confidence-building measures, including monitoring conventional arms transfers and tracking down illegal arms trafficking within the former USSR could also be handled by international agencies, such as the CSCE Security Forum and the CSCE Conflict Prevention Center (provided the latter is expanded).

International mediation of disputes is extremely important. Informal talks could be organized, adopting, where appropriate, the 'Norway model' used by the Israelis and the Palestinians. A meeting of Azeri and Armenian parliamentarians in the Aland Islands (December, 1993) is another possibility.

Crisis Management
International organizations (primarily the UN, but also the CSCE) could engage in traditional peacekeeping in the areas of crisis of the FSU. This would largely include cease-fire monitoring (setting up observation posts to monitor compliance). One area where this appears possible is along the Dnester River and around the town of Bendery in Moldova. The deployment of multinational forces as a buffer between the conflicting parties is another traditional mission to be taken up. Both Abkhazia and Karabakh call for this kind of international involvement. Without such a presence, any eventual cease-fire agreement is likely to be broken.

If a peace agreement had already been reached, but the partners do not trust each other, the experience of the Multilateral Force in Sinai could be useful. It appears that Armenia and Azerbaijan may have to consider this option. While some new countries (Georgia, Moldova) and political groups (e.g. in Ukraine) at one time or another spoke in favor of inviting NATO forces as peacekeepers, this, even if it were feasible, would clearly be counterproductive. Not only would the Russian military see this as a challenge, but Moscow's overall strategic orientation could change as a result.

Regional arrangements could be a way to help manage conflicts threatening several countries. Thus, Central Asian nations should be encouraged to cooperate among themselves as a regional group within the CSCE framework. To make the regional approach credible, non-CSCE countries, as Iran in Transcaucasia and Pakistan in Central Asia, may be asked to join in.

Post-conflict Resolution
Some of the more recent patterns of action by the international community could be applied to some post-Soviet situations. Upholding law and order in areas torn by internal strife (such as Georgia or Tajikistan) would require mounting an international civil

police force, as in Namibia. Demobilization of local forces and their disarmament would have to be the prerequisite to national dialogue and reconciliation, especially in Georgia and Tajikistan. Central American examples (Nicaragua, Honduras) might be helpful. In seemingly intractable cases, establishing a temporary international protectorate for organizing elections (as in Cambodia) may be worthwhile option according to some analysts.[16]

International assistance in nation-building should be accompanied by clear insistence on observing human rights, protecting the rights of minorities and strengthening democratic institutions, including reforming the military along democratic lines. Also, compulsory dispute settlement through international mediation might be a condition for international aid and support.

Prospects of International Involvement in FSU Crises

One conclusion which may be drawn from the previous section is that international organizations are much more effective either before a conflict enters the crisis phase, or after the period of intensive confrontation has passed. Practical world-wide experience seems to suggest the same. Thus, conflict prevention and post-conflict dispute resolution in the former USSR are the two areas in which international organizations can do the most. Active crisis management, especially if it involves using force, is something these organizations are not well suited to do.

International organizations have important advantages over individual actors: consistency, impartiality, non-selectivity, non-politicization, universality or regionality (whichever is more appropriate), preference for dialogue over physical intervention. Their disadvantages, however, are just as evident: they are increasingly reluctant to become engaged in conflict resolution, and when they do, there is not enough coordination among them; their authority depends on the cooperation of their leading members, few of whom feel compelled to engage themselves. As far as the conflicts in the former USSR are concerned, it is the interaction between the various international institutions and Russia which is of paramount importance in managing post-Soviet instability.

When defining its national interests, Russia declared the former Soviet republics as zones vitally important to its security.[17] Among the 'sources of external military danger', Russia's new military doctrine specifically cites actual or potential hotbeds of local wars and military conflicts 'in direct proximity of Russian borders, . . . suppression of rights, liberties and legitimate interests of citizens of the Russian Federation in foreign states, . . . attacks on military installations of the armed forces of the Russian Federation in the territory of foreign states', and international terrorism. These dangers would be upgraded to 'direct military threats' if Russian borders, or those of its allies, came under attack; if armed groups were organized for the purpose of infiltration into the territory of Russia or her allies; or if foreign troops were deployed to the countries on Russia's periphery, unless they were peacekeeping forces acting under an international mandate with Russia's support.[18]

Russia's interest in stabilizing its immediate periphery is genuine. There is a real danger of a spill-over effect, as in the Caucasus region, for example, where the abandoned conflict in Karabakh has generated regional instability, producing hundreds of thousands of refugees, encouraging illicit arms transfers and providing training to would-be fighters in other local conflicts. By the same token, inter-ethnic wars in South Ossetia and Abkhazia have had a destabilizing effect on Russia's own North Caucasian frontier, contributing to provoke the first armed conflict within the Federation (between the Ossetians and the Ingushi) and putting into question Russia's territorial integrity. Russia is clearly worried about the potential spread of 'Islamic extremism' from Afghanistan and Tajikistan into Central Asia and Kazakhstan, which has a 7,200 km border with Russia that is totally unguarded and indefensible.

While the West has been concerned about the flow of immigrants from the FSU, it is Russia which, for the moment, has to shoulder the main burden. In only 12 months in 1992-93, Russia has received some 2 million refugees and economic immigrants. Officials from Russia's Federal Migration Service predict an influx of additional 4 to 6 million people before the end of 1995, of which 400 thousand are expected to arrive from Transcaucasia, 600 thousand from the Baltic States, and some 3 million from Central Asia.[19] Russia's own resources are admittedly inadequate for dealing with an influx of refugees/immigrants of such proportions.

Initially, the Russians were ambivalent about any outside participation in peacekeeping operations within the FSU. Plans for

Romanian and Bulgarian units to police the ceasefire in Moldova alongside with Russian and Ukrainian elements in July 1992 had to be abandoned at the last moment, probably because of the opposition from the military. Later, however, this position began to change. In late February 1993, Russia asked for a UN mandate to conduct peace operations in the former Soviet republics. In November of the same year, a similar request was addressed to the CSCE Council of Ministers.

Predictably, this raised a number of serious objections. Russia's actions from Moldova to the Caucasus to Tajikistan represented a radical departure from standard UN peacekeeping practices: Russian national interests were directly affected (and therefore there was no impartiality); Russian troops were often used to support one party in an internal conflict (and therefore the action was highly politicized); and the methods employed, for example, in Tajikistan, were all too reminiscent of the Soviet Union's previous Afghan involvement.[20]. It would be wrong for the international community to give Russia a free hand in the former USSR (minus the Baltic) in exchange for Moscow's unquestioned support of Western policies elsewhere.

The present Russian government, however, does not agree with this costly unilateralism. Russia remains a strong supporter of building up the peacekeeping capabilities of the UN, including the revitalization and reform of its Military Staff Committee, for both traditional peacekeeping and Chapter VII operations. The Russian foreign minister has made a reference to the possible creation of a clear political chain of responsibility from the UN and the CSCE to NACC, NATO, the WEU and the CIS. While Russia is especially interested in institutionalizing a UN-CIS link,[21] it disagrees with the UN Secretary-General's proposal that Russians help make peace in Asia and Africa, while Asians, Africans and Latin Americans are given a similar job in the former USSR.[22] This is not viewed as realistic: were Russian peacemaking forces suddenly withdrawn from Moldova and South Ossetia, a resumption of violence is considered likely. This does not mean that Russia remains averse to foreign troop presence (as peacekeepers) within the borders of the former USSR; troop contingents from neutral CSCE countries are welcome to take part in multilateral operations.[23]

Any UN/CSCE-Russia/CIS interaction in the field of peace operations should be based on a set of clear principles, including agreement of all parties to the conflict; impartiality; recognition of sovereignty and territorial integrity of states; multilateral nature of operations; continuous international monitoring. Operations should be authorized on a case-by-case basis, so that international approval is not perceived as a blank check, as some countries (as Estonia) fear. There is also a genuine interest in Russia for turning the CSCE into a full-fledged organization to promote regional security and stability. In particular, Moscow would like to see the mandate of the High Commissioner for National Minorities expanded. Thus, Russia is prepared to rely on international institutions—from the UN to the CIS—in an effort to protect the rights of ethnic Russian minorities in the former Soviet republics.

But it is the CIS which may become the prime 'subcontractor' of the international community when dealing with post-Soviet conflicts. The Commonwealth is not doomed to be an instrument of Russian domination; on the contrary, the new independent states may discover that they have a greater chance to air and defend their interests (also vis-à-vis Russia) in the CIS than in bilateral arrangements with Moscow. A CIS-wide approach to the twin issues of national minorities (including the 'Russian question', which is potentially most dangerous) and borders, combined with the institutionalization of multilateralism, could introduce more stability and predictability into the process of post-Soviet reorganization. At least equally important is the assumption that only stronger cooperation among the CIS member-states and coordinated reform policies could arrest further decline in economic well-being and living standards which is behind most conflicts. Two conditions are essential here: an active participation by non-Russian CIS members (primarily the more influential among them, such as Ukraine, Kazakhstan, Uzbekistan and Belarus) in the Commonwealth's conflict-resolution activities; and a realistic arrangement between the CIS, on the one hand, and the UN and the CSCE, on the other.

The results of the December 1993 parliamentary election in Russia have underlined one of the most important tasks of current international politics: to prevent Russia from sliding into self-isolation and new imperialism. Engaging Russia into ever closer cooperation with international security institutions could contribute substantially to meeting that goal.

Conclusions

International security institutions have both a duty and a potential
for greater involvement in conflict resolution in the former Soviet
Union. Failure to do so would not only undermine the credibility of
these institutions, but would likely contribute to a sweeping Balkanization of large parts of the ex-USSR, with all its adverse
consequences. As of the spring of 1994, however, the results of the
involvement of these institutions (primarily, the UN, the CSCE, the
European Union, the Council of Europe, NATO, NACC) in the
post-Soviet area have been modest. Clearly, they recognize the
danger of over-extension beyond their current capabilities. More
important, however, is the lack of interest on behalf of the leading
members of those institutions in the problem areas. Though the
institutions have some potential, their members have little will to
act.

Russia seems to be the only major power which feels its vital
interests endangered by the growing instability on its periphery. Its
actions in the 'near abroad', however, are far from the standards set
by the international institutions. Moreover, Russia has not yet
achieved internal stability, which accounts for the inconsistencies
and general lack of transparency in Moscow's policies. The
composition of the first State Duma reflects the growing danger of
Russian nationalism. Thus, Russia can and will act—but its
unilateralism adds to the problems. International passivity and
Russia's over-engagement do not offer an optimal solution to the
post-Soviet conflicts. Ways should be found to combine
substantially increased activity of the institutions with a markedly
more restrained and responsible Russian attitude.

Preventing new conflicts and the deterioration of existing
tensions should be given clear priority. Encouraging and facilitating
dialogue could be supplemented with 'soft' or 'hard' mediation.
The CSCE appears especially well-suited to preventive diplomacy,
and the Council of Europe is an appropriate venue for facilitating
democratic transformation of post-Communist societies.

In the field of conflict management, international institutions
(e.g. the UN and/or the CSCE) could commission Russia and the
new independent states of the CIS to engage in multilateral peace
support operations in the territory of the former USSR, provided
that these operations are closely monitored by the authorizing

institutions, which establish their own presence in the field (observers/monitors, liaison officers with CIS units, troop contingents, etc.).

In most cases, dispute resolution will require mobilizing substantial economic and financial resources. In the short to medium term this appears possible only if Russia and the new independent states agree, within the framework of the CIS Economic Union, on the terms of trade and a system of settling mutual accounts; realistically, this would also keep the markets of the former Soviet republics open to all of them. For any new arrangement economic arrangement to be viable, however, the initiative for its creation should come from outside Russia. In the long term, much will depend on the form that future economic relations between the former Soviet republics and the EU will take. A 'Fortress Europe' will surely perpetuate crises around its walls.

Finally, the institutions (e.g. the Council of Europe, NATO and the European Union) could make full use of the respect they command in the former Soviet republics to create incentives for eventual membership, on condition that certain standards are met and maintained. Realistic plans for gradual integration could be then drawn up.

Notes

1. *Kontseptsiya Natsionalnoy Bezpeki Ukraini* (Concept for the National Defense of Ukraine), Section 1, 1993.

2. See, for instance, the declarations of national sovereignty passed by the Supreme Soviets of Ukraine and Belarus in 1990.

3. See the article by the former President of the Russian Parliament, Khasbulatov, Ruslan: 'Vozmozhna li «balkanizatsiya» Rossii' (The possibility of the «balkanization» of Russia), *Rossiyskaya Gazeta*, 27 May 1993.

4. *Nezavisimaya Gazeta*, 13 November 1993.

5. *Polityka i chas*, 1993, No.8, p.25.

6. *Rossiyskaya Gazeta*, 28 August 1993.

7. *Izvestia*, 29 September 1993.

8. *Le Monde*, 24 december 1993, p.5.

9. See the Sochi agreement on Abkhazia; text in *Nezavisimaya Gazeta*, 29 July 1993.

10. See 'Kontseptsiya vneshney politiki Rossiyskoy Federatsii' (Concepts for the Foreign Policy of Russia) *Diplomaticheskiy vestnik*, 1993, Special Issue.

11. Baranovski, Vladimir: 'Ispytanie na razryv', (Rupture Test) *Moskovskie Novosti*, No.3, 17 January 1993.

12. Mlechin, Leonid: 'Konflikt rossiyskoy i amerikanskoy diplomatii iz-za Nagornogo Karabakha' (Conflict between the Russian and American Diplomacies over Nagorno-Karabakh), in *Izvestia*, 13 November 1993.

13. For the Uzbek point of view, see Tazmukhamedov, Rais: 'Uzbekistan v mirovoy politike', (Uzbekistan in World Politics) *Nezavisimaya Gazeta*, 20 October 1993.

14. *Partnership for Peace. Invitation and Framework Document*, M-1(94)2, (Brussels: NATO Office of Information and Press, 10 January 1994).

15. Report of the NACC Ad Hoc Group on Cooperation in Peacekeeping, *NATO Review*, 1993, August, pp.30-35.

16. Rogov, Sergei (Ed.): *Rol' OON i drugikh mezhdunarodnykh organizatsiy v uregulirovanii konfliktov na territorii byvshego Sovetskogo Soyuza* (The Role of the UN and Other International Organizations in the Resolution of Conflicts on the Territory of the Former Soviet Union), (Moscow: Center for international Security/Russian UN Association, 1993), p.14.

17. Chernov, Vladislav: 'Osnovnye polozheniya kontseptsii vneshney politiki Rossiyskoy Federatsii' (Basic Concepts in the Foreign Policy of the Russian Federation), in *Nezavisimaya Gazeta*, 29 April 1993.

18. *Osnovnye polozheniya voyennoy doktriny Rossii*, (Fundamentals of the Military Doctrine of the Russian Federation) adopted by Presidential decree on 2 November 1993. See also *Krasnaya Zvezda*, 19 November 1993.

19. *Segodnya*, 13 November 1993.

20. See, for example, a very critical report by 'Helsinki Watch' in *Nezavisimaya Gazeta*, 9 November 1993.

21. Kozyrev, Andrei: 'OON: trevogi i nadezhdy mira' (The UN: Anxiety and Hope of the World), *Rossiyskaya Gazeta*, 30 October 1993.

22. *Izvestia*, 29 October 1993.

23. See Andrei Kozyrev's speech to the UN General Assembly, reported in *Nezavisimaya Gazeta*, 22 September 1993.

5 Should NATO Be Enlarged to the East?

Jamie Shea

The question of whether NATO should enlarge to the countries of Central and Eastern Europe (C&EE), and if so, when and how, has become controversial. This issue has sprung to the fore for two main reasons. On the one hand, following the violent clashes in Moscow in October 1993, and the triumph of Vladimir Zhirinovsky in the December elections, the fear of many Central Europeans of a return to imperialist ambitions in Russia is more acute, and their need for security guarantees, or at minimum some kind of reassurance, is correspondingly greater. Visiting NATO Headquarters in December 1993, Polish Foreign Minister Olechowski reported that recent polls in Poland revealed that twice as many respondents feared for the sovereignty and security of Poland than just a few months before.

On the other hand, the growing influence of both far right and neo-communists in Russia, with the military forces gaining more sway over policy-making, gives the Alliance every cause to be cautious about enlargement for fear of alienating Russia, thus undermining the position of the democrats by giving ammunition to the communist-nationalist coalition. At a time when the democratization process is at a crucial phase, this is a risk which cannot be taken—no matter how much Alliance policy-makers dislike being held hostage to the vagaries of Russian domestic politics.

The subject of NATO enlargement has generated great debate. The best way to address it is to clarify some fundamentals first, and then give some idea about how a middle ground can be found between the *Scylla* of frustrating the aspirations of the C&EE states and the *Charybdis* of marginalizing the most important security variable, for better or for worse: Russia. The worst thing for the Alliance would be to do nothing; this would only precipitate the quest of C&EE states for alternative forms of security (which could well prove to be destabilizing) while comforting Moscow's perceptions that even a weak Russia can exercise an effective *droit de regard* over both the fate of Central Europe and NATO's decision-making.

In the Atlantic Alliance, one thing stands out: it has never been simply Atlantic. From its inception, Italy was included, giving NATO a Mediterranean dimension. In 1952, Greece and Turkey joined, thereby making it an Eastern Mediterranean Alliance. Moreover, the defensive perimeter has moved about a thousand kilometers to the East. In 1949, it was on the Rhine, as Germany was not a member yet. When Germany became a member, in 1954, the perimeter moved to the Elbe. More recently, in the wake of German unification in 1990, it moved to the Oder. The Alliance jumped from eleven original members to sixteen. Can one argue that these previous phases of the expansion of NATO have led to a loss of cohesion, or to a breakdown in NATO's ability to fulfil its fundamental task of territorial defense by providing security guarantees?

To the historical experience can be added a simple and unavoidable moral imperative. The Western community of democracies would have missed a historic opportunity to anchor the C&EE countries into their structures if they had not made it very clear that they are, in principle, willing to open the Alliance. This was done in January 1994, at the NATO Summit, when the Allies stated that they would 'welcome and expect' NATO's enlargement as a process over time. The fact that enlargement is not an immediate possibility is not an obstacle, but rather a positive inducement to initiate the process that will eventually lead to it. The perception of insecurity in C&EE countries is real. It cannot be dismissed even in the absence of declared hostile intentions.

Russia may no longer be a military threat for the West, because it is now 1500 kilometers away (at least in military strategic terms) from where it was in the days of the Cold War and the division of Europe. But the C&EE region is more vulnerable to instability and more sensitive to modest changes in the strategic balance than is the West. Security is not only about palpable threats, but also about perceptions. One has to *feel* secure to be secure. If one does not feel secure oneself, one is likely to engender feelings of insecurity in one's neighbors as well. To the extent that NATO can reduce this sense of a security vacuum, it will lift some of the pressure it is currently under to provide security guarantees—thereby winning the time it needs to devise an acceptable formula, both internal and external, for enlargement.

In any case, it is apparent to Alliance policymakers that, whatever decision they make on enlargement, they cannot escape responsibility for the security of their Eastern neighbors. Integration is already taking place little by little. If one looks at the current dynamics of cooperation, there are now plans for joint peacekeeping training and exercises and even for cooperation in defense planning within the framework of the fourth annual workplan of the North Atlantic Cooperation Council (NACC). There is agreement to discuss air defense, and common endeavors are under way in fields like civil emergency planning, armaments cooperation and resource management. Thus, there is going to be—if these programs are fulfilled—a *de facto* integration of these C&EE countries into Western security structures, from the bottom upwards as it were, over the next few years.

The distinction between the rights and duties of members and non-members is going to become blurred. A kind of NATO I and NATO II is almost inevitable. Once the Alliance has accepted, as it did in Copenhagen nearly three years ago, that the security of C&EE states is its 'direct and material concern', it is committed to provide some form of post-aggression response even if it eschews pre-aggression guarantees or military deterrence. The closer the interaction, the more C&EE states will expect that response to be a firm one and the more NATO states will feel duty-bound to provide it. If this creeping integration is inevitable, it is best for the Alliance to recognize it from the outset and to try to steer the process consciously. In other words, it would be better if the aspirants to NATO membership were admitted in normal peacetime circumstances (in ways which minimize the prospect of new instabilities) than if a situation developed whereby NATO would steer clear of accepting responsibility for potential members only to dramatically reverse this policy if instabilities spin out of control and engender real military threats. The Central and Eastern Europeans may suddenly be faced with such a threat, and NATO may have to extend security guarantees in the middle of a crisis, knowing that such a precipitate step would be as likely to escalate as to defuse that crisis.

World War I started because security guarantees had to be clarified in the middle of a crisis, most notably from Britain to Belgium. In World War II, it was from Britain to Poland. In both cases, a political guarantee was extended against the background of inadequate military arrangements. Not surprisingly, such an ambivalent commitment is all too easily misinterpreted by potential aggressors as evidence of weakness, when in reality democracies tend to uphold their treaty commitments, even if not always enthusiastically. The consequences proved disastrous (in 1914 and 1939). If the extension of guarantees would have most probably have to be accepted in a crisis situation anyway, then it is best that this be planned beforehand and made abundantly clear. There is still time and scope to design offsets and alternative arrangements for those who can neither be given a binding guarantee in the near term nor be confined to a security vacuum.

Objections to NATO's Expansion to the East

There are six basic objections to the near-term enlargement of NATO. The remainder of this chapter will consider each in turn.

The EU/WEU Alternative

The first objection posits that it is best if these countries join the European Union (EU) and the Western European Union (WEU) first. In other words, the argument runs, if the EU is prepared to accept them, then, but only then, so should NATO. This has numerous advantages, most notably it means that NATO's member-ship does not have to be enlarged for perhaps another fifteen years. This leaves plenty of time to work out a *modus operandi*. Also, NATO would then be providing a security guarantee to countries which would need it less and would be less likely to call on it. This is because the EU criteria are so demanding in terms of democrati-zation, treatment of minorities, economic market reforms, and political stability, that any EU member to join NATO would already have largely stabilized its internal and external environment through its own efforts.

In a sense, what is being argued is that sound economics create security and that security comes from a momentum of economic development and a certain *per capita* standard of living. It is indeed self-evident that security and social stability come as much from an opening of Western markets as from the extension of Western security guarantees. But realistically this will be a long time coming, and, as Keynes memorably said, . . . in the long run we will all be dead.

After World War II the founding fathers of the Alliance saw things rather differently; to extend military security was to create a climate of confidence and stability which allowed governments not to overspend on weapons, or to shut themselves off from their neighbors, but to use their scarce resources for infrastructure renewal, for education, and for social reform. This created a climate of confidence for investment and for undertaking projects in the safe knowledge that things were going to be stable in the years ahead. Today, there is little evidence in Central and Eastern Europe for believing that the process of economic reform will continue in the absence of some kind of security umbrella.

Therefore, the notion that these countries should join the EU first, and only thereafter NATO, is fundamentally wrong. They are not in the same situation as the neutral and non-aligned countries of Europe (Austria, Sweden, Finland and Switzerland), in terms of economic, strategic, or historical experience. They have not found security and prosperity by occupying the middle ground between great powers. For them, independence means the choice and practice of alignment, not that of keeping a distance. To the extent that these countries have a security umbrella, they are more likely to stay the course and meet the criteria for membership of the European Union over time.

Maintenance of NATO Cohesion

The second argument is that of cohesion. This hinges on the belief that NATO performs well with sixteen members, and that seventeen would create disruption. It would be comparable to an Arab sheik who has sixteen wives but would become dysfunctional if he took on an additional one. Somehow, sixteen is portrayed as a kind of magic number which ensures cohesion whereas seventeen is its antithesis. Why, or how, is the question.

Cohesion in the Alliance has always been based not on numbers, but on the sharing of common democratic values. In fact, the Alliance of sixteen genuine democracies that has existed in recent years (since the return of democracy to Portugal, Greece and Turkey) has enjoyed greater legitimacy, and has even been able to assume a more active and outward-looking role, than the Alliance of eleven of the 1950s that was indeed smaller but more narrowly focussed and had some non-democratic countries in its midst.

Avoidance of Instability

It is alleged that enlargement would produce instabilities. Instead of exporting security to C&EE states, their insecurity would be brought into the Alliance. This translates into a dilemma for NATO: either it takes them in, and tries to deal with their problems, or the latter will grow and affect NATO anyway, sooner or later.

There has been much commentary of late pointing out that the new kind of security problems (refugees, organized crime, drugs, the spread of regional conflicts and the proliferation of weapons of mass destruction) cross national boundaries with ease and undermine neighboring states far more readily than the old type of security problem (for instance, thirty Soviet motor, rifle, and tank divisions in Central and Eastern Europe) which largely proved self-deterring and produced an automatic counter-reaction from NATO. Thus, if one is not actively spreading security, one is increasing one's vulnerability to insecurity. The situation cannot be frozen in a timeless balance of calculable forces. It is rather like the image EU Commission President Delors evoked of riding bicycle: if you are not perpetually going forward, you'll fall off.

Extending Security Guarantees?

The fourth objection is one of the strongest against the expansion of NATO: it has to do with the extension of security guarantees (as provided in Article 5 of the Treaty) which membership would imply. Are we willing, *du jour au lendemain,* to guarantee the security of other states, especially when defense budgets and the political will to undertake additional commitments tends to decline?

NATO has never provided a legally binding security guarantee committing its members to the use of force in mutual defense. When the Alliance was founded in 1949, US Secretary of State Dean Acheson was asked to testify before the Senate Foreign Relations Committee. He was asked by Senator Vandenberg whether NATO's ratification meant that American troops were going back to Europe, and answered 'no'. Had he said 'yes', there would probably not have been a NATO to begin with, because Congress would not have ratified the Washington Treaty. In other words, the Americans clearly accepted NATO because it did not commit them to a binding security guarantee.

Instead, it was seen as providing political reassurance, and if push came to shove, the Americans would provide air support and logistics. It was the Korean War which produced US ground troops in Western Europe, not the Washington Treaty. NATO's security guarantee has always been much more a question of day-to-day cooperation, joint exercises, and military integration than of binding obligations. The credible guarantee has been the practice of 'doing' security together, not the legal document. The WEU Treaty is far more explicit on mutual military guarantees than is the NATO Treaty.

Thus, in many respects, to the extent that NATO 'does' security with C&EE countries, through military contacts and exchanges, such as the joint manoeuvres initiated by the US, the UK, France, Denmark and Germany, it is providing a security guarantee. NATO countries are willy nilly taking on obligations that go beyond the standard notion of collective security, even if they stop short of giving formal guarantees before they join.

For example, a potential aggressor would have to ponder carefully the degree of interaction a C&EE country has with NATO before it attacked. Country X may not have a formal security guarantee from NATO, but it is very friendly to NATO: they do joint exercises and peacekeeping operations, their military work closely together, and they are a part of the same air defense and communication systems. Would an aggressor attack that country? Most probably not, because clearly the Alliance would have a moral commitment to defend it. And no matter how reluctant democracies are to accept moral commitments before a crisis, they usually do so when the crisis is upon them.

What is important for an effective security guarantee is not how much confidence a Pole, a Czech, or a Ukrainian has in it, but how much credibility it has in the eyes of the potential aggressor. What is inadequate for one may be perfectly adequate for another. Military cooperation without a formal security guarantee may therefore ironically be more valuable than the converse.

There is another point to be considered here. Is NATO really worried about country X in Central Europe attacking country Y, both of which would be NATO members? This is an eventuality that has long preoccupied the Alliance in view of the strained relations between Greece and Turkey. To whom would the security guarantee apply? Here, the WEU offers a useful model. When Turkey became an associate member two years ago, Greece, which at the same time became a full member, was persuaded to sign a protocol saying that the Article Five guarantee of the WEU Treaty would not apply in the case of a Greco-Turkish conflict: the security guarantee applies only against aggression by non-members, and not to internal disputes within the alliance. NATO could take the same approach.

Differentiation and Marginalization

The fifth objection is an even more serious one: it can be summed up in the words differentiation and marginalization. Just as the EU, which cannot take on board five, or six, or even seven new members simultaneously, neither can the Alliance. Whether it is best to take on one or two members, or perhaps three, or the four Visegrad countries *en bloc* is open to debate. This is an issue which still has to be addressed. There are currently eight C&EE countries that have expressed an interest in joining NATO (although, as of mid-1994, only Albania and Lithuania have formally applied).

What happens to those that do not become members of NATO? Last year, Foreign Minister Zlenko of Ukraine, in Brussels, expressed his concern that if Poland became a NATO member, the Russians might interpret this as implying that countries further to the East, such as Ukraine, were left in their sphere of influence. By choosing certain countries as members, the impression could be given that others are not of immediate concern, and that therefore a new Yalta, albeit more porous and less dangerous, would be implicitly accepted. Thus, from a Ukrainian perspective, there is more security if NATO rejects enlargement than if it embraces it.

This feeling is also shared by the Rumanians, the Bulgarians and others. It proves not that enlargement is undesirable but simply that it would be destabilizing at this time. Moreover, if NATO is enlarged simply to those the Alliance members want, provided they meet the democratic criteria, but also those capable of contributing to the Alliance (because it is in its interest to take countries that are able to provide to some degree for their own defense, and that are not just net recipients of security), then a broad number of countries could promote their claims with some justification. Romania, for instance, has gone very far along the road to restructuring its armed forces and is even developing a rapid reaction force, specifically designed for peacekeeping. It has shown itself to be very willing to participate in such missions under NATO authority. Moreover it was the first country to sign the Partnership For Peace (PFP) which NATO offered C&EE states after its January 1994 Summit in Brussels. Romania could thus feel all the more slighted (and it would not be alone in this) that NATO's preference would go to the Visegrad grouping for political reasons, notwithstanding its own military efforts.

There is the clear problem of identifying the basis or criteria NATO will say 'yes' to some potential new members, and 'no' to others, particularly when those it says 'no' to could perhaps be more able and willing to contribute both to the common defense and to the Alliance's new crisis management and peace support tasks. This is a problem to which there is no easy solution.

The Russia Factor

The sixth, and final, difficulty is Russia. Last autumn, President Yeltsin sent a letter to the 'Two-plus-Four' governments (those involved in negotiating the Treaty on German Unification in 1990, i.e. the US, the USSR, the UK, France and the two Germanies themselves) expressly ruling out the enlargement of NATO. He made it clear that Russia would not welcome this, proposing instead a joint Russian-NATO security guarantee of the C&EE countries and suggesting NATO should develop a privileged relationship with Russia.

This letter can be interpreted in two ways. One is as a Russian search for a new Yalta, in which large countries or groupings strike a deal over the heads of smaller ones. The Congress of Vienna springs to mind in that the two main power centers (NATO and Russia) would have amicable relations across a kind of 'Finlandized' zone in Eastern Europe, where Poland might be close to NATO but not formally an ally, while other countries might be close to Russia but not part of a reconstituted Warsaw Pact. This would create a zone of enforced neutrality—even limited sovereignty—which would be unacceptable to the C&EE countries and destined to create the very tensions and instabilities it is designed to repress.

But the letter could also be interpreted as a sort of *cri de coeur*, an urgent plea not to leave Russia out, or to seek to exploit its (presumably transitory) phase of weakness. It could be a warning to NATO to do nothing to make things more difficult for Yeltsin in the short term with the incipient promise that such restraint would bring dividends in terms of a stable Russian *Westpolitik* in the long term. Russia's predicament is clear: it is more 'Western-looking' today than it has been at any time in its history, and yet geographically, it is farther away from Europe. There is the belief among some influential Russians that the addition of Central Europeans to NATO would make manifest what they have always suspected the organization of being, namely an anti-Russian alliance. However, NATO is not an anti-Russian alliance. During the rigidity of Cold War confrontation, NATO could never have dispelled such a misconception among Russians; today it can, particularly given its cooperative efforts in peacekeeping and crisis management activities, its political and military dialogue with Russia, and its strategy to maximize political and military reassurance.

If Russian reform fails, anything NATO did for European security would be a second best option. Having worked for decades to overcome the divisions of Europe, NATO is not about to create new ones. Moreover, there is a perception in Russia that if, for example, Poland were to become a member of NATO, it would use its historic fear of Russia to lobby for the Alliance's resources, strategy, and thinking to be directed towards maintaining the balance of power and even containment of Russia. Thus, in Russia's eyes, an enlarged NATO would be paradoxically a traditional NATO; in Western eyes the purpose of enlargement would be to facilitate the emergence of an entirely different NATO, focussed not on deterrence but on crisis management and pan-European cooperation.

Perhaps one way of preventing C&EE and Russia from going off on different tracks is, as has sometimes been suggested, to have Russia as a NATO member, or at least as a treaty-linked partner. Yet here another dilemma arises. On the one hand, one does not want to give the Russians a *droit de regard* over European security. Is it for Moscow to say who does what? Is NATO not an independent organization? On the other hand, what happens in Russia will determine what happens to European security. Russia will continue to be a great military power, almost under any scenario, for a long time. It is a member of the UN Security Council whose compliance, if not active support, is needed for the enforcement operations and collective responses provided for in Chapter 7 of the UN Charter to such challenges as nuclear proliferation. This in itself will require NATO to develop a special relationship with Russia as an outgrowth of its participation in PFP. Russia still has thousands of nuclear weapons. What most fear is either chaos or the return to an authoritarian government, neither of which can be discounted, even if the Western preferred outcome is still possible: a democratic Russia at ease with itself, at ease with the West.

The dilemma can only be solved over time, and as political circumstances change. A democratically mature Russia would understand that its own process of reform depends upon having as much stability as possible around its borders. It would thus be a net beneficiary rather than a net loser following an expansion of NATO. But another factor is essential: in tandem with NATO's enlargement, a pan-European security system should be constructed to take into account Russia's legitimate security interests and give it a role commensurate with its great power status (while at the same time disciplining that power by making it subject to international rules and transparency, notably in Russia's attitude toward the former USSR).

The Partnership for Peace

It is in this respect that PFP has its full significance. It allows for a gradual opening up of NATO structures and buys the Alliance time to win Russia's confidence. Although there is no formal link between PFP and enlargement, the first new members to join the Alliance will obviously be those who, through their full participation in this program, will have demonstrated their ability to contribute to the common defense, and to carry out the necessary military reforms at home. The possibility of sending military representatives to a PFP coordination cell attached to NATO's integrated military command, of establishing liaison offices at NATO Headquarters, and of joint defense planning, training and exercises will vastly enhance the sense of security of partner countries without introducing a formal special status *vis-à-vis* the

Alliance which might alienate Russia.

Russia itself can use PFP to develop closer military links to the West and even to gain Western help and support for its peacekeeping activities. In short, NATO would not have to discriminate against candidate members; the latter would choose how fast and how far they wish to go in developing their military co-operation with NATO structures. The fact that this would also involve a certain financial effort on the part of potential members would help distinguish between those who are willing and able to engage themselves permanently in the Alliance from those who looking for a security guarantee for a minimal return. The principle involved would thus be equality of opportunity, but differentiation of outcome.

Countries which join the Alliance through a long-standing participation in PFP will be fully operational members from the outset, without the need to go through a prolonged learning curve and the negotiation of special arrangements, as happened after Spain's accession in 1982. The process of familiarization which the PFP offers would make it easier for the Alliance to extend security guarantees because partners will have demonstrated not only their willingness to defend themselves militarily, but also their resolve to address their security problems in an open and cooperative spirit. Alliance parliaments would also gain time to look upon PFP partners as countries that share the same values and interests, and that should therefore be protected. In addition, the evolution of the European security and defense identity, by shifting the burdens of conventional defense within the Alliance, will make it easier for the US Congress to accept an expanded defense perimeter in Europe. The PFP will also give the Allies time to integrate new members into the command structure.

As an alternative to enlargement, the PFP would undoubtedly represent a failure of imagination and nerve of the West. But as a means of progressive enlargement it can serve simultaneously to satisfy the aspirations of the Visegrad countries and to build up the practice of cooperative security which is vital to the emergence of a pan-European security structure. This in turn would satisfy the aspirations of Russia and other East European states. In particular, by reaching out to Ukraine and the Baltic states, the PFP will make it clear to Russia that NATO is interested in the countries of Russia's so-called 'near abroad' and will not countenance either a

NATO/Russian condominium or a Russian Monroe Doctrine.

What is required of the Alliance is flexible and creative diplomacy as well as determination not to be deflected from the goal of eventual enlargement. By not having named countries or established a timetable at the 1994 Summit, the Alliance gave the Russians time to adapt to this goal and seek the best offsets. At the same time, stating that NATO will open up indicates to Moscow that the Alliance takes its own decisions and does not give Moscow the key to this issue. By moving to devise a concept for enlargement and a timetable, once PFP is fully operational in 1995, NATO will both reassure the Visegrad aspirants and induce Moscow to consider how to adjust to the inevitable. NATO countries must not become so comfortable with the PFP that they forget it is a transitory regime.

Finally, a related issue is the development of the North Atlantic Cooperation Council (NACC) to play a more important role in conducting political consultations to complement the essentially military cooperation under the PFP. Given its pioneering work in developing cooperation in peacekeeping and the expertise that it is developing in regional issues, the NACC could eventually become the security arm of the CSCE. The fact that the neutrals are not in the NACC (although Finland is an observer) does not have to be an obstacle to such an evolution, as Austria, Sweden and Finland already participate in the NACC *ad hoc* group on peacekeeping. Moreover, they have indicated that they wish to join the PFP. The real concern for the Alliance is that in such an evolution the NACC might become an autonomous body, with its own secretariat and decision-making structure, that loses the special link to NATO (which in the eyes of the Central Europeans is its main advantage). Perhaps that is why Russia recently advocated just such a development, suggesting the CSCE and NACC should become the directing bodies of NATO.

In conclusion, there are no easy options for dealing with the security problems and aspirations of Central and Eastern Europe. But the fact that their aspirations cannot be satisfied does not mean that their problems cannot be dealt with. The disappointment of the Visegrad countries at not being offered immediate membership is more evidence of their understandably inflated expectations than of a lack of Western responsiveness. Facile notions like a 'security vacuum' only disguise the large-scale military cooperation that is already taking place and that will give C&EE countries special consultative rights vis-à-vis NATO through the PFP. This will convey a special responsibility, if not a binding security guarantee. This is no minor privilege.

This being said, the C&EE countries are entitled to ask NATO to clarify its intentions on enlargement. Moreover, politics are such that if there is no agreement on the end, there is little agreement on the means. Knowing that they are heading towards an enlargement will oblige NATO governments to come up with the resources to make the PFP work. Given the straightened financial circumstances, this will be difficult enough, but without expansion as a goal, it may be almost impossible. And if NATO does not provide the initial seed money, its NACC partners will see little reason to make the far larger financial sacrifices necessary to convert their defense structures to NATO standards and interoperability requirements. There is no pain without gain—or at least a convincing prospect of it. An American philosopher, Nathan Cummings, once said that nothing is achieved if all possible objections have to be overcome. Striking the right balance between the competing aspirations of its NACC partners will be a difficult task for the Alliance for some time to come, but getting it right is the key not only to its own future but also very much to that of a secure, prosperous Europe.

6 European Security Outside of Europe

Karl-Heinz Kamp

The end of the Cold War has significantly changed the security settings not only in Europe, but also beyond the traditional boundaries of NATO. With the Soviet menace gone, conflicts and crises on the European periphery and bordering areas are now of tremendous concern, despite their geographical remoteness. Traditional terms, like 'in area' or 'out of area' have become less and less applicable to the real security challenges because they allude to preferences and hierarchies which no longer exist.[1] The disintegration of more or less solid political structures and the sharp increase in the number of willful players in the European political orchestra have led to a significant decline in political stability in large parts of the former Warsaw Pact and to a constant flow of weapons and military equipment out of the former Soviet empire. Technical progress tends to sustain some of the adverse repercussions of the end of the Soviet empire, such as weapons proliferation. Since long range missile capabilities are now being developed in many Third World countries, conflicts there and the threat of weapons of mass destruction can no longer be regionalized.

This 'new world (dis)order' puts substantial pressure on the existing European security alliances like NATO or the WEU, and calls for modified processes of crisis management and decision making. In contrast to the Cold War situation, contemporary conditions allow a wider range of behavior by Alliance partners, which might increasingly be driven by 'national interests'. Western nations will be less inclined to subordinate national preferences and national pride to a collective effort, as previously required by strategic imperatives and sustained by US leadership. Hence, policy differences will be more common and will prove more difficult to resolve. This does not necessarily suggest that Western allies will renationalize their defenses and their strategic thinking or that they will return to the conflictual patterns of the past. But cooperation, while still possible, will be more problematic in the years to come.[2]

This article will outline the problems of risks and dangers affecting European security from outside, and will suggest to cope with these challenges. But first of all the term 'outside of Europe' requires some clarification, since the political definition of 'Europe' is still in doubt. For the purpose of this analysis, the regions on the Eastern periphery of Europe, notably Russia and the Ukraine, will be considered 'outside of Europe', at least with regards to threats and risks. Though parts that region belong geographically to Europe, political instability and unpredictability combined with the unlimited availability of all types of weapons would be likely to turn any major crisis in that area into a threat to European security organizations.

A second explanation appears necessary with regard to the main actors providing European security. Since the major security institutions in Europe, NATO and WEU, are still 'Western' organizations, this chapter will focus primarily on the problems of Western European security. Such a distinction might be regarded as preliminary and somewhat artificial since several Eastern European countries (particularly those of the Visegrad group) are getting increasingly involved in 'Western' security structures.[3] These countries have clear prospects of membership in the European Union, and will develop close ties to transatlantic security structures, which may lead to a formal membership in NATO. In addition to these more visionary prospects, concrete and pragmatic security ties to some Eastern European countries have already been fostered.[4]

These tendencies to broaden the scope of European Security, it seems justified to focus on Western Security because the number of Eastern European candidates for membership in NATO, EU, or WEU is still limited. Furthermore, any new member of one of the institutions mentioned above would automatically be 'Westernized', since membership would require the fulfillment of the (Western) political, economic or military standards of these organizations. The Visegrad countries are already actively fostering the process of 'self-Westernization'.

Based on the above definitions, the first section of this chapter identifies some of the crucial threats to European security which may develop outside the continent. This is followed by an analysis of how effectively European security institutions have dealt with recent security challenges, the Gulf war, the conflict in Yugoslavia[5] and the UN-Operation in Somalia. Finally, conclusions will be drawn about the European ability to take on external threats, and suggestions will be made for improving European capabilities for multilateral crisis management and military action.

Because the demise of the Soviet Union does not herald the disappearance of major threats to European security, many in West European now tend to regard virtually all areas in the world as being of 'strategic importance' and suggest that all deserve attention and engagement if a crisis should occur. According to this view, any case of conflict or armed aggression not only weakens the stability in the region concerned, but affects European security at least indirectly.

Dealing with all these challenges to world order would certainly overburden Western Europe. There are neither sufficient resources nor adequate public support to address issues in every trouble spot in the world. Rather, Western Europe must be selective, considering individual security interests, public attitudes, costs of required actions, and the availability of partners for cooperation. It is therefore difficult to foresee the circumstances under which Western Europe, will be prepared to take action through its security institutions. Hence the description of security challenges from outside of Europe will concentrate on those threats and risks for which European responses are more urgent and therefore more likely.

One feasible way of analyzing possible security challenges is to consider them under two broad headings: primary security challenges and secondary security challenges.[6] Clearly it is difficult to reach a consensus on the classification of a given threat according to these headings since the taxonomy of risks and challenges depends at least partly on the individual perceptions of the particular countries. A primary challenge for a Southern European country might be considered as a secondary one by a northern member of the European Union.

Secondary Security Challenges

Considering these difficulties, secondary security challenges will be defined for the purposes of this study as those which might have an impact on Europe, but which would affect European security only in an indirect manner:

• Northern Africa, particularly in the Maghreb. Given the geographic proximity of this area, the political upheaval there and the prospect of an influx of emigrants to Europe could have severe repercussions on broader European security interests;

• Turkey, a NATO member, occupies a central, strategic position on a potential arc of crisis that stretches from southeastern Europe and the Balkans to the Central Asian republics of the former Soviet Union (FSU);

• India and Pakistan considered nuclear weapon states, as it is presumed that they possess unassembled nuclear warheads. An military clash between India and Pakistan over Kashmir might conceivably escalate in a nuclear exchange. That would not only have cataclysmic consequences for the region concerned, but it would also end the 'nuclear taboo' which has existed for nearly five decades, leading to unpredictable consequences for world security;

• the Korean peninsula, where not only two heavily armed adversaries face each other, but North Korea reportedly has a reasonably developed nuclear program, with sufficient nuclear know-how and some 20-25 kg of weapons grade plutonium. If these suspicions prove to be true, it would demonstrate that even members of the Nonproliferation Treaty (NPT)—like North Korea[7] and Iraq—are able to pursue clandestine nuclear weapons programs, despite of intense inspections by the International Atomic Energy Agency (IAEA). The case of North Korea—if it can not be solved satisfactory within the NPT regime—is likely to further aggravate the subliminal crisis of the concept of nonproliferation. A collapse of the NPT would have lasting implications for European security.

Notwithstanding the undeniable relevance of challenges outlined above for the security landscape of Europe they are not of utmost concern to Europe in the sense that they are not likely to compel a unilateral European reaction. This is much more probable with regard to primary security challenges, that it, those which potentially threaten the very survival of Western Europe, and which will therefore receive a more extenxsive treatment here.

Primary Security Challenges

In this category attention should be focussed on two main issues: first, on the spread of former Soviet nuclear arsenals within the CIS and the danger of a proliferation of these weapons in the trouble spots close to Europe, particularly in the Middle East; second, on the challenges to Europe's vital economic interests, specifically with respect to the European dependence on the oil supply from the Gulf region.

Nuclear Risks Arising From the Disintegration of the FSU
The nuclear posture of the former Soviet Union still creates a major security concern for the CIS, its neighboring states and for Western Europe. The disintegration of the nuclear superpower USSR has led to the emergence of independent states with nuclear weapons on their soil: Russia, Ukraine, Kazakhstan and Belarus.[8] What they all have in common is a high measure of political instability combined with a disastrous economy and a grim perspective for the management of the transition towards prosperity and democracy. Further, the relations of two of the successor states, Russia and the Ukraine, are characterized by sharp tensions, which might end up in open hostilities. In light of these unfavorable parameters, nuclear weapons in these countries could become a serious threat to European security. This stems not so much from the (rather unlikely) danger of a direct nuclear strike of one of the republics against a neighboring state or against Western Europe, but much more to the overall implications of an insufficiently controlled nuclear posture, particularly because details of the size and structure of the Soviet military nuclear legacy are not yet fully understood.

The present problem of 'nuclear smuggling' into European countries is one repercussion of this situation, given the perceived international demand for nuclear weapons technologies, criminals in the CIS and in Eastern Europe might seek to fill the supply side of the international market by illicitly exporting nuclear material to European countries. Although recent reports of some 100 arrests linked to attempts to smuggle nuclear technology out of the Soviet successor states and into Germany are highly exaggerated, the illicit flow of nuclear materials into Western Europe must be taken very seriously.[9] Uncontrolled proliferation of nuclear material and critical technology-components, as well as 'loose nukes' within the CIS are challenges which not only increase the danger of unauthorized nuclear detonations, but also give rise to the threat of political blackmail and nuclear terrorism by extremist groupings all around Europe.

Even more disturbing are the dangers deriving from an uncontrolled proliferation of CIS nuclear weapons and nuclear know-how into highly fragile regions like the Middle East. Vast nuclear arsenals require perfect security and safety arrangements, which are quite difficult to achieve even under stable political conditions. If, in the wake of further economic and social decline of the CIS republics, only a fraction of one percent of the more than 30,000 nuclear weapons of the CIS would find its way to some of the rogue nations in Middle East, it would have a dangerous impact on European security. Given the radicalism of countries like Iraq, Iran or Libya their leaders could conceivably use nuclear weapons to foster their claim to regional supremacy. The Libyan missile attack against the American radar station on the Italian island of Lampedusa in 1986[10] clearly indicated the new vulnerability of European territory to threats from abroad.

Western Economic Survival and the Security of the Gulf Oil
The Middle East region contains 66 percent of world oil reserves, almost all of which are concentrated in the Persian Gulf.[11] Oil currently accounts for approximately 45% of the EU total energy requirement, but only one fourth of this comes from indigenous oil production, mostly from the North Sea. Hence, for Western industrialized countries there is no more vital resource than oil.[12] This crucial dependence of Western economies on the continuous flow of Gulf oil is unlikely to abate; despite improvements in overall energy efficiency and the use of other energy forms, worldwide oil consumption is expected to increase steadily.[13]

At present, there is not much danger of a complete cut-off of the Western oil supply, because the strategic oil reserves of the West will last for a few months.[14] Therefore, short term disruption of oil supplies might be endured without serious consequences. What is crucial is the maintenance of reasonable and stable oil prices. As long as supply and prices are chiefly regulated by market forces and by a largely ineffective oligopoly (e.g. OPEC), Western countries can live with their dependence; however, if oil prices spiral upwards as a result of a major change in the political or military constellations in the Gulf, the consequence would ultimately be disastrous—a collapse of the European economic, political, and social system.

Lessons From Recent Crises

Clearly, neither 'primary' or 'secondary' security challenges can be dealt with unilaterally, as it would overburden the political and military resources of any single European country; indeed, it could be too much for a single security institution. It is necessary to create a European 'security architecture' composed of different institutions—some of which already exist, some which needed to be established. To this end, multilateral consultations between the NATO General Secretariat, the EC Commission and the WEU General Secretariat as a first step towards a 'framework of inter-locking institutions'.[15] The suggestion is that NATO, WEU, CSCE, and UN should be orchestrated so as to make use of the specific abilities and qualifications of each institution. Moreover, the national preferences of Europe's major players should be properly coordinated to avoid duplications of capabilities and missions.

But the organic development of such a security structure in Europe has not yet been achieved, primarily because none of the respective organizations has evolved sufficiently enough to meet the new requirements of a completely different security environment, and because few European states have begun to adequately redesigned their national security priorities and structures. These failures became obvious in the recent crises on the European periphery and abroad: the Gulf war, the case of Somalia, and the Yugoslav conflict.

The Gulf War

The war of coalition forces against the Iraqi aggression in the Gulf was not only the first test case for the 'new world order'—a phrase coined by former US President George Bush—but also an indication of European ability to address conflict outside of Europe.

First of all, the Gulf war clearly revealed how a geographically remote crisis can quickly become a major menace to Western security interests. The Iraqi aggression was a 'primary' challenge in two ways: it threatened Europe's vital economic interests by implying the probability of a militarily predominant Iraq with a strong anti-Western attitude, controlling significant parts of the Western oil supply; and Iraq's apparent struggle for nuclear weapons encompassed vital threats not only for the region concerned but for the West in general. Nuclear capabilities in the hands of a 'rogue nation' like Iraq has been one of the worst-case scenarios that the long-established nuclear nonproliferation regime has tried to prevent.

Despite these severe implications of the Gulf crisis for European security, the institutional performance of Western Europe was poor. In the weeks prior to the attack of the Gulf coalition against Iraqi forces, the EC did not come to the fore. Some members of the Community took unilateral initiatives to free their citizens captured as hostages by Iraq; others, for example France, made uncoordinated peace proposals at a time when military action against Iraq was seen as inevitable. Even the WEU, which synchronized some operations of European naval forces in the Gulf, did not play a significant military or political role.

Nevertheless, some European countries made considerable individual contributions to the military success of the coalition against Iraq: France provided 20,000 troops, 350 tanks and 40 aircraft to the ground war operations; Great Britain sent 42,000 troops, more than 350 tanks, and 80 aircraft in the campaign against the Iraq.[16] Germany on the other hand, was still paralyzed by its domestic debate on the deployment of the German armed forces in 'out-of-area' operations and was not only unable to send armed forces to the Gulf but had also a bitter public debate on even deploying *Bundeswehr* soldiers within the NATO territory.[17]

The operations 'Desert Shield' and 'Desert Storm' demonstrated three other realities. First, it was a successful demonstration of forming and sustaining an *ad hoc* coalition composed of participants both from the region affected and from distant countries.[18] It is worth noting, however, that the process of coalition building was facilitated by a number of favorable circumstances, which may not necessarily pertain any future crisis. Saddam Hussein had not only committed a major aggression, but he had turned his pugnacity against his former allies. At the same time, Iran, seen as the *bête noire* in the region during the first Gulf war from 1980 to 1988, adopted a remarkably low profile and refrained from burdening the cohesion of the coalition. Furthermore, the end of the Cold war had *de facto* eliminated the Soviet Union as a major player in the region, and President Mikhail Gorbachev and Foreign Minister Eduard Shevardnadze cooperated with the Western coalition despite fierce resistance within the Soviet leadership.

Second, the crisis proved the ability of NATO to furnish deterrence, crisis management, and military action far beyond the traditional East-West pattern. Though NATO was not involved in combat operations as an organization, it provided the necessary framework for political and military coordination and for essential logistical support. While twelve NATO nations provided military forces to the coalition, NATO's formal role was limited to the defense of NATO territory in the Southern Region and of maintaining ships and aircraft in the Mediterranean Sea (in accordance with Article 6 of the North Atlantic Treaty) against military and terrorist threats. Beyond that formal task, which was implemented by deploying the Allied Mobile Force-Air (AMF-A) to eastern Turkey and by keeping up sophisticated early warning capacities in the region, NATO provided critical intelligence and command and control reporting, and coordinated major transportation needs through the Supreme Headquarter Allied Powers Europe (SHAPE) in Mons, Belgium.

Third, it showed clearly that both the success of the *ad hoc* coalition and the effectiveness of NATO was only possible because the United States as a superpower took the lead by keeping the alliance together and by preparing the political setting for a rapid agreement within the UN Security Council on legitimizing military action against the aggressor.[19] Hence, the American contribution to the success in the Second Gulf War was not limited to the military realm but included a substantial diplomatic effort.[20] Furthermore, it encouraged the benign behavior of China, while offering it a unique chance to break the ice in the frozen relations since the massacre on Tiananmen Square. It also put severe political and economic pressure on those countries, such as Yemen, which supported Iraqi positions.[21]

Somalia

If the crisis in the Persian Gulf represents an exemplary case of handling European security challenges from outside of Europe, the crisis in Somalia is just the opposite. The initial Western engagement in this country, which was fostered and legitimized by the United Nations, was not driven by Western perceptions of an existing or emerging threat, but primarily by humanitarian considerations. The complete breakdown of political, economic, and social structures had led to destitution and misery all over the country. Reestablishing governmental structures and ending the anarchy was seen as the only chance to prevent thousands of people from starving to death. A Western military engagement promised the option of quick emergency aid at a low risk of failure or of Western casualties.

In addition, some of the Western participants in the UNOSOM mission combined a self-serving purpose with their readiness to provide humanitarian assistance for the troubled region. For Germany for instance, a military engagement in Somalia offered an opportunity to further erode the political gridlock of the 'out-of-area' debate, which has been dragging on for years. To break that deadlock the German government pursued a step-by-step approach, taking minor but decisive steps to broaden the role of the *Bundeswehr*, notwithstanding the constitutional limits cited by the opposition. The transfer of 1700 *Bundeswehr* soldiers to Somalia to provide logistical support for the United Nations 'Blue Helmets' was one of these decisive steps.[22]

The widespread optimism concerning the success of the Somalia operation, combined with expected political payoffs in some countries, and the sincere intention of providing humanitarian relief prevented a sober analysis of the strategic rationale of the mission, particularly in political circles of the West. The political and military objectives and the anticipated time frame for achieving these objectives remained somewhat ambiguous.[23] This lack of clarity was obvious from the beginning of the mission when the first disagreement came up among the UNOSOM partners and the UN headquarters in New York on how the occupation of parts of the country and the disarmament of marauding gangs should be exercised. Later, when the first casualties occurred, the domestic support in those countries engaged in Somalia declined significantly. Finally, the obvious success of the Somali General Aidid and his supporters against the US forces and the hasty announcements of a quick withdrawal of Western forces indicated at least a partial failure of the mission. Humanitarian intervention proved neither to be a riskless issue, nor to be a self-evident value to all players in the region. Somalia also highlighted another crucial condition of any military action (apart from individual and collective self-defense): specific national interests must be in line with the particular requirements of the operation.

The War in the Balkans

The third case considered here with regards to Europe's ability for an engagement in distant crises and conflicts is also not a perfect example of an external security challenge, first and foremost because it is *within* Europe (though some European countries are currently handling the issue as if it were not a European case). The reason the war in the Balkans is mentioned at all in this analysis is that Western Europe, particularly the EC, saw the Yugoslav conflict as a possible catalyst for a common foreign and security policy.[24]

When the Community took the first steps to intervene in the conflict on the Balkans in early summer 1991, the foreign minister of Luxembourg, Jaques Poos, declared that 'the hour of Europe had struck'.[25] But in contrast to this euphoria, the real capabilities of the EC for conflict management and war termination on the Balkans remained far behind. By late June 1991, the EC formed a *troika* of intermediaries, comprising the foreign ministers of Italy (Gianni de Michelis), Luxembourg (Jaques Poos), and the Netherlands (Hans van den Broek). But all the cease fires negotiated by the troika in the following months were broken after only a few hours—a fact that progressively diluted the credibility of the EC as an 'honest broker' in the eyes of the conflicting partners. Consequently, the EC activities in the Balkans were pursued according to a minimalist approach, largely limited to humanitarian aspects. It is worth noting, however, that this is less indicative of institutional shortcomings than of a significant lack of strategic interests in the Balkan region. In addition, there was no agreement among member states as to which party should be defined as the aggressor. Thus, it is incorrect to blame the EC (or, for that matter, any other institution) for its passivity, since it only reflects the indifference of its members.

In some respect, however, Yugoslavia did turn out to be a

catalyst for the cooperation between NATO and the UN. The fact that NATO provided the UN peacekeeping forces in Bosnia with material support and intelligence data corresponded with a new UN policy to make increasing use of regional organizations. In turn, NATO expected a new legitimacy for its own existence from the UN mandate. These positive tendencies notwithstanding, it must be recognized that the West generally engaged primarily in activism instead of effective crisis management. Concrete operations like the naval patrols in the Mediterranean or on the Danube river, or the establishment of no-flight zones, were still fundamentally symbolic.

Prospects for European Action Outside of Europe

In light of the examples outlined above, the prospects for an effective and coordinated European response to a security challenge outside of Europe look rather grim, and unilateral action by European countries would be even less effective.[26] Even if the WEU becomes the military pillar of a true European Union, it could not fulfil the high expectations of its proponents. Even the new WEU activity in military planning, hailed by some proponents as a significant step towards a military posture, is barely linked to the political realities—at least with regard to the Yugoslav issue. Until now, the West has never seriously intended to conduct significant military operations in the Balkans; hence, it has been easy for the WEU planning cell to develop ambitious contingency plans.

Without an external federator in the shape of a vital threat to all Western European nations, and an internal federator in the form of an allied superpower able to provide clear leadership, the WEU still remains ill-suited to provide sufficient security for its members. This is particularly true for the material side of this organization, even if it is be provided with true military capabilities by its members. A military campaign in a major crisis outside of Europe might require huge numbers of troops and military equipment. More than 860,000 troops from 17 countries have been involved in the operations in the Gulf, with some 530,000 US troops providing the bulk of the forces. In comparison, European capabilities for power projection over long distances are extremely limited. Even the more than 60,000 British and French forces involved in 'Desert Storm' relied on crucial US support. Nearly all armed forces of the EU countries, perfectly designed for past 'Central Front' European contingencies against the Warsaw Pact, do not have sufficient capacities in either transport or strategic intelligence, not to mention tactical ballistic missile defence assets—which may be of critical importance in any future conflict outside of Europe.

In light of the significant decline in the defence budgets of all major EU partners, most of the eloquently advocated political declarations for quickly restructuring European armed forces towards increased mobility and a greater 'out-of-area' capability will remain theoretical—at least for the near future. Consequently, the WEU will continue to be heavily dependent on the NATO infra-structure dominated by the United States. This implies a *de facto* American veto power in all major WEU operations. Therefore, in the short and medium term, the role of the WEU will be limited to that of intra-European coordination in those cases in which the United States does not intend to fulfil a leadership role.

If unilateral action by Western Europe is difficult to foresee, the fruitful cooperation between NATO and WEU remains essential. But a harmonious concertation of both organizations is hindered by the fact that the WEU's dual identity as the European pillar of NATO and as the defense organization of the European Union has led to different views on both sides of the Atlantic as to the priorities and tasks of these organizations.[27] Both institutions are in the process of adjustment to the new realities, but are following a different timetable.[28] NATO has committed itself to a course of continuous reform towards an unstated termination point while the EU is heading for political union. Building a European defence identity is regarded as essential to Community construction. In that sense, a common security organization becomes a means to a compelling political end. In light of this precondition, practical issues such as military needs and effectiveness are in danger of being subordinated.

A prominent case for the a subordination of military needs to political purposes is the Franco-German Eurocorps. The creation of this cooperative military unit on the basis of the existing Franco-German Brigade was unquestionably an important symbol for a successful Franco-German defense cooperation. In addition, it was seen as the nucleus of a European defence identity, though its military purpose and its relation to NATO were unclear for a long time.[29] Though this was clarified by the SACEUR Agreement in

June 1993 (which provided that the Eurocorps would come under NATO command in wartime), important problems remain. The most important is perhaps the dichotomy between plan to deploy the Eurocorps outside of Europe and the German constitutional restrictions for deploying *Bundeswehr* forces in combat operations outside of Europe.

The Franco-German Eurocorps is not only an example for a preference for political symbolism to military effectiveness, but an illustration for the tendency to embrace a 'function-follows-form' approach in the process of shaping a European defence identity. The idea that the process of constructing new organizational structures has to precede to the definition of tasks and purposes of these structures is a risky one. Shaping a security landscape in this order could seriously damage existing organizations, like NATO, without putting something similarly effective in its place.

These major deficiencies in developing a European and transatlantic security architecture need to be overcome if Western Europe is to act efficiently in conflicts outside of Europe. This requires a change in the perception of NATO and WEU as competing organizations—a view which still finds a great deal of support in some Western capitals. Any development of a European pillar without harmonizing European and American political interests risks widening the gap between Europe and the United States. While it is valid to suggest that the Europeans must prepare for the time when the US withdraws from Europe and sharply reduces its political commitments to its transatlantic allies, it could be a self fulfilling prophecy, in the sense that it might accelerate the process of European-American estrangement.

This is certainly not an argument against a closer European integration in the field of security policy and a greater self-reliance of the European Union. In light of the changed political realities in Europe, more independence and greater flexibility is indeed highly necessary, since there are many potential crises outside of Europe, which are of much more concern to the Europeans than to the United States. In these cases, a purely European reaction might be inevitable. Ultimately, military engagement or non-engagement will be determined by the interests at stake.

With regard to the primary challenges, however, an American engagement remains necessary to enforce European capabilities for crises management and military action. In light of the severity and the universal character of primary challenges, as outlined, a US engagement is not only indispensable but also very probable, since American vital interests are most likely to be involved. Such an option for a rapid and coordinated reaction of Europe and the United States must not be hampered by a creeping process of transatlantic alienation.

As to the WEU, steps to enhance its capabilities should be measured mainly in terms of net improvements to the Alliance effectiveness in meeting important security needs of the member states. The contribution of the institutional development of the WEU to achieving European political union should not be its primary yardstick.

As far as NATO is concerned, the step to further widening its geographical scope seems inevitable. If NATO has been and still is an organization to safeguard the security and territorial integrity of is member states, it has to be able to deal with all vital security challenges, regardless of their geographical origin. This must include peacekeeping missions as well as combat operations for peace enforcement. A legitimization of the military operations by the UN Security Council or by the CSCE is important, but the ability to take on a vital threat must be guaranteed.

The CSCE is unlikely to be able to reach consensus in a crisis given that it comprises more than fifty members with completely different political structures and cultures. In the United Nations much of the post-Gulf war euphoria about the prospects of collective security is irretrievably gone. Disagreement among the members of the UN Security Council is still likely to paralyze UN operations in significant political or military crises. It is worth noting that Article 51 of the UN Charter might be a sufficient basis for legitimizing collective military in cases such as the war against the Iraq.[30]

But the possibility of a further evolution of Western security institutions towards a greater effectiveness outside of Europe requires a readiness among the allies to adapt their national policies to the new requirements. For example, united Germany must be willing to accept a greater responsibility outside of Europe, France must allow a wider role for NATO, and the US must be less sensitive to trends toward autonomy in Europe's further development. Once the prudent political decisions have been taken by all allies concerned, Europe's military capacities to act outside of

Europe must be strengthened. Force multipliers (e.g. like airlift capacities, tanker aircraft, long-range surveillance capabilities) are worthless if the political decisions to act coherently and effectively cannot be taken.

Notes

1. Ruehle, Michael and David Law: 'Die NATO und das «Out-of-Area» Problem', (NATO and the «Out-of-Area» Problem), in *Europa-Archiv*, 15-16/1992, pp.439-443.

2. Brenner, Michael: 'Multilateralism and European Security', *Survival*, Summer 1993, pp. 138-155.

3. In February 1991, representatives from Hungary, Czechoslovakia, and Poland met in Visegrad (Hungary) to agree on close trilateral consultations on political and economic questions. See Spero, Joshua: 'The Budapest-Prague-Warsaw Triangle: Central European Security after the Visegrad Summit', *European Security*, No. 1/1992, pp. 58-83.

4. Hungary received some tacit security commitments by WEU and NATO for its support for the WEU patrol mission on the Danube river and for NATO's AWACS flights over Bosnia. See Kamp, Karl-Heinz: *Die Frage einer Osterweiterung der NATO* (The Question of Expanding NATO Eastward), (Sankt Augustin: Konrad Adenauer Stiftung, November 1993).

5. Yugoslavia is without any doubt a European case, and not an 'out-of-area' issue. However, it provides important insight for West European inability to find a common and coherent approach to take on a military conflict, which does not affect vital interests of most of the key players.

6. Curtis, Mark: 'Western European Security and the Third World', in Curtis, Mark et al. (Eds.): *Challenges and Responses to Future European Security: British, French and German Perspectives*, (Munich: European Strategy Group, 1993).

7. North Korea joined the NPT in 1985 but refused to come to a comprehensive Safeguards Agreement with the International Atomic Energy Agency (IAEA). In 1990 an agreement was negotiated but North Korea constructed a linkage between its adherence to the NPT and American tactical nuclear weapons deployed in South Korea. Finally, the IAEA Safeguards Agreement was signed by North Korea in January 1992.

8. The characterization of Ukraine, Belarus, and Kazakhstan as 'nuclear weapons states' may be controversial, since it is highly questionable that these republics have full operational control over the missiles they host. On the one hand, the Ukraine, for instance, indicates its ability to overcome the technical and organizational hurdles and barriers formally erected to prevent the unauthorized use of nuclear weapons; on the other hand, many Western analysts believe view that the Russian centralized control is still intact, and that none of the new states is technically able to operate a nuclear posture. See Campbell, Kurt M. et al.: *Soviet Nuclear Fission*, (Cambridge: Center for Science and International Affairs, Harvard University, 1991). But besides these largely technical disputes it is nevertheless necessary to bear in mind the political value of these weapons in a major crisis or conflict. One can argue that possessing nuclear weapons might give these republics a political 'leading edge' toward their non-nuclear adversaries in a crisis, whether they really can operate the weapons or not.

9. Many of the smuggling cases in Germany turned out to be 'false alarms'. A close examination of this issue reveals that there were nine attempts of nuclear smuggling detected in 1992. None of the discovered material in these cases was of military relevance. In most cases, the substances were stolen from medical facilities or from nuclear power plants.

10. In reaction to the American air attack on Tripoli and Bengasi, Libya shot two missiles at the US 'Logan' radar station on the island of Lampedusa, Italy, on 16 April 1986. Both missiles missed their targets without doing any harm to either American or Italian installations.

11. Saudi Arabia has roughly one fourth of the Gulf oil, Iraq 10 percent, Kuwait 9.5 percent, and Iran 9.3 percent.

12. Until the late 1980s another critical Western dependence was seen in the field of 'strategic minerals'. The concentration of key minerals (platinum group metals, chrome derivates, manganese etc.) in South Africa and the Soviet Union has lead to a West European import dependence of nearly 100 per cent. See Ra'anan, Uri and Perry, Charles M. (Eds.): *Strategic Minerals and International Security* (New York, Institute for Foreign Policy Studies, 1985). The demise of the USSR and the recent political changes in South Africa, however, have reduced the political impact of these dependencies significantly.

13. Wolff, Reinhard: 'Western European Policy Responses to Future Security Challenges' in Curtis, Mark et al. (Eds.): *op.cit.* p. 139.

14. Existing EU law requires each country to maintain oil reserves for 90 days, but there is a tendency in Europe and in the United States to keep up larger stockpiles.

15. Nerlich, Uwe: *NATO Between the Gulf War and Strategic Disentanglement in Europe*, Unpublished Paper (Ebenhausen: Stiftung Wissenschaft und Politik, 1991).

16. Taylor, William F. and Blackwell, James: 'The Ground War in the Gulf', in *Survival*, No. 3, 1991, p. 237.

17. When the German government announced the transfer of 18 'Alpha Jet' aircraft as part of the Allied Mobile Force (AMF) to Turkey in early January 1991 as a visible sign of alliance solidarity, it was met with significant criticism from the political left and among the public.

18. Even Morocco contributed 2000 troops; Czechoslovakia provided 350 chemical warfare and medical troops.

19. Garrity, Patrick J.: *Why the Gulf War Still Matters* (Los Alamos: Los Alamos National Laboratory, 1993) pp. 5-20.

20. See Beschloss, Michael and Strobe Talbot: *At the Highest Levels: The Inside Story of the End of the Cold War* (New York: Little, Brown, 1993).

21. Yemen voted together with Cuba against the crucial Resolution of the UN-Security Council No. 678/93. The U.S. reacted with an immediate cancellation of a US $ 70 mn aid package for Yemen.

22. Kamp, Karl-Heinz: 'The German Bundeswehr in Out-of-Area Operations - to Engage or Not to Engage', in *The World Today* No. 8-9/1993, p. 166.

23. This has been criticized by military officers, most notably by General Colin Powell.

24. For a more detailed treatment of the role of international institutions in the post-Yugoslav crisis, see the chapter by Maurizio Cremasco in this volume.

25. Brenner, Michael: 'The EC in Yugoslavia: A Debut Performance', in *Security Studies*, No. 4/1992, p. 568.

26. The author is indebted to Michael Ruehle for many points made on this issue.

27. One striking example of the transatlantic dissonances on the future role of the WEU was the famous 'WEU Demarche' of March 1991, signed by US Undersecretary for International Security Reginald Bartholomew, and directed to the governments of the EC-countries and to WEU Secretary General Willem van Eekelen.

28. Brenner, Michael: *op.cit.*, pp. 138-155.

29. This led to bitter complaints from the US. See Kirkpatrick, Jeanne: 'A Second European Defense Force - To Exclude America?', *The Washington Post,* 30 May 30 1992.

30. Article 51 of the Charter of the United Nations states that 'Nothing in the present Charter shall impair the inherent right of individual or collective self-defence if an armed attack occurs against a Member of the United Nations, until the Security Council

has taken measures necessary to maintain international peace and security'.

PART TWO:

National Perspectives

7 International Institutions and European Security: the Russian Debate

Alexander Konovalov

The events of October 1993 in Moscow led to new deep changes in the political landscape in Russia and introduced new uncertainties into the future of Russian foreign and security policy. The liquidation of the Russian Supreme Soviet, the prospect of new elections in the Federal Assembly, and a referendum on the new Constitution made all previous debates on foreign and security issues irrelevant to some extent, and called for a reassessment of the issues. The priority given to these issues is demonstrated by the fact that the first important documents issued after the October events there were *The Main Foundations of the Russian Federation Military Doctrine* (adopted by the presidential decree on 2 November 1993) and the report prepared by the Russian Foreign Intelligence Service on *The Perspectives of NATO Enlargement and the Interests of Russia* (introduced to the journalists on 25 November 1993). Clearly, the new Russia is just beginning to search for a national identity in foreign policy and security, and the debate on national interests is far from complete. Russia's attitudes towards international institutions, and its role in the multipolar world have yet to be understood and defined by the Russian leadership.

The debate on vital Russian interests: *«Eurasians»* vs. *«Atlanticists»*

The changes in the world environment, and in Europe in particular, have called for a reconsideration of Russian attitudes toward European international organizations. In the final years of the

USSR, the discussion was focussed mainly on relations with NATO and, to a much lesser extent, on the Conference on Security and Cooperation in Europe (CSCE). The other European security institution, the Western European Union (WEU), was given much less attention by the Soviet political elite, mostly because its mission was not understood and its military-political role was perceived to be insignificant.

The August 1991 events appeared to mark the beginning of extensive public discussion on new relations with NATO. Several days after the failed *coup*, prominent Soviet analyst Sergey Blagovolin suggested that the cooperation of Russia with the West will shape the character of the international climate for the foreseeable future. He identified the need for close relations with NATO, but stressed that the question of immediate Soviet membership in NATO is premature, because it presupposes a long and complicated process, involving a high compatibility of political structures and armed forces, and a developed system of a civilian control over the military sphere. Mr. Blagovolin concluded that Russian military posture and strategy should be oriented toward joining the West in the construction of a security belt which US Secretary of State James Baker had suggested should stretch from Vancouver to Vladivostok.[1]

After the break up of the Soviet Union, the first official formulation of the vital national interests of the new Russian state included a close partnership with the West. A month after the failed *coup* in Moscow, Russian Foreign Minister Andrei Kozyrev wrote that Russian foreign policy must be aimed at a historical goal: to transform Russia "from a dangerous and sick giant of Eurasia into a participant of the Western zone of common prosperity." He also stressed that Western experts should participate directly in the realization of joint programs in the economy and particularly in security and conversion programs.[2]

In January 1992 he published an article in which he formulated the priorities of the Russian foreign and security policy, and characterized the USA and other developed countries of the West as the "natural allies to Russia." Subsequently, the idea that "the Western democracies are as natural allies to democracy in Russia as they are enemies of totalitarian regime" was repeated by him many times.[3] This view determined the official attitudes of the Russian foreign ministry towards the development of closest collaboration with the West and the international institutions in security area in the initial period after Russia was recognized as an independent state.

But alongside the worsening economic and political crises, and the growth of opposition to the Atlanticist foreign policy, closely associated with Kozyrev, harsh debates and political clashes in the Supreme Soviet began to erode the pro-Western position of the democrats. The right-wing nationalists accused the democrats and their representative in the foreign ministry to be traitors trying to conduct a foreign and security policy in which real national interests were replaced with abstract notions of "human rights" and "human values".

Political opposition in the Supreme Soviet insisted that Russia should conduct an independent foreign policy, because by following Western demands Russia had already lost at least 17 bn dollars through the Western-inspired economic sanctions against Yugoslavia, Libya and Iraq. Such assessments were based on a primitive and non-professional analysis of potential income, and did not take into consideration either the military consequences for Russia's own security, or the tensions with the democratic world community which would have been unavoidable if Russia had continued to support those regimes. The cumulative effect of the changes in Russian foreign policy called for by the nationalists would have meant a catastrophe for the new Russia. Nevertheless, the leader of opposition block "The Russian Unity", N. Pavlov, who was active in the Supreme Soviet before the October 1993 events, stated in his interview to *Narodnaia Pravda* (People's Truth) paper: "As long as I have an opportunity to legally struggle against this pro-American, puppet regime, I'll do it in this way. But I'll take arms in hands if there should be a threat of aggression."[4]

In the Supreme Soviet, the same radical nationalists stated that, in accordance with its traditional policy towards southern Slavs, Russia should unconditionally support the Serbs in their conflicts in the Balkans. Amidst such political demagoguery, there were also serious attempts to describe the political identity and the vital national interests of the new Russia. These were primarily in response to the criticism against an overwhelming orientation towards the West and international institutions, at the expense of the Eurasian dimension in Russian foreign and security policy.

Many analysts stressed that Russian foreign policy, in addition to improving relations with the West, should concentrate on at least two other questions: the Muslim world to the south of Russia and China to its east. According to Sergei Goncharov, a Russian expert on the Far East: "Even in case of the most favorable development of Russian foreign policy toward the West, any confrontation, whether it occurs with Muslim states or with China, could bring enormous damage to Russian vital interests."[5] It is reasonable to think that if such conflicts take place in the next three-five years, when Russia is passing through the most painful and vulnerable stage of its internal reform, they can undermine democratic changes and promote the restoration of a totalitarian regime.

Goncharov points to several foreign policy options which could carry destabilizing consequences. For instance, he suggests that joining NATO or creating another formal military political alliance with the West would mean that Russia would join any Western actions to protest human rights violations in China. Western countries might expect a diplomatic protest by China, but this could mean growing tensions on the Russian-Chinese border. Furthermore, any formal politico-military alliance of Russia with the West would unavoidably lead to a reciprocal counter-alliance of leading Muslim countries, with the possible inclusion of China, and a new global confrontation with Russia in the eye of the conflict.[6]

This assessment is highly debatable, first of all because of the deep confrontation within the Muslim world, but it can not be wholly rejected. Goncharov concluded that Russia should strengthen its partnership with the West so as to enhance its position *vis-à-vis* the South and the Far East, while developing a partnership with both regions to gain more independence in dealing with the West. He also suggested that Russia should never join formal military political alliances which could be perceived as being specifically oriented against any given country; rather proposed that Russian foreign policy should be "a constructive non-alignment with a definite preference for the West."[7]

The previous Soviet Foreign Ministry was criticized for the Atlantic orientation of its policy. But current Russian foreign policy deepened this weakness and tends to exclude the South and East from its top priorities list. Such a Eurasia-centric approach towards the formulation of Russia's interests is not an attempt to revitalize either the communist or the imperial heritages. According to Aleksandr Rahr "criticism of the Eurasian approach has nothing to do with reactionary communist or imperial thinking. Eurasians wish to keep good relations with the West too."[8]

As for the consequences for the West of a possible strengthening of Eurasia-centric forces, Rahr concluded that a Eurasian reorientation of Russian foreign policy does not necessarily conflict with Western interests. For the USA, France and Great Britain, democratic Russia would be a decisive counterweight to the new world giants—Germany in Europe and Japan in the Pacific.[9]

During 1992, the Russian press published several other analyses by independent experts, who proposed recommendations for a more balanced approach to foreign policy. One such analysis the report *Strategy for Russia*, was prepared by the Council on Foreign and Defense Policy, a public nongovernmental organization. This document suggests that it is in Russia's interest to foster the preservation of NATO and the development of a partnership with it. It cautions, however, that a one-sided orientation toward the West would be counterproductive; and that Russia should also develop political and economic relations with important partners in Asia, as India, Saudi Arabia, Egypt, the United Arab Emirates, Israel, and Iran.[10]

The multidimensional nature of Russian vital national interests, was a key determinant of the position of the foreign ministry and even led to contradictions in the positions of its key figures. The most visible was a long indirect dispute between Foreign Minister Andrei Kozyrev, who represented the *Russia's Choice* group (headed by then acting Vice-Premier Yegor Gaidar) in the election in the Federal Assembly on December 1993 and the Russian Ambassador to Washington Vladimir Lukin, who was one of the leaders of *Yabloko* (The Apple). In an article published in September 1993, Mr. Lukin wrote about the negative consequences of a "romantic", pro-Western orientation in Russia's foreign policy: the rejection of communism and the acceptance of a role subordinated to the US in international arena were seen as the foreign ministry's tools to persuade the West to invite Russia into the family of civilized nations and to bring prosperity.

Lukin asserted that, since Gorbachev and Shevardnadze, and now with the new Russia, the West takes for granted that is will have an all too easy life, and that the West appears to be unprepared to a more independent Russian policy. Instead, he called for two main things from the West: first, recognition of the legitimate Russian interests in the region of the former Soviet Union (FSU), preferably with support to the integration processes there, and second, the elimination of all obstacles to full Russian participation in world trade and economic cooperation.[11]

The position of Foreign Minister Kozyrev in October 1993 was that for democratic Russia the choice in favor of partnership and, in perspective, union with the West is natural . . . But partnership and alliance never mean unification. Russia has always had and will continue to have its own interests."[12] In response, Ambassador Lukin stated: "I am sure that it is both possible and necessary to collaborate with the USA but not at the expense of our own . . . interests."[13]

In sum, the period between the break-up of the USSR in 1991 and the tragedy of October 1993 saw an evolution from what could be characterized as a «romantic pro-western Atlanticism», based on the assumption of a full convergence of the interests of all democratic states, to a more realistic understanding of the specificity of the new Russia's interests. This brought Eurasian elements into Russian foreign and security policy. The search for a reasonable balance between the positions of Atlantists and Eurasians in this period dominated debates on military security issues and the future role of international institutions in this area.

The Russian Debate on European Security Institutions

Internal debates on European security issues in Russia are focussed primarily on relations with NATO and on the role of the country in the future international security system; what little public attention is given to the CSCE is only in connection with NATO's offer of infrastructure and military capabilities to CSCE peace-keeping operations. Only with the formation of the European Union and the Eurocorps, did political analysts begin a debate on the resilience of the direct US military presence in Europe.

The idea of a close partnership with (and even participation in) NATO has strong proponents both in the academic community and among top officials; nevertheless, there are serious doubts about the possible role of Russia in this organization, even among the most committed to democracy and partnership with the West. In one of the first attempt in Russia to define the possible mission of Russia in NATO, analyst Alexei Arbatov wrote that "until now there has been a clear-cut distribution of missions in NATO: the United States was the security guarantor in case of Soviet aggression . . . Western Europeans, in turn, contributed to collective defense and provided the US with their territory for military bases and other facilities. Russia could hardly play a role in this arrangement. Its internal problems do not permit it to take on any military security obligations outside of the FSU. At the same time, Russia does not need any military protection from the USA. There is no neighboring state which could represent a serious military threat to Russia for the foreseeable future. All real security threats are linked with Russian internal problems, which NATO would be unable to solve.[14]

It does not seem realistic to expect that NATO membership would prevent a resurgence of the military capabilities of Russia, as it did with Germany. Arbatov went on to assert that when the situation in Russia is completely normalized, and it is ready to join NATO, this alliance will immediately become meaningless. It will then be necessary to set up a true system of collective security, which would include the US, European countries, Russia and its neighbors, Japan and others.[15]

Since Arbatov made the above analysis in March 1992, the political situation has changed significantly in NATO's military posture, and the North Atlantic Cooperation Council (NACC) has been created. It has become clear that none of the existing international institutions, strategic concepts, or military instruments, built for the Cold War confrontation are useful for the types of risks and challenges to international security which Europe is facing now. Conflicts in the former Yugoslavia and in the FSU are the most evident examples of this inadequacy. Furthermore, the Central and Eastern European countries (C&EE), whose security concerns were associated mainly with political instabilities in the FSU, have accelerated their efforts to join NATO, which, in their minds, should fill the military vacuum left by the dissolution of the Warsaw pact and the USSR, and provide them with security guarantees against the possible restoration of an aggressive regime in Moscow. Increasing tension in the FSU, and within Russia itself, could challenge world security and stability.

In a broader sense, the principal question is: should the future

European security system, if Europe needs a formal security arrangement at all, be based on the idea of a gradual enlargement of NATO to the Russian border? Until August 1993 the answer seemed clear: C&EE saw NATO membership as a desirable, but long-term goal; NATO was ready to collaborate with them but did not display any enthusiasm for their formal membership; Russia, preoccupied with internal problems, made it clear that it would never agree to NATO's expansion to the East. But there was an unforeseen and explosive event during President Yeltsin's visit to Poland in 1993. The Declaration he signed with Polish President Wałensa on 25 August 1993 stated that Russia would not be threatened if Poland joined NATO. This step in the Russian-Polish declaration marked a fundamental change in the Russian position.

On 4 October 1993, Polish Foreign Minister Skubishevskiy declared that "Poland cannot be secure, prosperous and civilized without close links with the European Community and NATO . . . We expect that NATO, in its January 1994 Summit, will set up a perspective for its enlargement . . . The Polish aspiration to NATO is irreversible, . . . [though not] . . . for the short term."[16] The wish to join NATO was also expressed by Hungary, the Czech Republic, Bulgaria and the Baltic states. In the fall of 1993, NATO modified its previous position with regards to the possibility of its enlargement. Secretary General Wörner stated that "it is time to propose a real perspective for the C&EE countries to join NATO." Similar views were expressed by many Western politicians. German Defense Minister Ruhe, during his visit to the Czech Republic, supported the idea of Poland, Hungary, and the Czech Republic joining NATO in the near future.[17]

Observers in Russia reacted negatively to this unexpected change; strong criticism was raised both by radical nationalists opposed to the pro-western, "Atlanticist" orientation of Russian foreign policy, and by those who had traditionally supported it. According to Sergei Karaganov, a member of the Presidential Council, (an informal advisory board),

> an inclusion of Poland, the Czech Republic and Hungary into NATO will not lead to a growth of the military threat to Russia. But the political and psychological consequences of such step would be devastating. It will inevitably produce negative reactions on the main part of the military

leadership, whose influence in society is growing, and will be rejected by politicians of different orientation . . . Anti-Russian feelings might grow within NATO when the Eastern Europeans there air their worries about the imperial policy of Russia . . . The West should avoid a military isolation of Russia . . . We can not and should not prohibit our neighbors from joining the alliances they choose. But Russia must make it clear that NATO enlargement would deepen its isolation and would directly threaten its democratic development . . . Russia should also insist on joining NATO at the same time . . . our partners should understand that the choice is either to invite Russia in NATO, or to openly isolate her.[18]

The foregoing demonstrates that the main concern about NATO enlargement was the possibility of the restoration, in a new form, of confrontation in Europe. In Russia, however, there were even stronger reactions; an analyst from "EPY Center"—an organization headed by Grigoriy Yavlinskiy, the leader of the political group Yabloko, doubted Karaganov's conclusion that NATO's enlargement will not increase military threat to Russia. In the view of this analyst, the "extension of an alliance which was set up as a counterbalance to the communist USSR closer to our current borders would definitely worsen our military strategic posture."[19]

Holders of this view asserted that a NATO enlargement to the East would interfere with the Russian national sphere of interest. They believe that the Baltic, Polish, and even Balkan interests are part of Russia's history, and that it would be strange to hope that Russia will reject its aspiration to the Baltic which it inherited from Ivan the Terrible and Peter the Great. From this point of view, Russia is still under the illusion that "everybody will love and help Russia only because it defeated communism [but] the Western approach is much more pragmatic. ... events will force honest and responsible politicians to look at the West through the prism of Russian national interests."[20]

Such criticism resulted in significant changes in the Russian position on the issue of NATO enlargement. Less than a month after the signing of the Russian-Polish declaration, Yeltsin sent a confidential letter to the leaders of the US, UK, France and Germany. In this letter he argued against a possible NATO expansion to the East, which would conflict with the article on the non-enlargement of NATO membership set in the "Two-plus-Four" Treaty on Germany unification.[21] Instead of NATO enlargement to Eastern Europe, Yeltsin proposed they be granted mutual security guarantees simultaneously by Russia and the United States. The news of Yeltsin's letter had barely been made public when most analysts agreed that the paragraph in the Russian-Polish Declaration saying that a decision by Poland to request NATO membership would not contradict "either the European integration process, nor Russian interests"[22] should be considered as an aberration, and an example of poor improvisation in the foreign policy area made by some of the presidential closest aides or by Yeltsin himself.

These fluctuations in Russian foreign policy put its partners in a very uncomfortable positions. C&EE countries recognized Yeltsin's letter as an attempt to interfere with their legitimate right to join any international organizations, and to decide how to ensure their own national security. NATO made it clear that it would not follow orders from Moscow. As US Defense Secretary Les Aspin stated: "We are not afraid of the Russian threats and are not going to grant anybody the right of veto on NATO enlargement, but this enlargement should not create more problems than it solves."[23] At the same time, the leaderships of NATO countries took Moscow's main argument against NATO enlargement very seriously, particularly as it linked this step with increased indirect support for the right-wing nationalists.

Later events in September-October 1993 in Moscow confirmed that this concern was well-founded. The bloody clash between Yeltsin and the Parliament proved that the internal situation is weak and vulnerable. Many observers in Russia agreed that the October events were the decisive factor which forced Western leaders to change their initial plans towards C&EE formal participation in NATO. Even Germany, which was the main proponent of this participation, has changed its mind. German Foreign Minister Kinkel called on the preservation NATO in its current membership.[24]

Given the climate, NATO *Partnership for Peace* (PFP), announced by US State Secretary Christopher during his visit to Russia in October 1993, was seen by Moscow as a step in a right direction. This plan proposed a broad spectrum of bilateral contacts between C&EE countries and NATO (including joint military exercises, coordination and planning), but did not give them security guarantees or full membership. Christopher stated that the US proposals would create the conditions necessary to speed up the process for Russia's entry into NATO.[25] In other words, the United States and other NATO countries recognized that Russia must not be isolated, but integrated into any future European security system.

"The Prospect of NATO Enlargement and Russian Interests"

The most impressive Russian contribution in the debates on the possible enlargement of NATO was provided by an organization which traditionally does not intervene in public debates. In November 1993, Academician Evgenii Primakov, Head of the Russian Foreign Intelligence Service, publicly presented a report entitled *"The Prospect of NATO Enlargement and Russian Interests"*. The report is divided into two parts; the second part is completely devoted to analyses of NATO enlargement from the perspective of Russian interests. The report states that Russian concerns on possible NATO enlargement might have been assuaged if guarantees had been given either on a faster change in the Alliance's missions, or on the widening of its political functions. But these guarantees were lacking."[26]

Furthermore, the report suggests that, it C&EE states joined NATO, they would be engaged in the resolution of conflicts among themselves and certain domestic issues. The Alliance would thus have to postpone its plan to take up peace-keeping missions elsewhere. The absence of proper coordination between the transformation of NATO missions and its geographical expansion could lower the chances of finally overcoming the divisions on the continent and could lead to a return to "bloc" politics.

Geostrategic Aspects
As for the geostrategic aspects of the problem, the report analyzes C&EE arguments to support their membership in NATO. One such argument is that NATO's expansion will bring a zone of stability closer to the Russian borders; another is that C&EE participation in NATO will open the way for Russia to join later. But according to

Russian experts the mechanism for partnership is still vague. The report quotes Wörner's speech in Madrid on 29 October, in which he said that together with common defense, the main goal of the Alliance is keeping a strategic balance in Europe. This is interpreted as a continuation, under a new form, of the Cold War functions of NATO. If so, NATO's enlargement to the Russian border would demand either a Russian military build-up, or its acquiescence to a new and disadvantageous security situation.[27] The other new NATO mission mentioned by Wörner and analyzed in the report is the projection of stability to C&EE and Middle Eastern countries. The report states that if the PFP . . . means the inclusion in the Alliance's zone of responsibility of the Middle East, this could be interpreted in Russia as the setting up of a security system alternative to the collective arrangements of the CIS. It also states that the extension of NATO responsibility area to two regions directly neighboring Russia on the West and on the South could raise some suspicions.[28]

Military Consequences of Enlargement

On the military consequences of NATO's enlargement, the report states that it would be wrong to suppose that the geographical extension of NATO will be used as a play-ground to attack Russia or its allies. But this does not mean that such an enlargement might not pose new dangers for Russian military security interests. The report rejects speculations that Russian generals are trying to use their growing influence on the Russian government by exaggerating these dangers. But the report outlines consequences which would logically follow from NATO's enlargement: a review of Russian defensive concepts, a reorganization of the TVD (Theater of the Military Actions), the creation of additional infrastructures, the redeployment of huge military formations, and changes in operational planning. This would constitute a military reaction to changes in the military strategic environment, but would have nothing to do with political assumptions about NATO's intentions. The state budget wold be burdened by this military reorganization and the defense power of Russia would be weakened. Furthermore, the programs of arms reduction and defensive reorganization of the armed forces might be jeopardized. Finally, if the Russian government is unable to provide the armed forces with the necessary financial, human and material resources, discontent could escalate to the extent that it would undermine the Russian leadership.

Border Issues and Arms Control

The report considers a hypothetical case in which Romania joins NATO and tries to use it to support Romanian claims on Moldova. The report also stresses that a NATO enlargement could undermine several arms control treaties, and primarily the Conventional Forces in Europe (CFE) Treaty, which was based on idea of definite balance between two groups of European states, and which would become completely irrelevant if NATO absorbed the C&EE countries.

Internal Consequences of NATO Enlargement for Russia

Given that stereotypes are difficult to change, the report suggests that an extension of NATO might be perceived in Russia as a threat approaching the borders of the Motherland, and that this could rekindle anti-Western activities and provide arguments to opponents of the current reformist government.

Final Recommendation

Though Russia does not have the right to dictate whether C&EE states should join NATO or other international organizations, Russia must have a voice in NATO enlargement and the transformation of its missions, since "Russia should now conduct a multidimensional policy of active cooperation with all international institutions which are able to contribute to the construction of a collective security system in Europe."[29]

The recommendations of the report were confirmed by Galina Sidorova, Adviser to the Russian foreign minister, who stated that the position of both the foreign ministry and the president can be defined by three principles: NATO is not a threat to Russia; each state has a legitimate right to ensure its security in whatever way it likes; NATO enlargement without Russia would be counterproductive and harmful to Russia.[30] The assessments of foreign intelligence analysts, the foreign ministry, and the presidency coincided, except on one point. In November, a statement by the foreign ministry seemed to support NATO enlargement if Russia joined too, but the Foreign Intelligence report definitely recommended a collective security approach in which NATO would be an integral part but not a dominant power.

On 26 November Yeltsin's press office made the following statement: "The concerns expressed by Mr. Primakov are shared by the armed forces, Russian citizens and political forces concerned with the strategic interests of the state."[31] This was confirmed in December 1993, in Brussels, during the NACC session, when Russian Foreign Minister Kozyrev stated that "the idea of quick enlargement of NATO has been buried."[32] The PFP proposal was transformed as well. Moscow proposed to transform NACC into an independent organization, which would encompass NATO, WEU, CIS and other regional organizations in what could then be seen as a new forum for discussion on the future European security architecture.

In January 1994, at the Brussels NATO Summit, the PFP was adopted. This was well accepted in Russia at the official level because it gave Russian foreign policy a chance to put off the problem of NATO enlargement *sine die*. It seems that the PFP should be assessed not as a NATO strategic initiative, but as the Alliance's response to at least two external forces: pressure by the C&EE countries who wanted to join NATO as soon as possible; Russia, as any enlargement of NATO would be in conflict with its vital national interests. The PFP program was a reasonable compromise and evidence of NATO readiness to take legitimate Russian interests seriously.

But by March 1994 it became clear that Russia had to make a decision soon. More than sixteen European states, including several from the FSU, showed interest in joining PFP. The ministries of defense and foreign affairs, and the security council of Russia announced on 17 March that Russia "can join PFP before the end of March"[33]. Foreign Minister Kozyrev was more cautious about the schedule, but confirmed that Russia had decided to join. This became a subject for special hearings in the Defense Committee of the State Duma. These hearings, together with the expert assessments published in the Russian press, demonstrated that Russian legislators and at least some independent analysts had serious concerns about the consequences of such a decision.

The PFP initiative was presented at the NATO summit in the form of two documents: a *Framework Agreement* and an *Invitation*. The former corresponds with the strategic interests of any democratic nation (the establishment of democratic civilian control over the military, transparency in the defense budget, etc.). But the *Invitation* states that NATO "would welcome expansion that would reach to democratic states to our East", and proclaims that that PFP "will play an important role in the evolutionary process of the expansion of NATO".[34] Russia, however, does not see the PFP as a forerunner of NATO expansion, but as an opportunity to block this scenario. As an alternative, Russia would prefer the foundation of a future European security system which would integrate NATO, C&EE countries and Russia.

Russian Proposals for Future European Security Cooperation
Foreign Minister Kozyrev stated that the basis for future European security cooperation should run along several tracks.[35] These arguments, which are summarized below, aptly reflect the currently prevailing Russian view on the future of European security and on the role of international organizations in it:

• The Euro-Atlantic cooperation must be developed by transforming the CSCE into an efficient regional organization and NACC into an independent body, closely linked with CSCE. This is necessary to coordinate the efforts of NATO, EC, Council of Europe, WEU, and CIS in strengthening stability providing peace-keeping operations, and defending minorities rights in Europe.

• Cooperation within the NACC should be extended, together with the participation of neutral European countries; NACC should be transformed into an independent body with a small secretariat. NACC could became a laboratory for peace-keeping planning, and for fostering transparency in the military activities of the military-industrial complexes, including those related to civilian conversion.

• A network of bilateral agreements should be set up to promote cooperation and consultation, not only between NATO states on one side and C&EE and FSU countries on the other, but also with other states in Europe, and between NATO and the CIS.

• C&EE states should be granted joint security guarantees by Russia and by Western European countries. Such a network of overlapping guarantees could be extended to all of Europe. Today,

Russia and the West have a very broad range of common risks and challenges in the field of international security, and this determines an enormous potential for the further security cooperation.

• European states should build up their peace-keeping potential, and should seek to provide for a more positive response to the new kind of conflicts now threatening European security. This should include practical support to Russia and the CIS in their peace-keeping missions in FSU territory.

In conclusion, it seems likely that the Russian position on international security matters, and on the role of international security institutions, will be shaped more and more by Russian vital national interests, which will not necessarily coincide with the interests of developed Western countries. This, however, should not be understood as a retreat from Russian commitments to democracy, but as a normal process of a new country in search for its own national identity.

Notes

1. Blagovolin, Sergey: "Does the USSR Need to Join NATO?", *Rossiskie Vesty* (The Russian Herald), August 1991, No. 16, p.11.

2. Quoted in *Nezavisimaya Gazeta* (The Independent Newspaper), 16 August 1993, p. 5.

3. *Ibid.*

4. Quoted in *Moscovskie Novosti* (Moscow News), No. 41, 10 October 1993, p. 6B.

5. Goncharov, Sergei: "Specific Russian Interests: What They Are", *Izvestia*, 25 February 1992, p. 3.

6. *Ibid.*

7. *Ibid.*

8. Rahr, Aleksandr: "Atlantists versus Eurasians", *Nezavisimaya Gazeta*, 8 August 1993, p. 4.

9. *Ibid.*

10. *Nezavisimaya Gazeta*, 19 September 1993, p. 5.

11. *Segodnia* (Today), 3 September 1993, p. 10.

12. *Moscovskie Novosti*, No. 43, 24 October 1993, p. 15A.

13. *Ibid.*

14. Arbatov, Alexei: "Russia and NATO: Do we Need Each Other?", in *Nezavisimaya Gazeta*, 11 March 1992, p.2.

15. *Ibidem.*

16. *Segodnia*, 16 October 1993, p. 5.

17. *Segodnia*, 16 October 1993, p. 2.

18. *Moskovskie Novosti*, No. 38, 19 September 1993, p. 7A.

19. Melnikov, Sergei: "NATO Is not a Friend to Russia", in *Novaya Egednevaya Gazeta* (The New Daily Paper), 22 September 1993, p. 5.

20. *Ibid.*

21. *Segodnia*, 14 October 1993, p. 3.

22. *Izvestia*, 2 October 1993, p. 3.

23. Translated from the Russian citation in *Izvestia*, 23 October 1993, p. 3.

24. *Segodnia*, 14 October 1993, p. 3.

25. *Nezavisimaya Gazeta*, 26 October 1993, p. 3.

26. *Izvestia*, 26 November 1993, p. 2.

27. *Nezavisimaya Gazeta*, 26 November 1993, p. 3.

28. *Ibid.*

29. *Nezavisimaya Gazeta*, 26 November 1993, p. 3.

30. *Segodnia*, 27 November 1993, p. 4.

31. *Ibid.*

32. *Segodnia*, 7 December 1993, p. 2.

33. *Segodnia*, March 18, 1994, p. 1.

34. *Partnership for Peace: Invitation*, NATO Press Communique M-1 (94) 2, 10 January 1994, p. 1.

35. *Nezavisimaya Gazeta*, March 3, 1994, p. 4.

8 International Institutions and European Security: The Ukrainian Debate

Alexander Honcharenko

Ukraine and European Security

Two years after the proclamation of Ukraine's independence, its role and place in the European security system are being debated in the international community with increased interest. This stems from the unique geostrategic situation of Ukraine; its significant economic, scientific and technological and military potential; its policy towards the nuclear weapons it inherited from the USSR; the unbalanced policy of the West for an unconditional and immediate nuclear disarmament of Ukraine; and, finally, the political developments in Russia and its growing imperialistic ambitions, which are reflected in the current unpredictable state of Ukrainian-Russian relations.

In the attempted October 1993 *coup* in Moscow, the victory of the so-called 'democratic forces' demonstrated that Russian democracy is different from Western democracy. It is evident that President Yeltsin paid a high price for the backing of the military during the *coup*, not only by supporting the military-industrial complex, but also by pursuing an aggressive policy in the so-called 'near abroad'—i.e. the territory of the former Soviet Union, (FSU). Yeltsin's policy toward the 'near abroad' also finds complete support in the overwhelming majority of Russia's democratic parties. This demonstrates that Russian pluralism ends where the national question begins. Russia's policy in the 'near abroad' may be understood if it is considered within a historical perspective. As the Russian national mentality has focused on permanent expansion for the last 500 years, decades will be needed to change it.

Thus, the success of Zhirinovskiy's Liberal-Democratic Party in the elections of December 1993 is understandable, but the more recent shift to the right in the positions taken by President Yeltsin and Prime Minister Chernomyrdin, are greater cause for concern. There is little difference between Russian 'conservatives' and 'democrats' with respect to the country's policy towards the 'near abroad'. In fact, the main difference may be only in their tactics.

The Russian ultimatum to the states of the 'Four-plus-Two' treaty (US, UK, USSR, France and the two Germanies) concerning the undesirability of NATO membership for the countries of Central and Eastern Europe (C&EE) was only poorly disguised.[1] The 'Zhirinovskiy card' that allowed the Yeltsin government to scare the West once again with the risk of another 'enemy of Russian democracy' (Ligachev, Lukyanov, Yanaiev, Rutskoy, Zhirinovskiy ... who will be the next?) coming to power proved the point of those who argued that, if Zhirinovskiy had not come to the scene, Yeltsin would have had to invent one.

In Azerbaijan, the externally fomented, anti-democratic, pro-Moscow *coup* led to this country's hasty decision to join the Commonwealth of Independent States (CIS). An analogous scenario in Georgia resulted in its occupation by Russia and in the transfer of key military bases, lines of communications and sea ports (including Poti and Sukhumi) to Russian control. The comments by Russian Foreign Minister Kozyrev that Russia was defending its legitimate interests in the 'near abroad', demonstrate that the political ambitions of the Russian Federation are to revive the old empire. Finally, despite protests from the Ukraine, and a resolution of the UN Security Council, Yeltsin and his new Parliament have no intention to give up territorial claims on Ukraine.

In light of the above, it is not surprising that in only one year (spring 1992 - spring 1993) the number of Ukrainians who support a full nuclear status more than doubled (from 15-18% to more than 30%). The vast majority (more than 88%) support the idea that any further steps toward a nuclear-free status would be possible only if Ukraine receives both full and legally binding security guarantees from all nuclear powers and compensation from Russia for the nuclear weapon material that Kiev would give up.[2]

The results of an October 1993 poll taken jointly by the parliamentary gazette (*Holos Ukrainy*), the Ukrainian Sociological Service, and the Center for Democratic Initiative, are even more striking. With regard to nuclear weapons, 66% of the respondents agree that Ukraine should maintain its nuclear arsenal in some form. Only 22% believe it should give it up; 6% had no opinion. Of the 66% favoring the maintenance of nuclear arms, 27% support keeping them only until Ukraine receives international guarantees that they will be dismantled; 33% believe Ukraine should take possession of nuclear weapons and then initiate global nuclear disarmament along with other nations; while 6% believe it should declare itself a nuclear power. This radicalization of public opinion also takes place in other spheres related to the problems of national security and military matters.[3] A break-through in this dangerous situation took place only in 1994, after President Clinton visited Kiev, and after the signing of the Trilateral Statement between the US, Ukraine and Russia. In this Statement, the US and Russia assured Ukraine of their readiness to provide it with security guarantees after the entry into force of the START-1 Treaty and Ukraine's accession to the Nuclear Nonproliferation Treaty (NPT) as a non-nuclear-weapon state.

The National Security Debate

Starting in mid-1991, a number of publications elaborated the basic priorities of Ukraine. National security was defined as the absence of threats to human rights and to the basic interests of a sovereign national state.[4] This definition substantially broadened the traditional approach to national security, not only by introducing additional dimensions in economic, ecological, cultural and other spheres, but also by declaring the unconditional priority of human rights over the rights of a state.

The proposed security agreements with the CIS countries (given Russia's predominance) could provide Ukraine with the same security that the Warsaw Treaty Organization gave for Hungary in 1956 and Czechoslovakia in 1968. Therefore, Ukraine has not signed any military agreement within the CIS, and remains an associate member. At the same time, the hastily proclaimed Ukrainian neutrality is an obstacle for its desire for integration into existing structures of European and international security. Also, the uncertain and inefficient programs of conversion, the strengthening of the armed forces and the restructuring of the security service also hinders integration into Western security structures. These and other problems were widely discussed in the academic circles of the country in 1991-1992, often with the participation of leading Western experts.

As a result of these debates, the basic external and internal threats to the national security of Ukraine were defined. The main internal threats have been identified as follows: (i) the collapse of economic reforms, social instability and disorders; (ii) ethnic and regional conflicts and civil war; (iii) a *coup* by the old nomenklatura, with the possible participation of the armed forces; (iv) ecological degeneration mainly as a result of a new Chernobyl-type nuclear power catastrophe. The main external threats were seen to be: (i) Russian expansionism and Russia's military machine; (ii) inter-ethnic conflicts, possibly fomented from abroad, and potential fragmentation of Ukraine; (iii) an economic blockade and blackmail—including the confiscation of Ukrainian nuclear fuel without compensation; (iv) territorial claims and Ukrainian involvement in interstate conflicts; (v) pan-Slavic ideology and Russian socio-cultural domination.[5]

At the same time, articles by Western analysts also addressed problems of Ukrainian national security. For example, one analyst wrote that 'how Ukraine affects Europe will be determined by how it consolidates its sovereignty. Critical challenges include economic reform, the institutionalization of democratic governance, and the establishment of national security structures.'[6]

It is too early to speak about the existence of a multiparty system in Ukraine. Though more than 30 parties are officially registered, in one of the latest polls, 72.5% of those surveyed could not identify a favorite political party. Of those who could, 9% favored the popular movement *Rukh*; 5% the Democratic Party; 4% the Communist Party; 3.5% the Green Party: and 2% each for the Party of Democratic Rebirth and the Ukrainian Republican Party. This poll shows very little change from a previous poll taken in June 1993.[7] Consequently, it is impossible to identify the political platforms of different parties or different social groups on national security problems, on issues of multilateralism in security affairs, or on the role of international security institutions. The spectrum of political parties may be divided according to four main orientations: right-wing radical, right centrist, left centrist and left-radical. The following paragraphs will analyze each in turn.

Right-wing Radicals

The main right-wing radical parties are the Ukrainian National Party, the Ukrainian Conservative Republican Party, the Ukrainian Agrarian Democratic Party, and the following movements: State Independence of Ukraine, Congress of Ukrainian Nationalist, Ukrainian National Assembly, Union of Ukrainian Youth. Their representatives maintain nationalistic positions and appeal to the historical attempts to build an independent Ukrainian state in the seventeenth and twentieth centuries. They are cautions about any international alliances, agreements and obligations in the sphere of national security; national security must be grounded on the basis of inner resources and national armed forces. Let us recall that the main reason of the disappearance of the Ukrainian national state in 1918 was the voluntary dissolution by the Parliament of the 250-thousand-strong national army. The majority of right-wing nationalists want a full nuclear power status. They regard nuclear weapons as an important factor of deterrence and the only reliable guarantor of independence, as any international guarantees are inadequate. The Ukrainian National Assembly, while preparing for the parliamentary debate on START-1, states that the 'nuclear status is the best guarantee of peace, security and stability . . ., an instrument for solving the problems of development of fundamental sciences, defense, national military-industrial complex, and for promoting geopolitical priorities and long-term national interests.'[8]

The attitude of these parties towards international security structures as a whole is generally positive, but they are skeptical given their demonstrated impotence in the conflict in former Yugoslavia. These parties support the idea of Ukrainian membership in NATO and other organizations as a means to ensuring national security, provided that certain conditions are met, such as Ukraine's full nuclear status and Russia's exclusion from NATO.[9]

Right-centrist Parties

The Ukrainian Republican Party, the Democratic Party of Ukraine, the Ukrainian Christian-Democratic Party, the movement *Rukh*, the Congress of National Democratic Forces, maintain a more balanced position. They stress the need to accelerate the achievement of national statehood, but deem it necessary to combine external and internal security factors by participating in international security structures. Their attitude towards nuclear weapons varies from demands to proclaim Ukraine a nuclear-weapon state immediately to support for complete nuclear disarmament on the condition of firm, legally binding guarantees of national security by the world community, large-scale economic assistance, and adequate compensation by Russia for the nuclear materials taken from dismantled nuclear weapons. Their attitude towards a military and political treaty with Russia is negative. They accept only limited bilateral economic cooperation with Russia and other CIS countries, and emphasize the need for ties with Western Europe.

Right-centrist parties regard membership in the European Union (EU), NATO or the Western European Union (WEU) as a long-term goal. They pay close attention to the elaboration of theoretical and practical options for regional security structures in Eastern Europe, particularly in the Black Sea-Baltic belt. They initiated a number of conferences and international consultations on these issues with the representatives of parties and public organizations of the Baltic states, Belarus, Moldova, Poland, Hungary, and the Czech Republic, among others.

Left-centrist Parties
The main parties with this orientation are the Party of Democratic Rebirth of Ukraine (PDRU), the Social-Democratic Party, the 'Green' Party, the Ukrainian National Democratic Party, the Liberal and Liberal-Democratic Parties, the political grouping 'New Ukraine' and others. These parties have liberal-democratic, cosmopolitan ideals and represent the interests of the middle class. They have the largest support in the Eastern regions, among the Russian-speaking population. They strongly support the idea of independence, but at the same time want to preserve the CIS as a confederation of truly independent states. They also support the establishment of closer economic relations with Russia and other FSU states. Pacifist, and anti-nuclear, their general orientation is aimed at a neutral, out-of-blocs and non-nuclear status of Ukraine.

The position of these parties has recently changed because of political developments in Russia. The PDRU, well known for its pacifist tendencies, stated that, if Ukraine agreed to give up its missile and nuclear potential, it should be guaranteed sovereignty and territorial integrity because of the situation in Russia; otherwise, the implementation of the provision in the Declaration on state sovereignty concerning its non-nuclear status should be postponed.

Left-radical Parties

These are the Socialist Party of Ukraine, the Communist Party of Ukraine, the bloc 'Civic Congress of Ukraine' and by a number of regional separatist organizations like 'Republican Movement of Crimea', 'Movement for the Revival of Donbass'. The ideological basis of these parties is Marxism. These parties are popular in the Eastern regions of Ukraine, in Crimea and among the Russian-speaking population as a whole. Abundant financial support of their activity from Russia determines their pro-Moscow orientation, which in a majority of cases is in opposition to the national-democratic movement and the government of Ukraine. Despite some differences, they all aim at revitalizing the old Russian empire. They call for full membership in the CIS; immediate and complete nuclear disarmament; joint military command and single military-strategic space with Russia. These parties also insist on lifting the ban on the activities of the Communist party, which is the third largest party in Ukraine and claims more than 120,000 members.

National Security Policy and International Institutions

During its first two years of existence, Ukraine has not had a consistent national security policy. This stems both from the objective difficulties discussed above, and from a number of subjective factors or, to put it bluntly, serious political mistakes made after independence. Among the latter, the hasty and not well thought-out proclamation of the non-nuclear and neutral status of Ukraine. An analysis of security doctrines and basic strategic concepts of developed countries suggests that a country with a geopolitical situation comparable to that of Ukraine has two options for ensuring national security. The first is based on building up its own armed forces, possibly including a nuclear deterrent. National security doctrines of nuclear weapon states maintain that nuclear deterrent forces remain the primary basis of their security. The second option is to become a member of a powerful military system of collective security, which should provide clear guarantees.

Having simultaneously proclaimed both its neutrality and its non-nuclear status, Ukraine has given up both options. Attempts to receive guarantees from other nuclear weapon states as a prerequisite for its denuclearization brought no results. This led to a sharp increase in pro-nuclear sentiments and resulted in a conditional ratification of START-1 by parliament.

In October 1993, parliament adopted, at its first reading, the 'Concept of National Security'. It provides for coordinated policies on internal, external, economic, social, demographic, military, and environmental issues, as well as on science, technology, migration and information. This requires the coordination of various state organs.

The National Security Council has been established to coordinate national security policy. It works out the basic directions of strategy and drafts programs of the state policy of ensuring national security; in war-time, it would function as the Council of Defense.[10]

Also in October 1993, the Military Doctrine of Ukraine was officially adopted. It has a strictly defensive character, the main strategic goals being the defense of state sovereignty, territorial integrity and the inviolability of borders. Parliament deliberated that total military forces at the present stage should be 450,000, including 200,000 for the army, 90,000 for the air force and 50,000-60,000 for the navy. This would involve 0.8% of the total population, which is about average according to internationally accepted standards.[11]

An important feature of the Doctrine is the absence of a defined enemy. The document states that 'Ukraine will consider a potential enemy any country which . . . creates a military threat, intervenes in its internal affairs, endangers its territorial integrity and national interests.' While proclaiming its desire to become a non-nuclear state, it links the elimination of nuclear weapons on its territory to legally binding guarantees.[12]

On 18 November 1993 parliament ratified START-1. From the beginning, both president and government linked the ratification of START-1 and the Lisbon Protocol to the ratification of accession to the NPT. They hoped to persuade the world to provide reliable security guarantees, resources for the destruction of nuclear weapons, and compensation for their nuclear component value.

Ukraine and European International Institutions

NATO and the Cooperation Council
The interaction and cooperation with C&EE countries, aims at filling the 'security vacuum' that emerged in this region after the dissolution of the Warsaw Treaty. This is the main thrust of NATO strategy, and an important condition for its political survival. The creation of the North Atlantic Cooperation Council (NACC) as the main coordinating body of this cooperation has allowed NATO to influence the policy of C&EE countries without assuming any formal military and political obligations.

But it should be kept in mind that NATO's analysts started considering Spain's accession to NATO twelve years before it was granted. According to Ukrainian press reports, NATO Secretary General Manfred Wörner has said that Hungary may raise the issue of its membership in NATO in near future, while Ukraine has to solve a lot of problems, including its neutrality, and that careful thought must be given to the kind of guarantees it might be given.[13] The cautious the approach of NATO nations towards Ukraine is understandable: on one hand, they do not want to jeopardize their relations with Russia; on the other hand, the political and economical situation in Ukraine makes it difficult for Western states to assess its prospects.

From the Ukrainian point of view, NACC activities are useful. Participation in them enables the country to raise current issues of foreign and military policy, to explain its positions, and to block proposals against its national interests. The most pressing issue—in particular relations between Ukraine and Russia—have also been discussed in the framework of NACC. An important role can also be played by NACC in building mechanisms for interaction between Western European military and political organizations and new regional structures like the Visegrad Group, the Central European Initiative, the Black Sea Economic Commonwealth and others; the NACC can also contribute to in creating an pan-European space of stability and security under the aegis of the Conference on Security and Cooperation in Europe (CSCE). The proposals put forward at the NACC ministerial meeting in Athens in June 1993 concerned broadening the NACC mandate, put forth by the US, closer coordination between NACC, the UN and CSCE (put forth by France, Poland, and Italy). The NACC's support for

President Kravchuk's initiative on the creation of zone of stability and security in Central and Eastern Europe could be a basis for practical steps in this direction.

The North Atlantic Assembly

Formally, the North Atlantic Assembly (NAA) is completely independent from NATO. This is the only forum in which the parliamentarians of Europe and North America work together. Taking into account that NAA is a link between NATO and the parliaments of individual countries, Ukraine sees the NAA as playing an important intermediary role in shaping the policy of NATO. After granting the status of 'associate delegations' to C&EE countries, including Ukraine, the NAA will strive not only to play the role of inter-parliamentary forum for the NATO countries, but also to become a factor for the promotion of democratic changes in 'post-communist' countries.

For this purpose, the Assembly organized a number of special seminars and programs for parliamentarians and scholars (to which Ukraine participated) which addressed such issues as parliamentary democracy, disarmament, security and prospects for cooperation in Europe. Ukraine regards strengthening of links with the parliamentary structures of NATO countries as one of the most important directions of its foreign policy.

The Western European Union

Unlike NATO, the WEU wishes to develop relations with Ukraine, as well as with other countries of Central and Eastern Europe, on a bilateral basis. WEU Secretary General van Eekelen stressed the desire to develop relations with Ukraine. This shows that though Western states have not quickly granted Ukraine and other C&EE countries full membership in their military and political structures, or formal security guarantees, it should not be regarded as a refusal to cooperate with them or to support their development as of the independent nations; rather, the decision is determined by a number of objective economic and political factors.

The CSCE and the EU

Ukraine takes an active part in the negotiations of the new CSCE Forum for Security Cooperation. At the Forum, Ukraine confirmed its position with regard to such basic principles as inviolability of borders, peaceful settlement of disputes, development of a multilateral confidence-building process, arms control and disarmament; and it stressed the importance of the non-military aspects of security. The country fully supports the adoption of a CSCE code of conduct in security, i.e. the codification of existing and/or new international norms to regulate the actions of states in order to ensure international and internal security. Special attention is to be paid to the issues of conflict prevention.

The EU for a European Stability Pact provides for a number of agreements between participating states. In essence, it aims at starting a process of building mutual understanding and cooperation to promote stability in Europe. The proper institutions to ensure respect for these principles should also be organized and their activities coordinated. The proposal as a whole has much in common with President Kravchuk's initiative on the establishment of a zone of stability and security in C&EE.

But the EU draft does not provide clear guarantees on the inviolability of borders. There is also a danger that, because of Russia's support for the EU proposal and the pro-Russian position of France, it may be turned into a new mechanism for restoring the political influence of Russia in the Eastern Europe with the tacit consent of the West. Thus, while generally supporting the idea of the Pact, Ukraine has certain reservations about the possible consequences of its implementation, and insists on further development to ensure equal participation of Eastern and Western Europe.

Ukraine's integration into Western European military and political organizations is necessary because of the objective needs for the protection of national interests. This process should coordinate the general dynamics of the creation of an pan-European security structure with the existing Western European organizations. Ukraine wants to take concrete steps towards membership in the EU and the Council of Europe as an important prerequisite for its full membership in military and political structures. The following paragraphs will examine Ukraine's attitude towards the main international institutions in Europe.

An Uncertain Future

The main obstacle to the speedy development of cooperation by

Western European states is the controversy of Ukraine's policy on nuclear disarmament, as well as its slow processes of democratization, reforms and transition towards a market economy. However, there are also some fears among the European NATO members of worsening relations with Russia if it establishes close ties to Ukraine; if Russia is distanced from cooperation with MATO, the very existence of the Alliance in the new strategic environment will be threatened.

In Ukraine, few in the various branches of government understand that NATO, WEU, NAA, EU, and the Council of Europe are not homogenous structures, that there is a great differentiation of views and positions of their members, and that they can not have a single, coordinated policy with regard to C&EE countries. Despite the difficulties mentioned above, active work towards the integration of Ukraine into existing European military and political structures is one of the most important means of ensuring its national security and sovereignty.

The peoples of C&EE are an integral part of Europe and of the European cultural tradition. From the historic, geostrategic, political and even moral viewpoint they have the full right to be an integral part of the new European system of stability and security. This was stressed on a number of occasions by the presidents of Central and Eastern European countries—Havel, Wałensa, Kravchuk and others. Moreover, it is evident that this very system in any of its possible variants is indivisible. Under present conditions there can not be a reliable security system in Western Europe without an adequate security system in Eastern Europe.

It is possible to build this comprehensive security system only through joint efforts by all European nations—efforts aimed at overcoming the residuals of the Cold War and uniting Europe; the creation of new spheres of interests and influence must be avoided. Regretfully, recent debates and events pertaining to security of the new Europe and the future of such organizations as NATO and WEU not only cause disenchantment of C&EE countries, but generate fears about the possibility of the emergence of new versions of accords similar to that of Yalta or the Molotov-Ribbentrop Pact.

It has been said that the history repeats itself twice: the first time as a tragedy and the second time as a farce. And the role of producer of this farce can be played by the governments of some

NATO countries led by the US. As for C&EE countries, they may be left with the role of scapegoat and silent spectator trying to no avail to find an answer to the question of what is their *raison d'etre* in the new Europe. Many begin to wonder: Do We Need Ourselves?

Fear of Russia by some Western countries has led to an unconditional surrender on the issue of a possible NATO enlargement to the East. This has dashed the hopes of C&EE countries for a speedy integration into the European security structures. The *Partnership for Peace* (PFP) plan put forward by NATO at its January 1994 Summit is only a poor surrogate for the initial good idea of full membership for some and associate membership for other C&EE countries in NATO.

The PFP reduces the plan for the creation of a comprehensive security system to possible consultations and technical cooperation between NACC and the CSCE, and puts the very existence of NACC into question. In light of the prevailing NATO desire to establish special relations with Russia, and to guarantee a special role for that country in the FSU, the PFP could result in a new division of Europe into the spheres of influence.

This policy is not only a mistake but is also extremely dangerous for both Eastern and Western Europe: for Eastern Europe it opens the way for Russia to recreate a new empire within the old borders of the FSU (with the possible exclusion of Baltic countries); for the Western Europe the consequences would be serious as Western concessions to the imperial forces of Russia can only slow down the uncertain development of Russian democracy. Four options for the implementation of NATO's expansion into C&EE may be envisaged.

• *Expeditious enlargement of NATO.* Full membership to the majority of C&EE countries in order to fill the 'security vacuum' in the region, and associate membership to other East European countries without special security guarantees.

• *Partial enlargement of NATO.* Possibly through associated membership and the simultaneous broadening of the NACC mandate, turning the latter from a discussions forum into an organism capable of adopting and implementing decisions in the sphere of its competence.

• *Bilateral Agreements.* These would be concluded, on the basis of the PFP, between NATO and C&EE countries, and would include a formal treaty of alliance with Russia, the definition of specific areas of cooperation, mutual security obligations, etc.

• *Creation of regional security structures.* These would be analogous to the 'zone of stability and security' proposed by Ukraine and other countries; bilateral agreements should then be concluded between these regional structures and NATO.

It is useful to consider the last two options more in detail. It would be a serious mistake to regard PFP exclusively in a negative context or even as a program of betrayed hopes. Despite its compromise (because of the absence of clear mechanisms and a time-table for the admission of new members to NATO, the lack of both the possibility of associated membership and of any security guarantees) in line with the West's desire to appease Russia, the program has a positive and strategically important potential for all C&EE countries.

By taking part in the program, Ukraine is associated with the construction of a new system of European security and is not left alone in the sphere of Russia's immediate interests. Any political, economic or military pressure on Ukraine will be regarded in the context of growing general pressure on Russia by PFP members, and will likely bring a corresponding reaction in the West. The existence of broad bilateral programs of cooperation with NATO and other partner countries will doubtless serve the interests of Ukrainian national security, and will promote its further integration into European political, military and economic structures. Finally, the system of consultations provided for by PFP, despite its undetermined character, offers C&EE countries an opportunity to be granted some operative political support or, at least, a greater degree of understanding by the West in case of crisis.

In view of the above, on 8 February 1994 the foreign minister officially signed a document on Ukraine's accession to the PFP. He stressed that the country supports the PFP as a reasonable and pragmatic initiative. Ukraine's accession signals the nation's return to the fold of European countries and could also well serve the purposes of preventive diplomacy. PFP offers C&EE countries certain strategic advantages. But its success or failure will be determined by the concrete mechanisms (yet to be worked out) of its implementation and, more importantly, by the development of the political situation in Russia.

As for the fourth option, President Kravchuk proposed the

creation of a 'zone of stability and security' in Eastern Europe. This idea, in certain respects, coincides with the principles put forth by President Wałesa of Poland (referred to as 'NATO-BIS') and by French Prime Minister Balladur (the European Pact of Stability). Though these initiatives have a common approach, the Ukrainian initiative best meets the principles of the Helsinki Final Act and other CSCE documents.

This does not imply the creation of military blocs. By no means is it designed against any other state; any country of the region can join it. The idea of regional stability and a security zone is aimed at complementing, not substituting the efforts of such institutions as CSCE, NATO, NACC, WEU. The creation of regional structures of stability and security in Europe could contribute to a better division of labor between NATO, UN, CSCE, WEU, and would place these structures within a general framework of interlocking institutions. Regional structures could also effectively prevent the undesirable duplication of existing military and political organizations, and could promote their transparency and coordination. Support for the idea of a Euro-Atlantic alliance and contributions to the strengthening of transatlantic links through regional security structures could play an important role in establishing a European defence and security identity, and promote the construction of the a comprehensive system of European security.

Notes

1. Fears of Russia among the political elite of some NATO nations confirm that it will be just as difficult to change the traditional Western mentalities it will be to change the historical Russian perspective.

2. *Visti z Ukrainy*, 15-20 April 1993.

3. *Holos Ukrainy*, 14 October, 1993.

4. Honcharenko A.: 'National Security of Ukraine', *Vecherniy Kiev*, 11 April 1991.

5. Honcharenko, A. (Ed.): *The National Security of Ukraine: History and Present*, (Kiev, 1993), p.42.

6. Brzezinsky, I.: 'Ukraine: The Geopolitical Dimension', *The National Interests*, Spring 1992.

7. *Update on Ukraine*, # 10, 21 October 1993.

8. *Vechirniy Kiev*, 15 January 1993.

9. Ukrainian Conservative Party leader S. Khmara, quoted in *Shliakh Peremogy*, 6 November 1993.

10. *The Concept of National Security of Ukraine*, (Kiev: Government Press, October 1993).

11. For France this figure is 0.9 and for Greece it is 1.9%. Further plans based on the assumption of a stable international environment stipulated deeper cuts of the armed forces to 200,000-250,000 men by the fall of 1998.

12. *The Military Doctrine of Ukraine* (Kiev: Government Press, October 1993).

13. *Holos Ukrainy*, 23 June 1993.

9 The Rise—or Fall?—of Multilateralism: America's New Foreign Policy and What It Means for Europe

Ronald D. Asmus

The paradoxical impact of the end of the Cold War is that it simultaneously vindicated American purpose and past policies, yet forced a rethinking of the assumptions that guided US foreign policy for nearly half a century. While liberating the United States from its overriding concern with the Soviet threat, the end of the Cold War has also compelled Americans once again to confront core issues concerning the definitions of their national interests and their role in the world. The result has been an expanding debate over American national security strategy in the post-Cold War world.

For the past four decades, the United States enjoyed a large degree of bipartisan consensus in national security strategy. That consensus is now crumbling as politicians, diplomats and defense planners, scholars and the broader public seek to grapple with the meaning of the end of the Cold War. In its place has emerged a burgeoning debate about the nature of the post-Cold War world and the desired US role in it. The current debate is rooted in very different assumptions concerning core questions: the nature of the international security system, definitions of American interests, *and* the best means to pursue those interests. If the United States is to find a new post-Cold War consensus, then an airing of these views and differences is a healthy and inevitable part of building that new consensus.

Although President Clinton is often criticized for not having a cogent foreign policy, the administration has indeed sought to define and implement a new conceptual framework around the principles of 'multilateralism.' The degree to which it succeeds or fails has enormous implications for the US role in and attitude toward Europe and European security institutions. This chapter begins with a summary of the parameters of the post-Cold War debate within the United States over the future national security strategy. It outlines the Clinton Administration's attempts to define and implement a new foreign policy around the principles of multilateralism—and the problems and criticism that attempt has encountered. This study concludes with a discussion of the implications of these trends for European and US attitudes toward European security institutions.

The End of the Cold War Consensus

The political beauty of the Cold War consensus which governed US national security strategy was that it provided an umbrella for disparate traditions in American strategic thinking. Geopoliticians, realists, liberal internationalists all rallied around the twin intellectual pillars of containment and deterrence in the face of what was seen by the *élite* (and accepted by the public) as the Soviet threat. The collapse of communism and the unraveling of the USSR have eroded that unifying element in American national security thinking.

The result has been a burgeoning debate over two distinct yet intertwined sets of issues: the nature of the post-Cold War international system. The US role within it. Different definitions of American national interests and perceptions of the desired American role flow naturally from varying assumptions on the nature of international politics and the possible threats that could arise to those interests.[1]

Perhaps the most important fault line divides those who advocate a narrow view of US national interests rooted in traditional categories of geopolitics and *Realpolitik* from those who promote a value-driven definition of US interests. To be sure, a tension has of course always existed in US foreign policy between the sober pursuit of power politics and the more idealistic promotion of universal values and democracy. But the Cold War consensus allowed these two traditions to coexist without the need for policymakers to worry much about whether they were containing the USSR because of geopolitical balance of power considerations, or for moral ideological ones. In theory, the rhetoric of American policy often leaned more toward the internationalist school whereas the actual practice of American diplomacy was often dominated by realist considerations.

This old divide has reemerged in the wake of the end of the Cold War. The collapse of communism has revealed the fault line between those for whom the Cold War was only about containing Soviet power, and those for whom it was also a struggle for democracy. For the former the collapse of communism and the unraveling of the USSR means that the US can retreat to a more traditional balance of power stance with US national security strategy primarily concerned about maintaining American sovereignty, strategic flexibility and independence, and preventing the emergence of a new hegemon threatening their definition of vital interests; for the latter, the new task is to foster democracy and expand multilateral institutions and cooperation and to build an expanded and more effective system of collective security in a changing and increasingly interdependent world.

To be sure, there are a good number of gradations between both camps as a function of the relative weights attached to these goals. Moreover, American foreign policy has always sought to find a middle ground between these two intellectual poles. Finding this new middle ground, however, may be much more difficult in the future as different understandings of American interests clash and compete for political preeminence, and as the downsizing of the defense budget forces policymakers to confront new issues and trade-offs.

There are four schools of thought in the current strategic debate: isolationism, selective unilateralism, multilateralism an collective security.

Isolationism
The *leitmotif* of this school is domestic renewal and strategic independence. This school claims that America's Cold War internationalist strategy has warped our sense of national interest and justified US involvement and entanglement in areas and issues of marginal utility to the United States while eroding America's wealth and prosperity. This school criticizes America's postwar strategy as too 'internationalist' and as having bankrupted the country.

Proponents of isolationism firmly see calls for preserving

'global stability,' a 'new world order,' or the pursuit of democracy as slippery slopes to new commitments and entanglements in the world which will only further burden the United States. According to Ted Galen Carpenter, director of foreign policy studies at the CATO Institute, goals such as 'global stability' or 'democratization' fail the test of solvency.

> It is unlikely that either objective is attainable at a reasonable cost, and it is even less likely that a hyperactivist US role can bring about such utopias... Each would entangle the United States in a morass of regional, local, and even internecine conflicts throughout the world; and more often than not, each would involve the United States in conflicts that have little or no relevance to America's own vital security interests. *Washington would become either the social worker or the policeman of the planet—or, in a worst case scenario, it would seek to play both roles. The United States will find itself with even more political and military burdens than it endured throughout the Cold War.* (emphasis added)[2]

The strategic alternative such isolationists offer is the classic agenda of realism and strategic independence. At the heart of a policy of strategic independence is a fundamental change in America's most important alliance relations and the liberation from American commitments in both Europe and Asia. The United States, they insist, is blessed with an unusual amount of geopolitical security rooted in geography. They argue, therefore, that forces in the world responsible for instability are unlikely to make the US the object of their enmity unless it gets involved in their disputes.

Selective Unilateralism

The *leitmotif* of this school is power—the preservation of America's strategic advantage after the Cold War and prevention of the emergence of strategic challengers. While it, too, places a high emphasis on preserving strategic independence, it believes that the United States has global interests. It sees the US as the sole superpower in the post-Cold War world and promotes a hard-headed approach to defend US sovereignty and maintain its strategic advantage in the years ahead. In a nutshell, unilateralists are opposed to abandoning any national sovereignty.

Unilateralists are deeply skeptical of collective security and the ability of multinational institutions like the UN to play an effective role in international security. Whereas isolationists advocate the abandonment of American-led alliance systems, unilateralists place a strong emphasis on maintaining strong bilateral ties with key actors and see US-led alliance systems as crucial for maintaining a balance of power in important regions and preventing the emergence of new hegemons in those regions. Many are concerned about the power potential of a Japan or Germany and justify an ongoing American role in these regions as necessary to contain Japanese or German power.

Unilateralists are straightforward in acknowledging their opposition to multilateral or collective institutions. They argue that no nation, alliance, or institution—including the UN—should have a veto over the sovereign decisions of the US government. Distrust of big government at home thus extends to distrust of large multilateral organizations such as the UN or the International Monetary Fund (IMF) which are difficult for the US to control. While shades of unilateralism can be found on both sides of the political aisle, such thinking is most clearly articulated among American conservatives. As Jeane Kirkpatrick put it: 'It is accurate, I believe, to say that a conservative would not have designed and worked hard to realize the UN—though many voted to ratify the treaty. The UN embodies many of the characteristics least attractive to conservatives.'[3]

Multilateralism

The *leitmotif* of this school is interdependence. It sees international politics as having been transformed by the spread of democracy and the globalization of politics and economics. Multilateralists argue that the security and welfare of Americans can be affected as much by actions and decisions of actors beyond US borders as by domestic actors. They see the United States and its allies as having emerged from the Cold War with a strong sense of shared values, goals and institutions. They want to build on that 'strategic capital' and establish more effective means of cooperation.

Multilateralists propose the expansion of a Western caucus

within a global community. While the UN is seen as key, the preferred strategy is to expand Western regional alliances to deal with new and common problems. The United States would not fear a strong Europe or Japan, but rather would encourage them to assume a larger international security role as full partners in this new Western global caucus.

While proposing a new form of burden and power sharing with other Western democracies, this school sees the United States as having a unique ability to help shape the elements of the post-Cold war system. As the lead power in regional alliances, the US leadership will be required to transform such alliances into new coalitions pursuing broader shared objectives. But this will also require a considerable retooling of traditional American thinking on such matters. As a recent Carnegie Endowment's National Commission report entitled *Changing Our Ways* wrote:

> Collective actions will also have costs. Working with others can be cumbersome and demanding. It is terribly difficult to build consensus and forge a common agenda among sovereign countries when there are differences in self-interest. The task is still more arduous with democracies whose governments—like ours are accountable to shifting public opinion . . .
>
> If we are to succeed with a new kind of leadership, we will sometimes have to yield a measure of the autonomy we have guarded so zealously during most of our history. It is not enough for the United States to say that we will pursue common goals on our own . . . The challenges of collective leadership will be especially demanding in the management of our relations with the other major powers. They feel freer to pursue their own agendas and are less willing to follow an American lead . . . Americans will need to change the way we think about the world and our role in it.[4]

Collective Security

The *leitmotif* of this school is justice and the rule of law—right backed up by might. World peace is indivisible; and aggression against any nation is viewed as a threat to all nations. The international community must insure that aggression does not pay and, therefore, may employ the force it deems necessary and appropriate to enforce collective security.

Proponents of this school argue that the end of the Cold War has liberated the UN from its Cold War paralysis and opened a window of potential global reform and renewal. They insist that the US should have a special interest in collective security because of its privileged position in the UN and because the alternative would be for the US to assume the role of the world's police officer. They see collective security as the only vehicle through which US leadership can preserve world order at a cost tolerable to the American public.

The New Political Lineup

Even a quick look at American political parties reveals that the fault lines in the emerging American debate do not always or easily correlate with the existing political lineup. Realists do not always correspond neatly to Republicans, nor are internationalist Wilsonians always Democrats. Each of the two major parties in the United States has its own checkered foreign policy traditions as well as its own internal divisions.

In the 1930s Republicans and conservatives were most prone to represent isolationist, protectionist views, largely as a counterpole to Franklin D. Roosevelt's internationalist foreign policy. But anti-communism altered that by forcing together disparate Republican and conservative viewpoints into a steady anti-communist internationalism. Old-line conservatives, libertarian conservatives, religious conservatives and neo-conservatives all came together in their desire to counter the Soviet threat. With the collapse of the communist threat, however, the conservative movement has splintered along centrifugal lines of ideology and culture. Pat Buchanan's 1992 Presidential campaign was as much about the challenge of new isolationist conservatism to postwar mainstream Republican foreign policy thinking as about domestic issues in the debate over the future of the conservative movement.

In many ways, former President Bush epitomized the convergence of the unilateralist and multilateralist traditions that underpinned the Cold War consensus. As president, George Bush always emphasized the need for the US to have the capability to act alone if necessary, yet he was also famous for his attention to maintaining America's alliances. Speaking at the Chicago Council on Foreign Relations in the spring of 1992, former Secretary of State James Baker rejected both the notion of the United States as a sole superpower and what he termed 'misplaced multilateralism.' Looking back upon the Bush Administration's accomplishments, Baker observed:

> American leadership and engagement made collective action possible. We did not have to do it alone, but without us it could not have been done successfully. . . . US leadership of collective engagement avoids the dangerous extremes of either fallacious omnipotence or misplaced multilateralism. The United States is not the world's policeman. Yet we are not bystanders to our own fate. Obviously we can hardly entrust the future of democracy or American interests exclusively to multilateral institutions, nor should we. Of course, the United States reserves the right to act alone, which at times may be the only way to truly lead or serve our national interests. Ours is a pragmatic approach, a realistic approach, but also a principled approach—for it promotes those common values that are essential for a democratic peace. It is in this way that we build a new and better world order: US leadership catalyzing collective action to protect and promote our core security, political, and economic values.[5]

If one American political party has been historically identified with the advocacy of internationalism, multilateralism, and collective security, it is the Democratic Party. Collective security was the watchword not only of Woodrow Wilson, but also of Franklin D. Roosevelt, who ensured that collective security principles were espoused in the Atlantic Charter, in subsequent key statements on American war aims during the Second World War, and ultimately in the Charter of the United Nations itself. From the 1940s to the 1960s the Democrats were united around strong anti-communism coupled with a Rooseveltian international outlook. Vietnam fractured that consensus, creating new divisions between 'Cold War liberal' anti-communists and 'anti anti-communists,' and set the party down a 20-year-long path of internal divisions and political disadvantage with the public, who perceived it as weak on national security and defense. Although the collapse of communism potentially removed a source of internal division within the Democratic Party, the Gulf War and the debate over the use of force was a reminder that such historical divisions remained difficult to overcome.

The 1992 primary campaign also showed the Democratic candidates to be spread across the political map on foreign policy issues. The Democrats had their own contemporary version of 'America first' in the 'come home America' theme voiced by Tom Harkin and, even more stridently, by Jerry Brown's isolationist campaign. Indeed, in light of the pressing domestic problems and the precarious fiscal situation facing the country, many Democrats quickly called for a more rapid defense drawdown to free resources for domestic programs.

More than any of the other Democratic presidential candidates in 1992, Bill Clinton based his campaign on an assertive internationalist and multilateralist foreign policy. In each of the three major foreign policy speeches delivered during his campaign, Clinton embraced a foreign policy agenda which moved the center of gravity in American foreign policy more firmly toward the promotion of democratic values and multilateralism. Although foreign policy never became a major in the campaign, Clinton emphasized that domestic renewal and foreign policy reform had to go hand in hand, and that domestic reform was a precondition for the United States to sustain an activist international role.

Speaking in Milwaukee in October 1992, Clinton delivered his harshest campaign critique of former President George Bush, accusing him of not being 'at home in the mainstream pro-democracy tradition of American foreign policy' and of pursuing 'a foreign policy that embraces stability at the expense of freedom.' Candidate Clinton clearly rejected the 'realist' tradition in American foreign policy:

> This approach to foreign policy is sometimes described as 'power politics,' to distinguish it from what some contend is sentimentalism and idealism of pro-democracy foreign policy. But in a world where freedom, not tyranny, is on the march, the cynical calculus of power politics simply

does not compute. It is ill-suited to a new era in which ideas and information are broadcast around the world before ambassadors can read their cables. Simple reliance on old balance-of-power strategies cannot bring the same practical success as a foreign policy that draws more generously from the American democratic experience and ideals, and lights fires in the hearts of millions of freedom-loving people around the world. Military power still matters. And I am committed to maintaining a strong and ready defense. . . . But power must be accompanied by clear purpose. . . . Bush's ambivalence about supporting democracy, his eagerness to defend potentates and dictators, has shown itself time and time again. It has been a disservice not only to our democratic values, but also to our national interests. For in the long run, I believe that Mr. Bush's neglect of our democratic ideals abroad could do as much harm as our neglect of our economic needs at home.[6]

Toward a New Multilateralism

Clinton is the first post-Cold War President of the United States. Clinton and his foreign policy team have sought to implement the themes of a new multilateralist foreign policy articulated during the campaign and in many of his speeches and those of his foreign policy team since assuming office. The president and his advisors have repeatedly emphasized four pillars upon which this new 'multilateralism' would rest: (i) elevating global economic growth as a primary foreign policy goal; (ii) promoting the spread of democracy and free markets; (iii) updating American-led alliances created during the Cold War as well as working to revitalize and reform the United Nations; and (iv) updating America's security arrangements and armed forces to meet new threats and challenges, including a higher emphasis on peace support operations.

In practice, this has meant, first and foremost, a domestic reform agenda coupled with a foreign economic strategy aimed at strengthening the global trading system. Clinton has made US economic recovery and the nation's economic security his top political priority. While emphasizing the need for America to get its own economic house in order, the president has firmly embraced multilateralism in his international economic policy. Since big budget deficits largely inhibit any significant use of fiscal policy to stimulate the economy, with the overhang of private and corporate debt simultaneously limiting the potential use of monetary policy, the Clinton team has made international trade strategy an integral part of America's overall growth strategy.

The clearest example of Clinton's commitment to these goals at the core of his national security strategy was reflected in his high-risk effort to obtain congressional passage of the North American Free Trade Agreement (NAFTA) and a successful conclusion to the Uruguay round of the General Agreement of Tariffs and Trade (GATT) talks. Similarly, Clinton's commitment to the second pillar of his foreign policy, namely the promotion of democracy, has been reflected in a commitment to aiding the democratic transition in Russia which has been elevated to one of the top priorities in Clinton's foreign policy.

Moreover, Clinton moved quickly to signal his support for reforming and revitalizing the United Nations, providing Ambassador Madeline Albright Cabinet status and making her a key foreign policy spokesperson. Already during the presidential campaign, Clinton had hinted at his willingness to consider a significantly expanded American military role in a reformed United Nations, especially a more active engagement in peace support operations. In congressional testimony in the spring of 1993, Ambassador Albright justified the Clinton Administration's support for a revitalized UN as an essential part of a broader strategy to build a new system of collective security in the post-Cold War world:

> In the aftermath of the Cold War, the security of the United States is no longer defined by the size and strength of our nuclear arsenals and military deployments on the front lines of the Iron Curtain. President Clinton has spoken often of this nation's security being defined by the strength of our economy, the adaptability of our armed forces to the new threats of the 1990s, and the spread of democratic government in the world. The security threat to America—a threat that only collective security can ultimately manage—is a world where weapons of mass destruction proliferate and ethnic and regional conflicts trigger massive

refugee flows, enormous economic dislocations, unacceptable human rights atrocities, environmental catastrophes and the senseless killing and maiming of millions of citizens. That world has already arrived. Unless we face up to it and create the institutions and resources necessary to share the burden of restoring international order, the United States will stand exposed to an endless raid on its resources, its goodwill, its soldiers, and, finally, its territorial integrity or the territorial integrity of its allies. Anyone in this room or elsewhere in this country who thinks that what occurs in Bosnia or Somalia or Cambodia is too distant to concern Americans—or has nothing to do with US security—has a very narrow view of economics, politics and morality and has not learned the lessons of history. The costs of these conflicts are staggering, and, ultimately, we end up paying large shares of those costs[7]

The most difficult and contentious component of Clinton's multilateralism has been the effort to multilateralize American military strategy and to update regional alliances for the post-Cold War era. The debate over the former has centered on 'how little is enough?' for the post-Cold war era; whether multilateralism reduces American strategic independence in unacceptable ways; on peace support operations and a renewed debate over the circumstances and purposes for which American armed forces should be used; and on the issue of command over US forces in multinational operations. The debate on enhancing collective security and updating regional alliances for the post-Cold War era has centered on a new commitment to the United Nations. Both during the presidential campaign and while in office, Clinton has backed an expansive idea of UN peacemaking. Although the details have never been published, the review of American multilateral diplomacy (Presidential Decision Directive 13 and the accompanying Presidential Review Document 13) are reported to envision a significant expansion of American involvement in UN efforts such as permanent assignment of US troops for UN efforts and intelligence sharing.

While this debate was and is, first and foremost, an internal US debate, it centers on core issues of American interests and the appropriate means to pursue those interests—issues with obvious and profound implications for Europe. Europe has also played a role in several other regards. Indeed, in the eyes of the new multilateralists, Europe and the US-European relationship was *the* testing ground for building a new multilateralist strategy with Europe as *the* natural partner for the United States in the post-Cold War world. A principle premise of multilateralism was that the alliances and habits borne of the Cold War would provide the foundations for an expanded and shared agenda and strategy between these power centers to address the challenges of the post-Cold War era. No two parts of the world seemed more interdependent, more used to working with one another, and more capable of defining such a shared agenda than America and Europe.

Moreover, after the Cold War, the US public seemed willing to embrace a multilateralist foreign policy. Public opinion polling conducted by the Chicago Council on Foreign Relations and the Americans Talk Security Foundation in the late 1980s and early 1990s documented a shift in favor of institutions like the United Nations and acting together with allies. Americans emerged from the Gulf war convinced of the value of multilateralism, of a growing role for the United Nations and of the need for collective action to meet new threats.[8]

Finally, the Clinton team assumed office with a significantly different view of the future of the US-European relationship. Above all, they were not afraid of a strong and more autonomous Europe, but welcomed it. Many of Clinton's closest aides on European affairs saw the Bush Administration as desperate to maintain NATO's dominance in Europe as a vehicle for American influence—with the commitment to a base force of 150,000 reflecting an outdated belief that West European reliance on American military power would give Washington sufficient influence in other areas as well. Above all, they saw the Bush Administration, while giving rhetorical support to both the European Community and the Conference on Security and Cooperation in Europe (CSCE), as being quite resistant to proposals to do more for European security. This was the case with in the thinly veiled American criticism of the initial formulation of a EC common foreign and security policy and such steps as the establishment of the Franco-German corps.

In contrast, Clinton and his advisors greeted the emergence of Europe as a more autonomous actor. While every US administration has claimed to support European political and economic unity and a more equal 'two-pillar' alliance, the Clinton team insisted that they really meant it. During the campaign and afterwards, Clinton stated that he welcomed a strong Europe and spoke of the challenges that this would pose for the United States. The Europeans, his advisors insisted, should be encouraged to take more responsibility for their defense. The real danger was not that they would act autonomously, but rather that they would not do enough. Greater American support for the CSCE was also considered an area in which US policy had to change.

Such a strategy was designed to increase Europe's self-reliance, but did not mean that the United States was abandoning Europe. Instead, the US role in Europe was seen as evolving into one of a balancer and conciliator rather than one of a protector or guarantor. Europe was becoming much more important to American interests as a future ally and partner in other areas. When Chancellor Kohl visited Washington in late March 1993, President Clinton painted the following vision for future US-German relations:

> During the Cold War, our two nations stood shoulder to shoulder in the common effort to contain communism in Europe. Today, we must be leaders in the great crusade of the post-Cold War era to foster liberty, democracy, human rights And free market economics throughout the world.[9]

The first test cases of Clinton's new multilateralism were two crises inherited from the Bush Administration—Bosnia and Somalia. Although Administration officials claimed—not entirely without justification—that they were dealt a 'bad hand' insofar as they inherited two difficult crises not of their own making, each of these crises has rapidly become closely associated with the president and with a failure of the administration's new multilateralism. The details of the Bosnian and Somali crises need not concern us here. What is important is to note the impact of these failures on the attempt to define a new multilateralist foreign policy, and on American attitudes toward European institutions.

Multilateralism in Practice

Bosnia became the first test case of Clinton's new multilateralism.

From the outset, his administration put itself at the forefront of efforts to resolve the Bosnian crisis—stating that important principles of international order, stability and democracy were at stake. Moreover, Bosnia was a first attempt to apply many of the principles articulated by the Clinton Administration—the importance of the UN, the utility of new instruments such as peacekeeping and peacemaking, the definition of a new 'out of area' role for NATO, the need to find a new division of labor and power within the trans-Atlantic relationship whereby the United States would remain engaged yet allow the Europeans a greater say in formulating and implementing strategy, etc.

As Bosnia quickly turned into a policy quagmire, and as it became clear that there was little if any political consensus within the West over how to resolve the crisis, the case of Bosnia quickly turned into an embarrassing illustration of how little shared sense of values, vision and political will actually existed both within Europe and between Europe and the United States.[10] As criticism over the administration's lack of success in its Bosnian policy mounted, senior officials increasingly blamed the Europeans, or the nature of the crisis or simply redefined American objectives in order to reduce the importance that would be attached to the Bosnian quagmire.

In May an unnamed senior State Department official, rumored to be Undersecretary of State for Political Affairs Peter Tarnoff, created a mini-scandal when, in a not-for-attribution speech at the Overseas Writers' club, he created the impression that the United States was now only willing to act multilaterally and that it was scaling back its international commitments. The tenor of Tarnoff's remarks was that with the end of the Cold War and the decline of the nuclear threat, economic interests were ascendant in American foreign policy and that the US could no longer be counted on to take the lead in resolving all regional disputes.[11]

Tarnoff's remarks created such controversy because they were assumed by many to reflect the 'real' thinking and unspoken agenda of the Clinton Administration—this was, in effect, so it was claimed, the new 'Clinton Doctrine.' Critics claimed that all the administration's activist rhetoric about a 'new multilateralism' was only a cover for organizing a US retreat from international affairs, the abandonment of leadership to the vagaries of ineffective international institutions like the UN, and an opportunity to dilute past definitions of what constitute 'clear and vital national interests.' Secretary of State Warren Christopher subsequently sought to clarify Tarnoff's remarks by suggesting that the United States would 'of course' still adopt a unilateral approach if necessary when 'vital' American interests were at stake, while a multilateral approach would suffice for crises involving lesser interests. Nonetheless, Pandora's box had been opened.

In a speech in late June, Senator Richard Lugar, a Republican moderate and one of the most respected congressional leaders on foreign policy, claimed that the Clinton Administration was in danger of pursuing a 'doctrine of diminished US leadership cloaked in multilateralism at a time when the number of security threats are increasing.'[12] As Lugar pointed out, the policy dispute over Bosnia was no longer just about Bosnia, but rather about allied unity and the willingness and ability of Europeans and Americans to adjust their Cold War political and security institutions to the changing geostrategic circumstances in and around Europe. Bosnia, he insisted, was a greater act of collective political failure as an entire political class had sought refuge behind the idea that nothing could be done to stop a war taking place on the one continent where everyone had assumed only a short time ago that war had been banished for good. Collective security in Europe had failed once again. The issue was no longer whether America and Europe would be standing side by side accomplishing great and new things in the new post-Cold War world, but whether they could act at all.

Lugar's speech was one catalyst in a broadening debate over the future of multilateralism, Europe, NATO and the nature of American 'vital interests' in the post-Cold War era. His claim that not only was multilateralism a failure in the one arena where its proponents had always said it would be most successful, namely US-European relations, but that Europe itself was in danger of unraveling and becoming a major foreign policy challenge in the decade ahead came on the heels of a distinct shift in the *Zeitgeist* of intellectual and political thinking in the US. This shift is reflected on bookstore shelves: several years ago the initial post-Cold War euphoria reigned, captured in books such as Frank Fukuyama's *The End of History and the Last Man* and Sam Huntington's *The Third Wave* which essentially forecast an optimistic international future; by early 1993, however, we witnessed the rise of a more pessimistic literature forecasting a decade of growing nationalism, fragmentation and geopolitical and geo-cultural confrontation—as reflected in Sam Huntington's article in *Foreign Affairs*, 'The Clash of Civilizations;' or in books like Zbigniew Brzezinski's *Out of Control.*[13]

By the fall this debate had spilled over into the realm of the future of European institutions. In another *Foreign Affairs* article entitled 'Building a New NATO' three RAND authors argued that Europe was in danger of unraveling in the years ahead and put forth a plan for alliance revitalization—a new strategic bargain between America and Europe, a basic overhaul of NATO's strategic rationale in order to export security into the new trouble spots along Europe's 'twin arcs of crisis' (including eventual expansion to include the new democracies of the East) to avoid the risk of the alliance collapsing and Europe unraveling for the third time this century.[14] By this point, the debate over multilateralism had extended well beyond Bosnia and encompassed the basic issue of whether the trans-Atlantic alliance had any future at all.

The second test case of the Administration's multilateral-ism—and debacle—came in Somalia. If the notion of the US-European relationship as the natural test case for successful multilateralism suffered a serious blow in Bosnia, the victim of the Somali crisis was another pillar of the administration's new multilateralist thinking, namely the commitment to expanding US military involvement under the auspices of the United Nations and through the vehicle of 'peacekeeping'—whereby this term had an increasingly elastic definition, including a variety of radically different missions ranging from truce enforcement to new forms of combat operations.

It is only a slight exaggeration to say that many of the noble goals articulated by senior Clinton Administration officials along these lines went down to political defeat in the American political context in the streets of Mogadishu. The US experience in Somalia seemed to confirm all of the fears and the worst nightmares of senior political and military officials about the problems inherent in peace support operations, inadequate command and control arrangements, etc. Following the deaths of some 17 American soldiers, the administration outlined the new rules in Somalia—new forces would be under US and not UN command; nation-building would not be included as part of the American mission; and US forces would be withdrawn by the spring of 1994.

One year after Clinton assumed office, the new fault lines in the American foreign policy debate were becoming clear and were crystallizing around two issues: multilateralism and peacekeeping. In the eyes of critics, multilateralism and the United Nations no longer seemed to be the vehicle to reduce US burdens, but rather appeared to be a recipe for either ineffective diplomacy or open-ended commitments in distant places where there were few prospects of success and where American interests were unclear. Senator Robert Byrd summed up a growing ground swell of opinion on Capitol Hill when he told President Clinton that he had 'sworn allegiance to the United States not the United Nations.'[15]

Similarly, in the wake of the Somalia debacle, 'peacekeeping' was transformed in the American political arena and strategic lexicon, almost overnight from a politically attractive form of preventive diplomacy that would contain the costs of US international engagement into a synonym for political trouble. The congressional reaction led to calls for rewriting the rules of warmaking and the War Powers Act for any future peacekeeping missions. Within the administration, there was a growing realization that the US cannot put American forces at risk unless the stakes are important national interests supported by the American people and their elected leaders; failure to do so would lead to the collapse of political support needed to sustain American forces in combat. One senior Administration official was quoted as saying it was 'a shock of reality that will force us into a serious reexamination of US involvement in any peacekeeping effort.'[16]

Implications for European Security Institutions

In the initial wake of the end of the Cold War, the problem of future European security was essentially seen as one of 'architecture' or institutional construction. This reflected the belief that Europe was, or at least was becoming, a stable continent after the collapse of communism, that the era of conflict and geopolitical competition was largely over, and that the key task for the future of European security was essentially to lock in and sustain those security structures that had worked so well during the Cold War.

Apart from the dangers of a reversal of reform in Russia, the great danger to European security, or so it seemed, was intra-

Western squabbling. The problems of European security were therefore seen largely in terms of maintaining domestic consensus and Western cohesion. The greatest concern for many was that intra-Western rivalry and competing claims for leadership and influence (above all between Washington and Paris) could potentially lead to the undoing of the American commitment to Europe. The result was the development of the concept of 'interlocking institutions' designed to ensure that everyone had their appropriate seat at the European security table and that an overlapping set of institutional safety nets existed to successfully resolve any future problems.

The focus of these efforts was much more to sustain the relevance of the old Cold War institutions in the eyes of practitioners and those of Western publics, than to apply them to the newly emerging security challenges. In retrospect, much of such thinking was short-sighted and, while at times creative, simply misguided. New architectural blueprints notwithstanding, Europe is faced with new security problems and the West's ability or lack thereof to deal with them is first and foremost an issue of political will and not an institutional one: whether we keep NATO relevant in the eyes of Western publics is not the point; the real concern is whether the alliance can stop war in the Balkans, or prevent potential conflicts from breaking out elsewhere in post-Cold War Europe.

Five years following the fall of the Berlin Wall, it is clear that the revolutions of 1989 not only toppled communism and ultimately unraveled the former USSR; they also unleashed a new set of dynamics that have upset the peace orders of Yalta and Versailles. War in the Balkans, instability in East Central Europe and the former USSR, growing doubts about the European Community's future and increased uncertainty over the future US role—all underscore the lack of a stable post-Cold War security order in Europe.

As a result, much of the discussion over future European architecture and interlocking institutions increasingly sounds somewhat artificial as we are confronted with much more basic strategic issues—the rise of nationalism and a security vacuum on Europe's periphery, the search for new alliances in East-Central Europe, new geopolitical jockeying and a partial renationalization in parts of Western Europe, nuclear proliferation, etc. The problem in European security is not a lack of institutions, but a lack of strategic vision and coherence along with political will. Without those elements, interlocking institutions become 'inter-blocking' institutions or decaying and impotent institutions; with these elements, even radical institutional changes become possible even though the details will always remain contentious.

Against this background it is understandable why Europe, which was envisioned as a key partner in a new multilateralist American foreign policy, did not become a major factor or priority in American thinking during the first year of the Clinton Administration; many of the initial assumptions regarding European security and Europe as a partner have proven overly ambitious or simply wrong. The absence of a senior European expert in Clinton's immediate entourage only encouraged the view that the 'Europeans' are (again) simply too difficult to deal with. Though this administration came into office more open-minded and (at least in principle) committed to reforming NATO, encouraging a strong Europe and the development of a European defense identity, and enhancing the role of institutions like the CSCE, it found itself increasingly frustrated and, so far, largely unable to formulate a European policy.

By the end of 1993, however, Europe had returned as an issue—not as an opportunity and a willing ally in new multilateralist ventures, but rather as a problem and a source of frustration. Bosnia, growing instability in Eastern Europe and the debate over NATO expansion, the strong showing of the Russian right-wing in the December elections—drew the Clinton Administration's attention to the importance of Europe and the need to define a new US-European partnership for the post-Cold War era in the run-up to the January 1994 NATO summit.

The president's successful performance at the Brussels Summit notwithstanding, many core issues in the debate over how to transform the Atlantic Alliance and forge a new US-European strategic partnership remain unresolved. The administration's proposals on a 'Partnership for Peace' and 'Combined Joint Task Forces' reflected its assessment of what the political traffic can bear, and do not necessarily imply a shared consensus) either in the Administration or within the alliance) on the new strategic challenges in Europe or how to address them. If NATO is ultimately to accept the challenge of expansion or a more ambitious role in so-called out-of-area conflicts on Europe's periphery, it will require a much more fundamental political and military restructuring.

For better or worse, NATO and alliance reform is the next test case of Clinton's multilateralism and the ability of America and Europe to define a new partnership to address the emerging security problems in and around Europe, and in a broader international context. Should this attempt fail, the ramifications will be far-reaching: in the United States, multilateralism will have failed; in Europe, the continent's future stability could be jeopardized.

For the Clinton Administration, 'multilateralism' remains the policy that reflects both American interests and the realities of a new and interdependent world. This involves the search for a new and creative way of meshing traditional American foreign policy objectives with allies in a world where the United States, while enjoying the title of the sole remaining superpower, nonetheless needs partners, allies and both the United Nations and other coalitions to pursue its objectives if it does not want to assume the burden of 'global cop.'

The problem, senior Administration officials insist, is not the conceptual basis for multilateralism, but rather 'growing pains' and the fact that it has thus far been poorly implemented in several very difficult crises. The answer, they claim, lies not in abandoning the theory behind multilateralism, but rather in better implementing it. Perhaps in part because of this realization, by early 1994, it was clear that the first reshuffling of the Clinton Administration's national security team was under way.

More importantly, officials point out that the Clinton Administration has been willing to take on the challenge of trying to reform and revitalize the United Nations, unlike the Bush Administration which spoke of a 'new world order' but failed to develop any new policies to help bring one about. Similarly, Clinton's performance at the January 1994 NATO summit demonstrated his commitment in principle to transforming the Atlantic Alliance, and encouraging a more integrated Europe as a stronger partner, as part of a multilateralist strategy for the post-Cold War world.

For the critics, however, multilateralism has more flaws. They claim it is a chimera—in many ways the worst of all possible worlds for it will simultaneously cede American sovereignty while engaging the United States in a potentially long list of new conflicts where American interests are unclear and where the ability to act decisively is diluted by the constant need to find a strategic common denominator. It is seen as reflecting a dangerous shift away from the post-war center of gravity in US foreign policy, a cover for a new redefinition of US national interests and a half-way house toward a new isolationism shrouded with internationalist rhetoric or an open-ended set of entangling commitments through the UN where few if any American interests are involved.

Writing in *Foreign Affairs* in early 1994, Paul Wolfowitz noted that the jury was still out on Bill Clinton's foreign policy, and suggested that the president could turn out to be either a second Harry Truman or a Warren Harding. Both Truman and Harding, he noted, took office at historic moments when great struggles had come to an end, old enemies had been defeated, and a new era was dawning. Both came to be judged very differently than they had been after their first year: after a difficult start, Truman was judged quite positively because he moved to a much clearer and stronger foreign policy; in contrast, Harding, after a successful first year, came to be judged quite negatively because his initial foreign policy successes were based on diplomacy and economic leverage without clear-cut security commitments, thereby producing a peace on paper that only contributed to the subsequent debacles of the 1930s. This leaves us to wonder about the answer to the question posed by Wolfowitz:

> Will Clinton's first year in office ultimately look like Truman's, a halting first step toward addressing the real dangers to US interests and acknowledging the need for American leadership to secure world peace? Or will his administration forge along in Harding's footsteps, indulging the comfortable conviction that the major threats to American security disappeared with the Cold War and that the United States can now protect its interests in the world with minimal effort?[17]

Notes

1. For further details, see Asmus, Ronald D.: *The New US Strategic Debate* MR-240-A (Santa Monica: RAND, 1993).

2. Carpenter, Ted Galen: 'The New World Disorder', *Foreign Policy,* Fall 1991, p.24.

3. Kirkpatrick, Jeane J.: 'Defining a Conservative Foreign Policy,' *The Heritage Lectures*, No. 458, February 25, 1993.

4. *Changing Our Ways* (Washington: Carnegie Endowment National Commission, 1992), p. 13.

5. From James Baker's speech before the Chicago Council on Foreign Relations, April 21, 1992.

6. *Remarks by Governor Bill Clinton, American Foreign Policy and the Democratic Ideal,* Pabst Theatre, Milwaukee, Wisconsin, October 1, 1992.

7. Albright's testimony entitled 'The New Opportunity to Build a Collective Security System' to the Subcommittees on Europe and the Middle East and on International Security, International Organizations, and Human Rights, House Foreign Affairs Committee, May 3, 1993 reprinted in *United Nations*, July-August 1993, pp. 65-6.

8. For further details see the chapter on 'US Public Opinion and the New Debate' in Asmus, *op. cit.*, pp. 79-96.

9. *The Washington Post*, March 27, 1993.

10. In private, some Clinton officials viewed intra-Western differences over how to handle the Bosnian crisis as reflecting a lack of shared values for two reasons: first, many were surprised at how quickly old intra-European rivalries could be rekindled and override a shared interest in resolving the conflict; second, the eagerness of some European governments to sign on to proposed solutions which many in Washington viewed as compromising core Western principles inevitably led to analogies being drawn with the

'appeasement' policies of the 1930s and to questioning of the degree to which America and Europe still shared common values. However, the fact that the United States was not willing to devote the political will and resources to implement an alternative strategy left it with the choice of supporting a plan it considered flawed in principle or simply letting the war continue.

11. See the coverage of the remarks in the *Washington Post*, 7 May 1993.

12. Lugar's speech at the Overseas Writers' Club in Washington on 24 June 1993.

13. Huntington, Samuel P.: 'The Clash of Civilizations?', *Foreign Affairs*, Vol. 72, No. 3, Summer 1993, pp. 22-49. See also Brzezinski, Zbigniew: *Out of Control: Global Turmoil on the Eve of the Twenty First Century* (New York: Macmillan Publishing Company, Inc., 1993).

14. Asmus, Ronald D., F. Stephen Larrabee and Richard L. Kugler, 'Building a New NATO,' in *Foreign Affairs*, Vol. 72, No. 4, September/October 1993, pp. 28-40.

15. *The Washington Post*, 8 October 1993.

16. As quoted in the *New York Times*, 12 October 1993.

17. Wolfowitz, Paul: 'Clinton's First Year,' *Foreign Affairs*, Vol. 73, No. 1, January/February 1994, p. 29.

10 The German Debate on International Security Institutions

Reinhardt Rummel

The security debate in Germany has been inadequate, in both quality and quantity, with respect to the magnitude of change in the international security constellation and the country's internal situation following reunification. Gone are the days of major populist demonstrations for or against the stationing of new weapon systems on German soil, of parliamentary clashes over differing concepts of *Ostpolitik*. Today the German people see security in terms of employment, ecology, public order and the fight against crime. With rapidly falling defense budgets and decreasing numbers of soldiers, defense is barely a subject of discussion these days in the former outposts of the two mighty ideological-military blocs. More pressing and threatening dangers have entered people's daily lives than the remote risk of a nuclear attack or a major conventional war on German territory.

But security emerges in more subtle ways in a number of issues which are high on the list of political controversies in today's Germany. For example, immigration is a pressing domestic and international concern: how can the country ensure against nationalist overreactions to large inflows of economic refugees from the East, and asylum seekers from the former Yugoslavia, Africa and Asia? How can the causes of migration in the refugees' countries of origin be reduced? Another issue is the current economic recession and its negative implications for the financial foreign and security policy of Germany. Preoccupied with problems stemming from inadequate adaptation to unification, Bonn is tempted to look inward while it is ranked among the major powers and pressured to behave accordingly.[1]

To the extent that there is an open security debate in Germany, it focuses on three questions, all of which have reference to the reform of international security institutions:

• Should the *Bundeswehr* be allowed to take on military roles beyond its obligations in the North Atlantic Treaty Organization (NATO) and the Western European Union (WEU); if so, what should its size and characteristics be?

• Should the European Union (EU) and NATO be enlarged toward the East, extending security guarantees beyond the Oder-Neisse river? As the large majority of the population agrees with enlargement the debate concentrates on how it should take place.

• Should Germany be admitted as a permanent member to the United Nations Security Council? This is a question discussed more by others than by the Germans themselves.

Changes in the German position may occur in the short to medium term, especially in case of a new coalition government after the October 1994 elections. The following paragraphs provide a brief overview of some of the major elements of 'the national security consensus', in which major shifts are highly unlikely in the foreseeable future; among these elements is the principle of multilateralism in German security policy.

Multilateralism: The 'Third Basic Law'?

Walther L. Kiep, a widely respected German politician, has referred to German relations with the United States as 'the second Basic Law of the Federal Republic'. The 'third' Basic Law seems to be multilateralism in German security policy. The two Germanys had already developed a multilateral foreign and security policy during the Cold War, at a time when neither Bonn nor East-Berlin had the option of a unilateral security policy, and both were happy with a growing role inside their respective alliances.

United Germany maintains that multilateral orientation, though it has more options since it regained full sovereignty with the 'Two-plus-Four' Agreements in 1990. This continuity may be explained by tradition: Bonn used to assert some of its national independence through multilateral security policy and through candid support of integration and cooperation in the Western institutions. Today, German leaders continue to favor collective action as their experience has demonstrated that this is the best way to achieve national security interests. Therefore, current German multilateralism also reaches into the Eastern section of the continent and seeks to expand the Euro-Atlantic security setup to Central and Eastern Europe (C&EE), including Russia.

Germany wants to become a 'normal' country, by way of articulation of its national security goals. But, what is 'normalcy' in this context?[2] Should it follow the example of France? Great Britain? Italy? Or does 'normal' mean focussing on national specificities?[3] In this regard, both the general public and the political *élite* are learning to establish a national process for foreign and security policy-making.[4] This leads to a temptation to move toward nationalist action, though the definition of national interest is supposed to prepare a national position for multilateral cooperation. It is not easy to guide this learning process in the right direction. Overreactions from outside the country which refer to supposed new dangers of an aggressive, hegemonistic Germany do not facilitate such a delicate exercise in self-confidence.[5] The four main parties, the Christian Democrats (CDU), their Bavarian CSU partners, the Social Democrats (SPD), and the Liberals (FDP) all endorse multilateralism in security affairs, although there are some differences of interpretation among them and among party factions.[6]

Beyond these four parties, on the fringes of the political spectrum, there are groupings which either do not take a firm stance, or assert nationalist sentiments. Franz Schönhuber, leader of the rightist Republican Party, has coined the populist phrase, 'Europe Yes, Maastricht Never'. But he has not come up with an alternative of his own.[7]

The Green Party is in favor of the United Nations (UN) and the Conference on Security and Cooperation in Europe (CSCE) as major security frameworks within which Germany should act; on the other hand, they are against a 'militarization' of the EU via a merger with the WEU, and are in favor of either leaving or dissolving NATO. At a special party congress in September 1993, the Greens (which are currently represented in the *Länder* and at the municipal levels, but not at the federal level), reaffirmed their pacifist tradition but took no other strong position on security matters. The congress revealed inner-party tensions, with the delegates from Eastern Germany proposing the acceptance of interventionist measures in cases of inhumane actions (such as in former Yugoslavia) and the delegates of Western Germany opposing them. The Western view prevailed. This leads to the assumption that the Greens would continue to view a strengthening of multilateral approaches to security via EU and NATO as negative, and would actually opt for a more 'nationalist' program. This can be of some relevance if a Green/SPD coalition might gain a parliamentary majority after the federal elections of October 1994.

Despite this deep-rooted multilateralism, Germany does have national interests,[8] ' . . . a triangle of economic, political and strategic priorities: free trade and open markets across the globe; prosperous and democratic neighbors; and not being on the front-line of a conflict . . . '[9] According to Wolfgang Ischinger, Head of Planning Staff at the Foreign Minstry: 'German foreign policy does not have to be reinvented.'[10] This is nothing new, it is just that with the end of the bipolar world the context of these interests has changed.

The prevailing view in the German defense ministry is similar:

> concrete action in the field of security policy has to consider constant political factors and parameters with a long-term effect: the geopolitical central location of Germany, its economic situation as an industrialized nation dependent on exports and firmly interwoven with the world economy and, last but not least, the experiences of German and European history.[11]

Based on the constitutional provisions of the Basic Law, German foreign and security policy is guided by five central interests, as stated in the German defense department's 1994 *White Paper*, which reads:

- Preservation of freedom, security, welfare and territorial integrity;
- Integration in the European Union;
- A lasting alliance, based an a community sharing values and similar interests, with the United States as a world power;
- The familiarization of our neighbors in Eastern Europe with Western structures in a spirit of reconciliation and partnership;
- Worldwide respect for international law, human rights and a just world economic order based on market

principles, for the security of individual states can, in the long run, be guaranteed only in a system of global security with peace, justice and well-being for everyone.[12]

As a member of major international security institutions (UN, CSCE, NATO, EU, WEU) Germany has a strong interest in their improvement and interaction. Bonn wants these institutions to complement each other, such that they form a strong security order in Europe and contribute to extending stability to C&EE and into the Commonwealth of Independent States (CIS). The two main institutions which have helped shape West German foreign and security policy over the past 40 years—EU and NATO—still form the primary setting within which Germany adapts and reacts to international challenges. Bonn is thus keen to keep these institutions dynamic.

The governing CDU/CSU/FDP coalition has undertaken steps to underline German entrenchment in multilateral security organizations. A few recent concrete examples may be enumerated here in addition to the fact that Bonn has been an active promoter of both the Maastricht process and the reform of NATO:[13]

- the establishment of two multinational corps with the United States;
- the establishment of the Eurocorps, with the participation of France, soon to be joined by Belgium and Spain;
- the proposed establishment of a German/Dutch corps in 1994;
- the participation of German personnel on AWACS aircraft in the Balkan region;
- the involvement of German medical personnel in Cambodia and the stationing of German army units in Belet Huen, Somalia, in conjunction with multilateral UN-missions.

Not all of these missions have been endorsed by the opposition parties. However, both the government and the opposition SPD supported the further deepening of the Common Foreign and Security Policy (CFSP) of the EU and the evolution of NATO. In their view, both processes are now closely interlinked, since the United States has recognized Europe as an equal partner in the Alliance and there are plans to strengthen the WEU as the European pillar of the Alliance. Thus, the EU/WEU will be capable of strategic action, while avoiding costly duplications. Defense Minister Volker Rühe has emphasized the need for 'Europe' to become militarily more capable; and the establishment of the Eurocorps is a step in this direction. As he stated in a speech given at the 34th Meeting of Commanders in October 1993: 'The Eurocorps is available for NATO use; under the control of the WEU it is the core for a European Defence. It is an important step towards an all European defensive capability.'[14]

This in no way implies a move away from a close alliance with the United States, or a break with NATO. Rühe later went on to say that it is necessary for the West Europeans and North Americans to be able to act independently, but not separately, depending on the situation. It will allow the Europeans to assume greater responsibility for their security and to take action in contingencies where NATO does not commit itself. The rationale here is that all substantive efforts toward a European defense identity relieve the burden on America and simultaneously lay the foundations for a lasting American commitment in and to Europe, which is essential to the preservation of the strategic balance.

Thus, the Eurocorps is a major strategic and political tool which is intended to serve three goals:

• the establishment of a central building-block for European defense;

• the development of an instrument for a Common Foreign and Security Policy; and

• the strengthening of the European foundation of the trans-Atlantic bridge.[15]

These three functions of the Eurocorps help Bonn manage its perennial problem of keeping relations with Paris and Washington both compatible and constructive.[16] It is therefore no surprise that all major German parties have been interested in specifying the division of labor between NATO and the WEU, and have welcomed the concept of a Combined Joint Task Force (CJTF) as deliberated at the January 1994 NATO Summit.

The CJTF allows for the possibility of overcoming some of the problems of incompatibility and duplication between the WEU and NATO. It is a pragmatic solution, acceptable to WEU members (France and Spain) which prefer to remain outside NATO's integrated military structure. The central idea of the CJTF consists of a mobile headquarters which, in a sense, is ranked above Western defense organizations and which will be assigned forces for specific missions on an *ad hoc* basis. Given the undecided question of the *Bundeswehr's* participation in international peace enforcement (see below), the CJTF initiative has not been a major item in Germany's security debate.

Collective Security: German Participation in Doubt?

The domestic debate in Germany regarding European security and the institutions designed to carry out action during crisis management is concentrated on two different levels, a practical one and a constitutional one. Germany must take on a larger share of responsibility in world affairs. Since the nature of world affairs has changed, it is necessary for Germany's role to change as well. Yet, many in Germany tend to avoid engaging in the political debate on the merits of alternative strategic options; instead, they refer to the Basic Law to justify their positions; they look for help to Karlsruhe, the seat of the Constitutional Court.

This is exemplified by the controversy over whether and under what conditions the *Bundeswehr* should be engaged in military missions other than (traditional) collective defense; and if so, whether the Basic Law needs to be amended to clarify the conditions under which such intervention would be legally acceptable.[17] As Karl-Heinz Kamp has pointed out, the answer depends on whether article 87a or article 24 is referred to. Article 87a, states that the orientation of the Bundeswehr is strictly defensive:

> (1) The Federation shall build up Armed Forces for defense purposes. Their numerical strength and general organizational structure shall be shown in the budget.
> (2) Apart from defense, the Armed Forces may only be used to the extent explicitly permitted by this Basic Law.

As Kamp further discusses in his study, the Basic Law does not explicitly define 'defense'. Article 51 of the UN Charter says that, in case of an armed attack, states can defend their integrity, individually or collectively. He also notes that a narrow interpretation of Article 87a could justify the use of force only if the Federal Republic is attacked itself. Then, even military assistance to other nations under attack, as intended in NATO, would only be possible if Germany were also the victim of military aggression. A different interpretation is possible if Article 24 is taken into account. It says in paragraph (2):

> For the maintenance of peace, the Federation may enter into a system of mutual collective security; in doing so it will consent to such limitations upon its rights of sovereignty as will bring about and secure a peaceful and lasting order in Europe and among the nations of the world.

If the Basic Law allows the Federal Republic to a system of mutual collective security, it must also be possible to take on all the obligations resulting from such a membership. This includes military and non-military duties. Obviously, Germany's Basic Law leaves room for interpretation with regard to a possible out-of-area mission of the Bundeswehr. Whether one comes to a more restrictive or a more permissive reading depends on which Article in the Basic Law is emphasized in a legal interpretation. It is this very ambiguity which has provoked a great deal of the inner-German dispute on the future role of the armed forces.[18]

The very fact that large parts of the political *élite* hide behind legal interpretations of the Basic Law indicates the reluctance of the German body politic to face the new nature of security in Europe. Germany faced an entirely new situation in 1989. Suddenly, old rules no longer applied. Given its size and economic strength, Germany was expected to take on a greater share of the burden in ensuring world peace. Given its historical heritage, however, the German commitment has not been as clear-cut as others might have wanted. In the past, Germany was able to rely on the bipolar Cold War to renounce responsibility for security outside of the NATO Treaty area. Its geographic location made it *the* battle zone in Europe, and therefore its allies did not pressure Germany to become involved in areas outside of Europe. Since 1989, these old arguments can no longer be applied.

The position of the CDU/CSU has been fairly straightforward regarding Blue Helmet missions. They want the Federal Republic to participate at all levels or, more precisely, to establish the option for this choice, but also do not see the need for an amendment of the Basic Law in order to this end. The FDP, on the contrary, has insisted on an amendment to the constitution and has appealed to Karlsruhe. Meanwhile, the government has slowly implemented policies and sent the *Bundeswehr* on various missions, both to set a precedent and to accustom the population to international activity of the *Bundeswehr*. From the Gulf mine-sweeping in 1988, to the Somalia mission in 1993/94, German participation and risk-taking has gradually increased.

The consensus within the coalition has been quite strong, although signs of a rift appeared in the fall of 1993 over the question of the continued participation of a *Bundeswehr* contingent in Somalia. While the defense minister announced its early recall, the foreign minister stated that the soldiers would remain for the whole planned duration of their mission. For a week it seemed as though there was no clear inter-ministerial division of responsibility with regard to the Somalia contingent—another sign that Germany was entering the uncharted waters of its new range of political action. The foreign minister accused the defense minister of interfering in foreign policy and called him a 'lout and a boor';[19] the defense minister claimed to be acting in accordance with the chancellor.

Within the SPD, the division of opinions has been accentuated. The party head, Rudolf Scharping, and the head of the parliamentary fraction, Hans-Ulrich Klose, represent partly diverging positions: Scharping wants to allow Blue Helmet missions, but only if there is a 2/3 majority in parliament; Klose goes further and would steer SPD policy more in line with that of the governing parties, allowing all types of UN missions and other combat missions[20] while Scharping initially agreed to peace keeping missions, but not to peace-enforcement (which would mean engaging in an open conflict).[21] Klose has stated that if Germany is a member of an international institution such as the UN then it must accept all obligations of such membership. He is against a partial German participation in UN missions, his argument being that the declaration of human rights as stated within the UN Charter cannot be superseded by individual national interests. He fears that if Germany shows itself to be incapable of fulfilling international commitments, it will not be given a permanent seat in the Security

Council (see below). Scharping's position has approved that of
Klose on the point that UN soldiers should not seek to engage in
combat but should be ready to defend themselves. Scharping has
gone one step further, stating that it would be unacceptable for a
constitutional amendment to be formulated such that Germans
would only participate in certain UN missions.

In opposition to Scharping and Klose is a group of SPD
politicians led by Oskar Lafontaine, Gerhard Schröder, and
Heidemarie Wieczorek-Zeul. They have vowed to torpedo any
attempt to implement a constitutional amendment so that additional
(military) missions may take place. The SPD wants to reduce the
military element in German foreign policy in general. At the
congress in November 1993, it proposed

- to reduce the *Bundeswehr* to 300.000 by 1996 and even
  further if the security situation is favorable;
- to consider armed forces based wholly or partially on
  volunteers (the former option, in which the draft would be
  abolished altogether, could be implemented over a period
  of five years; the latter would bring the reduction of
  conscription to a 6 month tour and could be implemented
  more quickly);
- to reduce the costs of military planning and arms
  acquisitions;
- to focus on a further cooperation with European partners;
- to affirm the view that not all countries need to have the
  same military capabilities and that rationalization and
  specialization need to occur Europe wide.[22]

After the government decided to send German warships into the
Adriatic in 1992 as observers of the UN mandated embargo against
Serbia, the SPD went to the Constitutional Court claiming that this
use of the *Bundeswehr* was unconstitutional. A final ruling has not
yet been made.

Enlarging Western Institutions: How Not to Be a Frontline State?

Most Germans are still haunted by the period when the Iron Curtain
ran right through their country. At that time, there was little that
East or West Germany could do about it. *Détente* and *Ostpolitik*

were means of easing a conflict which would not be solved between adversarial blocs. This experience has a great influence on current German policy toward the East. Germany does not want to be squeezed into such a position again; rather, it wants to take its natural geographic place, which is in the center of Europe, not at an artificial borderline of European subregions.[23] Hence the German interest is developing a network of connections with Eastern Europe such as those with the West, or to simply extending Western institutions to the East.

Despite the end of East-West antagonism, the security landscape in Europe presents an inconsistent picture: on the one hand, the process of integration in the West continues; on the other hand, centrifugal tendencies go as far as fragmentating states in the East. Most Germans are aware of this new security situation. Their former role as a front-line state has changed since the end of the Cold War.[24] Given the many crises in Eastern Europe, however, Germans get the feeling they continue to live at a front-line, albeit one which is characterized by open borders and major imbalances in wealth, stability and political culture. German policy toward Eastern Europe therefore tries to reduce these imbalances, and to relocate Germany in the middle of the continent. All political parties are unanimous on this point: after German unification, European unification is the next strategic goal.

To this end, the Federal Republic has been reestablishing good relations with Eastern neighbors, providing emergency aid and medium-term support for the countries in transition to market economy and democracy. It has worked together with Western organizations such as the International Monetary Fund (IMF), the Organization of Economic Cooperation and Development (OECD, including the G-24), the European Bank for Reconstruction and Development (EBRD), the G-7, NATO, EU and WEU, to transfer Western ideas and assets to the East. There has been relatively little debate in the German public, in principle, on massive financial contributions. Certainly, the tremendous burden of reintegrating East Germany has caused a discussion of how much Germany can afford, but the answer has tended to be that there is no choice: progress toward the completion of the unification of Germany and the unification of Europe must go together. There is also the feeling that there is no time to be lost: just as German unification (at least in legal terms) was a matter of a few months, the unification of

Europe should be speeded up in order to take advantage of this historic opportunity.

This widespread view is reflected in Bonn's leading role in promoting the enlargement of both EU and NATO to the East, and in intensifying ties with all those who are not candidates for accession (especially Russia and Ukraine). The EU's Europe Agreements and Partnership Agreements are both major contributions to this end. They allow for economic cooperation and political dialogue on a regular and structured basis. The SPD, in particular, has favored a concept of security which would stabilize East European democracies through the opening of Western markets, even if this runs counter to West European economic interests. The aim here is to help to build up stronger economies and more stable political systems in the countries in transition, while drawing them into an international interdependent network.

Germany has also established defense agreements with all former Warsaw Pact members. This cooperation goes beyond mutual information to common exercises and beyond security dialogue to exchange of officers. These contacts form a substantial part of the activities of the German defense ministry and of the *Bundeswehr's* in 'security diplomacy' and seem to submerge many of the traditional tasks of politicians and military experts. As the January 1994 NATO Summit indicated, membership for the East Europeans is not yet contemplated, though the Partnership for Peace (PFP) concept allows countries to be virtually as closely connected to NATO as they wish. The PFP has been endorsed by all major parties in the *Bundestag*, but some claim it has not gone far enough.

German Defense Minister Volker Rühe supports a quick expansion of NATO to include Hungary, Poland, and the Czech Republic. Foreign Minister Klaus Kinkel and Chancellor Kohl are far more cautious. They fear that moving too quickly would upset Russia. Similar considerations are being made in the opposition parties. Kinkel's position on enlargement represents a general German consensus: perspective member countries enter the EU first, then become members of WEU in accordance with the Maastricht Treaty, and, finally, via the link between WEU and NATO, they become members of NATO as well.

The sequence could be as follows: first the EFTA members, followed by the Visegrad countries, the Baltics and, finally,

Bulgaria and Romania. In Kinkel's view, though neither Ukraine nor Russia qualifies for membership, a wide ranging partnership should be extended to them as they cannot be excluded from European security. Furthermore, Russia must become the eighth member of the G-7.

Those in the opposition (Greens and the left-wing SPD) who do not want to strengthen NATO, put the emphasis on a more prominent role of CSCE, especially in crisis prevention and peacekeeping. They prefer to enhance the link between NATO, NACC, PFP and CSCE, with the latter in a directing position. The CSCE should be strengthened in many areas: security partnerships, conflict prevention, peace maintenance measures—including the creation of CSCE Blue Helmets and the establishment of a CSCE security council. Some of these propositions derive from 'old thinking' which revealed during the Cold War when the CSCE represented the core of cooperative security. It is popular in East Germany and among pacifists in the Green Party and the SPD.

United Nations Security Council Permanent Membership: Neither Push Nor Pull?

When Germany became a UN member in 1973, it committed itself without reservations to the associated rights and duties, and it was involved in all of the organization's political, economic, legal, social and humanitarian functions. One of the core objectives of German foreign policy remains to help maintain world peace. Bonn is aware of the sharp rise in the demands placed on the United Nations, as well as of the massive increase in the number, scope and cost of peacekeeping measures in recent years.[25]

Germany considers the humanitarian dimension to be a focal point of its United Nations activities. Bonn is active in the Middle East, in Africa, in Southeast Asia, in the Gulf region and in former Yugoslavia, providing humanitarian aid, transport and medical care, monitoring disarmament and repatriating refugees.

But, the UN is overburdened.[26] One of its problems is that the composition of the Security Council is outdated. In this context, a debate started on German permanent membership in it. The debate did not start in Germany and no official application has been presented, but at the 1992 UN General Assembly, Foreign Minister

Kinkel stated that Germany would apply for permanent membership if the world community considered expanding the Council. Possible German membership has been discussed widely among observers and experts in the world. Often the issue has been connected to Japan's pressure for membership. Some American analysts have rated Japan and Germany as emerging superpowers and have concluded that both of them should take on more worldwide responsibility.

The German government has adopted a low-key approach, in part because it does not want the world to expect still more contributions from Germany. With the financial burden of unification rising, and the decision on international *Bundeswehr* missions pending at Karlsruhe, the government does not yet feel prepared for security Council membership. Moreover, Bonn has felt that it is not the right moment to take this step so shortly after unification, which has stirred fears among neighbors of a new hegemonistic Germany.

The German public neither welcomed nor opposed Kinkel's statement in New York. It seemed to be a proposition which was as modest as it was self-evident: the united Germany as one of the world's economic giants deserves a seat at the table along with France and Britain. Moreover, as none of the opposition parties seriously questioned the proposal, the wider public had no reason to argue against permanent German membership in the Security Council. This changed when almost a year later, in June 1993, the General Secretary received comments from the UN member states on the enlargement issue. Most of the reactions had been in favor of a Security Council reform, but for different reasons and with a different design than the one given by the German diplomacy. The subsequent debate in Germany has largely been confined to academic circles.

The arguments for and against are summed up in two articles in a major German foreign policy journal, *Europa-Archiv*.[27] The pro-membership advocate, Karl Kaiser, regards Germany's membership in the Security Council as a necessary means for the country's adaptation to a new level of international responsibility. The opponent of membership, Wolfgang Wagner, looks at the subject from the point of view of the majority of UN member states and concludes that the world does not need more veto-powers in the Security Council, especially not from the industrialized countries.

The Kaiser/Wagner debate demonstrates that, in the security area, multilateralism interferes with integration and efficiency. Wagner makes the point that the German application shows that Bonn does not want a common foreign and security policy of the EU; Kaiser claims that while engaging in collective security in the UN Germany must eschew action in the EU, NATO or WEU and thus reduce the efficiency of the organizations which are supposed to implement the Security Council's decision.

Karl Lamers, foreign policy spokesman of the CDU in the *Bundestag*, makes it plain that the efficiency of the Security Council must not be hindered, even if this means that Germany does not acquire permanent membership: 'If the price for Germany's permanent seat in the Security Council is the membership of numerous other countries, like Brazil, Nigeria and Indonesia, all with veto-power, then it is too high.'[28] Under such circumstances, decision-making in the Security Council would be hampered, as would European influence in it. Therefore, Lamers proposes that Germany cooperate with France and Great Britain under EU rules.[29] He regards a common EU policy in the UN as more important than a permanent German seat, while both Foreign Minister Kinkel and Chancellor Kohl aim at a German veto-right status.

Part of the political debate on this topic has been directed at the reform of the UN in general. At its congress in November 1993, the SPD made it clear that the party emphasizes on the improvement of the UN in general. This would include:

• strengthening of the position of the Secretary General over that of the Security Council;

• unconditional acceptance by UN members of the decisions of the International Court of Justice (so that the principles of sovereignty and non-intervention could be superseded in cases of massive violations of human rights);

• changed membership for the Security Council so that all world regions feel equally represented—the FRG should have a permanent membership;

• limits to the veto-power in the Security Council;

• additional financing of UN activities and sound management;

• establishment of an environmental security council;

• a reduction of the burden on the UN by strengthening regional agreements and organizations.[30]

Such a laundry-list of reforms is used by most politicians in the opposition who denounce a combat role for German troops under a UN mandate or command. First UN reform, they argue, then UN military missions for the *Bundeswehr*. Knowing that such a fine-tuned reform of the UN will never occur, they are reasonably sure that Germany will not have to commit combat forces to the UN for quite a while.

In Quest of a Conclusion: Beyond Germany's *Einbindung*

As stated at the beginning, most of the security debate in Germany these days is conducted at the fringes rather than in the center of the broad political mainstream. There is not much of a strategic discussion of a kind academics are keen to initiate.[31] The situation may best be described as one of 'bi-partisan' foreign and security policy. No fundamental ideological rifts run through the electorate. The only area of major controversy, the combat mission of the *Bundeswehr* in cases of collective security, does not really stand the test. Even if the Constitutional Court allowed such missions, the political mood of the German people is against it.[32]

A legally confirmed option to use force under the mandate of the UN will not be taken up by the majority in the *Bundestag*, whether the government is led by the CDU or by the SPD. In practical terms, Germany is likely to remain an ally with small military contributions to collective security operations. It will try to make up for this by many quasi-military and non-military means in order to participate in allied peace enforcement actions. Bonn's (self-)exclusion from the management of crises and the solution of conflicts in Europe is more likely than a militaristic rush into a leading peace-enforcement role. Both Chancellor Kohl and shadow-Chancellor Scharping exclude sending German soldiers to regions like the former Yugoslavia, 'for historic reasons'.[33]

Outside interest in the internal German debate on international security institutions is motivated by the need for Germany's contribution and the fear of German nationalism. In both cases the strategic demand is to 'tie in' the Germans (*Einbindung*). Bonn's partners will be disappointed in both respects. Given its historical political and current economic constraints, Germany is likely to contribute less than others had hoped, and will be less inclined to break out of multilateralism than other countries would in the same situation. A 'Red-Green' coalition (SPD-Green) government would not come into existence if the price were leaving NATO, as urged by the Greens' program. Germany has become a team player by conviction; its population has internalized multilateralism, not for reasons of altruism but for the sake of efficient foreign and security policy in an interdependent world. In this sense Germany is likely to follow its own special path (*Sonderweg*).

Notes

1. For a description and an analysis of the current difficult German situation, see Kielinger, Thomas: 'Germany: the Pressured Power', in *Foreign Policy*, No. 91 (Summer 1993), pp. 44-62.

2. Young, Thomas Durell: *The «Normalization» of the Federal Republic of Germany's Defense Structures*, (Carlisle, Pa.: Security Studies Institute, 1992).

3. For a discussion of Germany's 'normalcy', see Schweigler, Gebhard: *Die Rolle des Vereinigten Deutschland in Europa: Möglichkeiten und Grenzen* (The Role of United Germany in Europe: Opportunities and Limits), unpublished paper presented at Japanisch-Deutsches Zentrum Berlin, 23 September 1993.

4. For a discussion of this learning process, see Rühl, Lothar: 'Einige Kriterien nationaler Interessenbestimmung' (Criteria for the Definition of National Interests), in Heydrich, Wolfgang et al.: *Sicherheitspolitik Deutschlands* (Germany's Security Policy), (Baden-Baden: Nomos Verlag 1992), pp. 741-759.

5. This dilemma is well treated in Asmus, Ronald D.: *Germany in Transition: National Self-confidence and International Reticence*, (Santa Monica: Rand Corporation, 1992).

6. In early 1994, opinion polls rated German parties as follows: CDU/CSU 40.6%, SPD 34,9%, Greens 9,7%, FDP 8,2%, Republican Party 3.2%. See the *Frankfurter Allgemeine Zeitung*, 13 April 1994, p. 5.

7. For a closer look at the program of the Republican Party, see Veen, Hans Joachim et al.: 'The Republikaner Party in Germany. Right-wing menace or protest catchall?', *The Washington Papers*, No. 162, (Westport: Praeger, 1993).

8. For a sober account of German interests, see Lübkemeier, Eckhard: 'The United Germany in the Post-bipolar World', *Report* No. 56, (Bonn: Friedrich-Ebert-Stiftung, 1993).

9. 'Germany and its Interests', *The Economist*, 20 October 1993, p. 20.

10. Quoted in *The Economist*, 20 November 1993, p. 20.

11. See *White Paper 1994: The Security of the Federal Republic of Germany and the Bundeswehr Now and in the Years Ahead*, Abridged Version, (Bonn: Federal Ministry of Defense, April 1994), p. 7.

12. *Ibidem.*

13. The restructuring of NATO has received a fair amount of attention in Germany. The previous rationale for NATO membership (the American nuclear guarantee and the German non-nuclear status) still exists, but the loss of the overarching Soviet threat has left a logical vacuum which has not been filled. Defense Minister Volker Rühe was very clear in a speech to the German Commanders of the *Bundeswehr*, on 7 October 1993: multinational crisis management must become the main function for NATO. This, certainly, implies the hope that the debate within Germany will lead to a better understanding and acceptance of the new type of collective security challenges, which demand German military involvement in properly legitimized multilateral crisis management.

14. Speech given by Volker Rühe at the 34th *Kommandeurtagung der Bundeswehr*, 7 October 1993.

15. *Ibidem.*

16. For the Bonn-Paris relationship, see Schmidt, Peter (Ed.): *In the Midst of Change: On the Development of West European Security and Defense cooperation*, (Baden-Baden: Nomos Verlag, 1992). On the Bonn-Washington link, see Rummel, Reinhardt: 'German-American Relations in the Setting of a New Atlanticism', in *Irish Studies in International Affairs*, Vol. 4 (1993), pp. 17-31.

17. For an overview of the differing interpretations of the Basic Law concerning the utilization of the *Bundeswehr* in the framework of the UN Charter, see Scientific Service of the German Parliament: *Internationale Verwendung der Bundeswehr im Rahmen der Charta der Vereinten Nationen* (International Employment of the German Armed Forces in Accordance with the UN Charter), Info-Brief No. 132, Bonn 1993.

18. Kamp, Karl-Heinz: 'The German Bundeswehr in out-of-area operations: to engage or not to engage?', in *The World Today*, Vol. 49, No. 8-9 (August/September 1993), p. 167.

19. *The International Herald Tribune*, 17 November 1993, p. 8.

20. In this regard he is supported by 'right-wingers' in the SPD who want the party to go further than Scharping proposed, making peace making missions possible, and making troops available for the CSCE and UN.

21. This position (Blue Helmets yes, waging war no) contradicts a declaration of the Euro-Social Democratic Congress of 5 November 1993, (in which Scharping participated), which favored peace enforcement by military means.

22. *Frankfurter Allgemeine Zeitung*, 18 November 1993, p. 3.

23. A new debate has started recently (initiated by Professor Zitelmann) on the question of whether Germany's ties with the West during the Cold War demonstrated a historic rule or exception.

24. For a comprehensive and sober description see Diel, Ole: 'Eastern Europe as a Challenge to Future European Security', in Curtis, Mark et al.: *Challenges and Responses to Future European*

Security: British, French and German Perspectives, paper prepared for the European Strategy Group, 1993, pp. 15-68.

25. The rise in missions has been steep since 1988, when the UN peacekeeping forces were awarded the Nobel Peace Prize. From the end of World War II until the beginning of 1988, a mere 13 peacekeeping missions were conducted. In the following four years, agreement was reached to start another fifteen. In 1992 alone, the number of troops employed in peacekeeping operations rose fourfold. At the beginning of 1993, more than 80,000 Blue Helmets from seventy states were employed in a total of thirteen peacekeeping missions.

26. Some of the crucial deficiencies of the UN are being dealt with in Schoettle, Enid C.B.: 'Kein Geld für den Frieden?' (No Money for Peace?), *Europa-Archiv*, Vol. 48, No. 16, (25 August 1993), pp. 453-462.

27. See Wagner, Wolfgang: 'Wer braucht wen: Die UN die Deutschen? Die Deutschen dieses Privileg?' (Who Needs Whom: The UN the Germans? The Germans this Privilege?), *Europa-Archiv*, Vol. 48, No. 19 (10 October 1993), pp. 533-540; and Kaiser, Karl: 'Die ständige Mitgliedschaft im Sicherheitsrat. Ein berechtigtes Ziel der neuen deutschen Aussenpolitik' (A Permanent Seat in the Security Council: A Just Goal of the New German Foreign Policy), *ibidem*, pp. 541-552.

28. See *Frankfurter Allgemeine Zeitung*, 23 October 1993, p. 4.

29. Lamers' concept is that the EU establishes common positions which are presented to the Security Council by either Paris or London. Such a solution would be a temporary one until the EU itself becomes a member.

30. Extracts from *Antrag des SPD-Parteivorstandes zum Bundesparteitag 'Perspektiven einer neuen Außen- und Sicherheitspolitik* (SPD Proposals to the Parliamentary Group for a New Foreign and Security Policy), 13 September 1993.

31. For such an attempt, see Stares, Paul B. (Ed.): *The New Germany and the New Europe*, (Washington, D.C.: The Brookings Institution, 1992).

32. For some analytical hints in this regard, see Peters, Susanne: 'Germany's Future Defense Policy. Opening up the Option for German Power Politics', *German Politics and Society*, No. 26 (Summer 1992), pp. 54-74.

33. 'Even after the question of conformity with the constitution has been settled, Germany's contribution towards the preservation of peace will continue to be primarily political and economic, and not military. Germany will not employ armed forces unless it is engaged in combined action with allies and partners within the scope of a United Nations mission. Germany will conscientiously examine every single case against the background of its values and interests, political objectives, risks and potential consequences, and—conscious of its responsibility in the eyes of history—reach a decision.' Ministry of Defense, *White Paper*, *op.cit.*, p. 12.

11 International Institutions and European Security : A Turkish Perspective

Nur-Bilge Criss

The world order is increasingly being reshaped along the lines of the classical system of balance of power and concomitant spheres of influence. While the merits of this are debatable, it is indisputable that no clear *modus vivendi* has been established in international relations. During the euphoria connected with the collapse of communist systems, expectations ran high. Some even welcomed 'the end of history': liberalism had triumphed. But subsequent events indicated that liberalism had only begun to penetrate societies where it had previously been repressed. Meanwhile, history has reasserted itself with a vengeance, and the question of how to manage international security remains open.

A comprehensive definition of post-Cold War security has emerged. Conceptually, it comprises defense, human rights and democracy, and economic development. Hence, the trend in Turkey, like in other Western countries, has been to look for solutions to conflicts through the Council of Europe, the United Nations, NATO and the CSCE. At the regional level, one component of Turkish foreign policy has become interdependence through economic cooperation, reflected in the Turkish promotion of the Black Sea Economic Cooperation project, and its participation in the Economic Cooperation Organization (ECO) with Iran and Pakistan since 1988 (later joined by the Turkic republics of Central Asia).

This policy continues though expectations of the ability of other international institutions to resolve conflict have been somewhat disappointed. For example, there is no consensus at the operational level, to direct international action toward the conflict in Bosnia-Herzegovina. But if there has to be a justification for the *raison d'être* of these institutions, and if they are not to be judged by history as being paper tigers (as was the League of Nations) interlocking institutions need to exert as much influence as they can, and must avoid becoming entangled in their own bureaucracies. This may be easier said than done, especially if there is no political consensus or political will by the member states. In fact, the institutions should not be judged too harshly; their failures are to be ascribed, at least in part, to the politicians of member governments.

The Turkish posture towards international institutions and security may be analyzed at least from four perspectives:
• the European security linkage;
• its efforts to balance its Atlantic and European links;
• its objective of furthering democratization while struggling against th terrorist activities of the PKK (Kurdish Workers' Party);
• its regional security concerns, (which brings the issue right back to the European security linkage).

This chapter will analyze these four perspectives within the framework of multilateralism and/or the national approach in foreign and security policy, the various 'interlocking' institutions, and the enhancement of regional security through the Black Sea Economic Cooperation initiative.

Collective Security / National Security

Turkey has practised both a multilateral and a national foreign and security policy. Throughout the history of the Republic, it has had a collective security approach on its North and West axes (e.g. the Balkan Pact of 1934, the Montreaux Convention of 1936, and the accession to NATO in 1952). In regard to its northern security, Turkey did not settle for either the Truman Doctrine or bilateral relations with the US. Nothing short of becoming a member of NATO sufficed. There were other reasons for wanting NATO membership, such as Turkey's European vocation, a desire for a strong institutional link with the West, and the fact that Greece had become a member (in that order). But the driving motive behind this desire was Turkey's adherence to multilateral security arrangements on its north-west axis.

Turkey's policies toward East and South, on the other hand, have been based on bilateral relations. The only exception to that was the Sadabad Pact of 1937 between Turkey, Iran and Iraq for the purpose of collective security against rebellious Kurdish tribes. The major reason for this unilateral approach to the East and South may be that Turkey did not perceive a military threat from those directions. Secondly, it did not wish to get involved in Middle Eastern quarrels; it clearly does not have an obsessive historical interest in the area. Therefore, if and when Turkey got involved in a Middle Eastern crisis, it was only indirectly. When it allowed the use of the Incirlik Base by the coalition against Iraq in 1991, it was an exception. While the debate still continues in the country as to whether this policy was in the best interest of Turkey, the majority supports the decision for joint action with the allies. The aftermath, and the repercussions on Turkey's national interest are another matter, but this issue will be taken up in a subsequent section on regional security and European security links.

Adopting a purely national approach to foreign and security policy has never been popular with Turkish policy makers. In 1979, when the leader of the then Republican People's Party, Bulent Ecevit, suggested a new national security policy, the propsal was not upheld: those academics and journalists who supported Ecevit's idea simply reflected the residual disappointment with the multilateral approaches which followed the infamous Johnson letter of 1964 (in which US President Lyndon Johnson wrote to the Turkish Prime Minister Ismet Inonu that if Turkey took unilateral action in Cyprus and thereby provoked Soviet aggression, NATO would not be obligated to defend Turkey), the US arms embargo (following the 1974 Turkish military action in Cyprus), and pressure throughout the 1970s to limit cultivation of hashish. But the direction of Turkish foreign policy did not change.

Turkey has never advocated a primarily national approach in foreign and security policies even under the most adverse circumstances, and it is not likely to do so in the future. This cannot be accounted for by dependency theory; the pillar of Turkish foreign policy has been firmly anchored in the international system and international law.

While the major political parties agree with the traditional foreign policy approach, the radical (ultra-nationalist) right and left call for a nationalized foreign and security policy. The pro-Islamic Welfare Party proposes an Islamic defense pact.[1] Some members of this party go further, proposing the abolition of Turkish currency and the adoption of Saudi currency, and the establishment of an Islamic Common Market. The rhetoric of all three radical groups claims there are conspiracy theories against Turkey, presumably concocted by the West and Israel. But because Islam is not a coherent force, particularly not in Turkey, this stance cannot be taken seriously.

Since 1989, Turkey has been focusing more on international institutions such as the UN, CSCE, WEU, and CE, but not at the expense of NATO. The Atlantic link is of crucial importance for Turkey, because European institutions alone cannot solve conflicts and their collective leadership is not leading to consensus, at least for the time being; NATO is still the most experienced and comprehensive security institution and consistently the most tangible institutional link that ties Turkey to the West.

Turkish strategists and decision-makers seem to be intensely disappointed with UN performance in Somalia. General Cevik Bir, who served as the Turkish Commander of the UN forces there, argues that without a decision-making mechanism such as that of NATO, UN military missions are doomed. In the absence of political and military strategies, disarming the belligerent parties was not entirely successful.[2]

General Bir's assessment is reminiscent of Turkish Foreign Minister Hikmet Cetin's proposal at the UN General Assembly at the end of September 1993, that the UN Security Council needs restructuring. This would mean enlarging the Security Council membership with semi-permanent seats. The membership could rotate among certain states based on geographical location, economic potential and a record of contribution to international security. It is not clear how this proposition is assessed, but the fact remains that the UN should be restructured to meet the new challenges of the post-Cold War era.

Although Turkey recognizes the importance of the CSCE, policy makers see two major deficiencies with the organization. First, decision making is by consensus. Secondly, and perhaps more serious , CSCE decisions are not binding. In this sense, the CSCE remains a mere instrument of good-will, but its psychological impact should not be underestimated. The test case is the recent CSCE decision that the Russian Federation should not play a unilateral peacekeeping role in the Caucasus. Russian officials, however, reiterate that, while Russia would not insist on a unilateral peace-keeping mission in the Caucasus, it was not averse to taking part in such a mission if requested. This remains to be seen, for Azerbaijan already rejected a Russian-only force.

In addition, it is quite premature to consider the WEU as an instrument of enforcement for the CSCE or the EU. Turkey would have preferred a stronger role for the WEU so that there would be a balance between the Atlantic link and Europe, but this is not yet the case.

European and Atlantic Links

Since 1947, Turkey has identified the West with NATO, and NATO with the US. The role of the US was not diminished after, the events of 1989, and it seemed that Turkish foreign policy was more balanced between Western Europe and the US. By December 1993, however, Turkish perception was that Western Europe was treating it like a second class partner by denying it full membership in the WEU. In fact a serious imbalance was introduced when the WEU granted Greece full membership in order to pursue political harmony within the EU, but gave Turkey only associate member status. Article 5 of the WEU treaty reads that an attack against one of its members will be treated as an attack against all. Turkey had already announced that if Greece extended its territorial waters to 12 miles in the Aegean, Turkey would regard it as *casus belli*. Given Papandreau's hardline against Turkey, there is an increasing risk in this regard—a risk that concerns not only Turkey, but Western Europe as well. The CSCE guarantees, in the absence of an enforcement mechanism, remain far from convincing as far as Turkish policy-makers are concerned.

Turkey had applied for full membership in WEU in 1987 at about the same time as it applied to the EC. It did not wish to be left out of a European security system because full integration within Europe would not be possible, without it. At the time, a debate developed within the WEU: on the one hand, France and Germany argued for the establishment of a Eurocorps, and for making the WEU the security arm of the EC; on the other hand, Britain and Italy argued that the WEU should become the European security pillar within the Atlantic Alliance. Accordingly, NATO membership would be an automatic criterion for membership in the WEU. In the former case, Turkey would have been left out of the European security system. Therefore, President Turgut Özal, who spoke at the 1991 WEU Assembly, supported the latter position.

Özal's basic premise was that NATO members were being artificially divided between those who belonged to EC and those who did not. This division placed Turkey in a situation whereby it shared the responsibility for European security, but did not have a voice in the new European architecture to which it belonged.

Turkey accepted this situation because it could not afford to stay out of the system altogether. Secondly, it realized that EC and WEU membership went together, and decided to treat its associate status as a step toward full membership. Finally, the WEU association reiterates the transatlantic link that Turkey is so keen on maintaining. The *Document on Associate Membership of WEU of the Republic of Iceland, the Kingdom of Norway and the Republic of Turkey* clearly states that 'the association of these three countries represents a significant step in the strengthening of the European pillar of the Atlantic Alliance, and thus of the transatlantic link itself.'[3]

By November 1993, WEU Secretary General Willem van Eekelen assured Turkish journalists that 'the WEU without Turkey is out of the question. Besides, there is not a significant difference between full and associate membership in the WEU.'[4] The subject had come up in connection with the East European countries' application to EU (European Union, which entered into force on 1 November 1993) and upon the question of their simultaneous acceptance to the WEU as associate members. Just one week after Van Eekelen's statement, Turkish Foreign Minister Hikmet Cetin, made headway in convincing his Western European colleagues that associate members, could also potentially contribute forces to the Eurocorps.[5]

In January of 1994, German Foreign Minister Klaus Kinkel and his British colleague, Douglas Hurd, visited Turkey, mainly to discuss regional security. As reported by the Turkish Foreign Affairs Undersecretary Ozdem Sanberk, both Germany and Britain committed themselves to search for ways to accommodate Turkey as a full member in WEU though it does not have the same status in EU.[6]

As for possible NATO enlargement Turkey may object, because it would imply getting directly involved with problems in Eastern Europe. Thus, Turkey now finds itself exactly in the same situation as those countries which had objected to Turkey's entry to NATO, and for the same reasons. Turkey will probably not be averse to new NATO missions in that region as long as they are on an *ad hoc* basis, but if NATO were to become a permanent military tool of the UN or CSCE, it may be incompatible with Turkish national interest. If NATO were routinely assigned to act according to UN Security Council decisions, Turkey would not welcome such a development, because, once again, it would not be a part of the decision-making process.[7]

In addition to NATO, the Council of Europe (CE) is perhaps the only other institution to which Turkey pays close attention. Turkey has been a member of the CE since 1949. Between May 7 and November 1992, Turkey assumed the interim leadership of CE. The most significant activity that Turkey undertook then was to begin a dialogue between CE and CIS, by visiting the five Central Asian Republics with the CE's Secretary General Lalumière, and by hosting a number of meetings in Istanbul on transition to democracy.[8]

Current Issues of Security

While there is a a myriad of concerns in managing post-Cold War transitions at the geographical core of Europe, stability in Europe cannot be divorced from regional security concerns. There are a number of potential threats to security and economic stability:

• loss of prestige and credibility of international institutions as a result of their mismanagement of the Bosnian tragedy;

• the disruption of the land transit route through Turkey;

• disruption of Middle Eastern oil flows;

• growing radicalism, promoting anti-Western culture;

• spread of of fundamentalist terrorism;

• proliferation of armaments, and especially the danger of nuclear proliferation in the Middle East;

• overt rightist extremism in Russia and with its assertiveness about keeping its 'near abroad' under its sphere of influence.

In the early 1990s, Turkey has faced three main security questions: Has Turkey become strategically marginalized, now that its full membership in EU is postponed indefinitely? Would and/or should Turkey not be concentrating solely on the Middle East and Central Asia? Would more visible Islamic lifestyles affect Turkish foreign policy, and if so, how? According to Ian Lesser, Europeans now see Turkey's strategic importance largely with respect to the Middle East, and this has made its integration into European security arrangements more difficult. As a result of the Gulf War and Turkey's cooperation with the coalition Europe has begun to see Turkey as a barrier rather than as a bridge.[9]

Turkey perceives itself as a frontier country, which means that the Balkans, the Black Sea and the Caucasus are of immediate concern both for its security and for that of Europe. A second area of potential threat is the Middle-East.

Turkey's concern with the Balkans stems partly from its Ottoman cultural heritage, the existence of ethnic Turks in the region, and the presence of Muslims of different ethnic backgrounds (e.g. the Slavic Bosnian Muslims). It also has strategic concerns as the Balkan airspace and land routes are the major transit links between Turkey and Central Europe. Given that the Yugoslav crises have already disrupted a major geographical linkage to Europe, Turkey has pursued an unusually active diplomacy in all international fora, but especially through the CSCE, to impose preventive measures for potential clashes in Macedonia, Kosovo, Vojvodina and Sanjak. In addition, in 1993, the Turkish Eximbank extended credits amounting to US $125 million to Romania, US $50 million to Bulgaria, and US $15 million to Albania. A US $2.5 billion highway construction project from Albania-Macedonia-Bulgaria-Turkey proposed by the latter will soon be discussed at a meeting of Ministers of Construction and Development of the four countries.[10]

It appears that Turkey can establish a constructive relationship with all but two Balkan countries, namely Greece and Serbia. The Greek fixation with a 'Turkish threat' serves solely domestic consumption purposes, and may well be short-sighted. Turkey is likely to continue its traditional policy of inviting Greece to all its North and Western initiatives (for example Greece was invited to the Black Sea Economic Cooperation (BSEC), even though it is not a Black Sea littoral state).

Although Turkish policy-makers are well aware that Serbia is too important to ignore, mending fences seems to be contingent upon a just peace in Bosnia-Herzegovina. A second impediment to establishing better relations with Serbia is the diplomatic opposition of Greece, Serbia, and Russia to lifting the arms embargo against Bosnian Muslims. That Western countries support this stance is completely unwarranted, especially since Serbia has continued to import oil, food and even weapons from Greece, Russia, and Romania.'[11]

It would be naïve to expect Bosnian Serbs to stop at the borders of Croatia once they achieve their objective in Bosnia-Herzegovina. Turkey is actively promoting an alliance between Bosnian Muslims and Croats, and is trying to convince its Western allies to do the same, mainly within the framework of international institutions.[12]

Turkey is also trying to promote confidence-building between the Albanians and Macedonians, especially by involving both in the same institutions. Nevertheless, the complexity of the Balkan situation and current trends do not point to an immediate solution: on the one hand, states which try to contribute to peace and stability in the Balkans by using international organizations and by proposing projects of regional cooperation are often viewed by their rivals as attempting to extend their sphere of political influence; on the other hand, the byproduct of policies aimed at cooperation may be the integration of an arc of instability into a peaceful framework of international relations.[13]

Based on the principle that interdependence promotes security, in 1990 Turkey initiated a project on regional cooperation called the Black Sea Economic Cooperation (BSEC), which currently comprises Albania, Armenia, Azerbaijan, Bulgaria, Georgia, Greece, Moldova, Romania, the Russian Federation, Turkey, and Ukraine. This is not meant to be an alternative to the existing institutions of Europe, but has been conceived and developed as an integral part of Europe's new architecture, and is considered as an instrument directed to the European and world economy.[14] In the past, trade relationships between member states were not only bilateral, but state-controlled. The BSEC intends to transform them into multilateral trade relations based on private sector initiatives.

The application and acceptance of Greece, an EU member, to the BSEC, is indicative of the fact that this project is complementary to other European institutions, the goal being the diversification of economic and trade relations. Greece will probably assume the interim chairmanship of BSEC. Furthermore, Salonica has been designated as the headquarters of the Black Sea Investment and Trade Bank. Two points of contention remain: in the early 1990s, Turkey lifted visa requirements for Greek citizens, but reciprocity on this matter is still not achieved. And, the current

Greek government at times seems to support Kurdish terrorism. Nevertheless, the BSEC serves as yet another forum for dialogue between the two.

The BSEC also serves a similar function with Armenia although there are two major problems upon which constrains this relationship. One is the conflict between Armenians and Azerbaijanis, and the second one is the existence of PKK terrorists on Armenian soil.

The most promising relationship within the framework of regional economic cooperation has developed between the Russian Federation and Turkey. The total volume of trade between them jumped to US$ 1.3 billion in 1989 and to US$ 1.8 billion last year (1990) after a steady level of about only US$ 600 million for years.[15]

As Oral Sander argues, a common feature of Russia and Turkey is that their Europeanness has been questioned (if not sometimes totally rejected) by the European countries both geographically, historically, and culturally . . . The 'Europeanness' of the two countries was somewhat reluctantly acknowledged for brief periods only when their armed services were needed to avert military threats.[16] However, in the post-Cold War era, both countries have been trying to redefine their respective identities. Turkey is definitely committed to a European identity, and would only welcome Russia if the latter succeeded in adopting and maintaining a similar identity and using its influence in the Balkans, Northern Black Sea and in the Caucasus as a factor of stability.

European and Regional Security Linkages

In 1990, Ian Lesser wrote that 'Turkish observers are almost unique in the Alliance in stressing the continuing Soviet threat to their territory [and that] the prevailing Turkish view of CFE [the Conventional Forces in Europe treaty] is distinctly conservative.'[17] In 1994, Turkey is no longer unique with regard to its concern about the resurgence of power politics in Russia, which profoundly affects its so-called 'near abroad' (i.e. the newly independent states of the former Soviet Union). Though it was an exaggeration both in 1990 and today to expect a direct threat to Turkish territory from Russia, Moscow's heavy-handed approach towards Eastern

European countries that have expressed a desire to join NATO, and its coercive actions to establish spheres of influence in Soviet successor states, do seem to imply a resurgence of power politics for spheres of influence—and in a worst-case scenario, renewed Russian expansionism. Many were pleased that Turkey and Russia no longer shared borders and had acquired buffer states between them; however, this turned into much disappointment when Russia behaved in a way that reminded the regional countries that it was still a great power and intended to remain one. This disappointment was greatest among those who thought that the demise of the communist systems would lead to total independence from Russia, ironically at a time where interdependence was on the rise elsewhere in the world.

This attitude was compounded by zealous Turkish politicians who talked about 'a Turkic world from the Adriatic to the Wall of China'. while their visions stemmed partly from rejection by Europe, it also had much to do with the fact that their generation had grown up without any knowledge or information about Russian/Soviet or Central Asian history, let alone Marxism. This criticism is not meant to belittle the relationships that have been established between Turkey and the Turkic Republics. For example, that the Central Asians Turkic republics accepted the use of the Latin script is a major leap forward. Politically speaking, however, the Russian factor has reasserted itself and Turkey has had to focus on Russia once again.

If politics is the art of the possible, then the tacit agreement between the West and Russia that Moscow would leave the Baltic states and Eastern Europe alone in exchange for a relatively free hand in the Caucasus and Central Asia, was a possible solution. But, fine-tuning of these positions is in order: the West is in search of a political piano-tuner in Russia. An interesting precedent in this respect might be set in Georgia. The Russian Ambassador to Turkey has announced that since Georgia does not have regular armed forces yet, Russian soldiers, on Georgian payroll, would be protecting Georgia's borders.[18] This may look like a purely professional and mutually beneficial arrangement: it will finance otherwise unemployed Russian soldiers whom Moscow finds difficult to maintain on payroll, and end Georgian President Eduard Shvardnadze's pain in trying to keep the country intact. But it also keeps Georgia in the Russian political orbit.

That the Georgian leader had no choice is not a secret. Clearly, this is an interim solution. Questions remain, however, as to whether the Russian military would ever leave if Georgia feels that there is no need for them, or whether Georgia will be allowed to build up its own forces. Or will the 'near abroad' serve as a source of unemployment insurance for the Russians in the foreseeable future? If the price of handing over one country's security to another prevents parochial nationalism and subsequent civil wars, is it not worth paying? After all, it would appear that Russian military regulars as mercenaries in the Caucasus might be more successful than the performance of international organizations elsewhere in the world.

Azerbaijan is a somewhat different case, because Aliev enjoys a stronger position than Shevardnaze does, thanks both to recent Azerbaijani military successes *vis-à-vis* Armenia and to the country's oil wealth. The brutal intervention of the Soviet army in January 1990 in Baku was perceived in Turkey as retaliation against the Azerbaijanis for ethnic violence (some Armenian residents had been killed by unemployed Azerbaijani mobs who had been exiled from Erevan the year before).[19] But very little attention, if any, was paid by Turkish media or scholars to the fact that in addition to ethnic violence, some Azerbaijanis had attacked the border between Iran and the Soviet Union the same month (the Soviet Union was formally disbanded at the end of 1991), and destroyed border fences.

Perhaps the Red Army and KGB had overreacted to the situation. But what seems clear is that attention should not be focussed only on thnic violence; Azerbaijani agitation on the Iranian border should also be taken into account. This incident alone could have involved the Soviet Union in an armed conflict at a time when it could ill afford it. No one in Turkey paid attention to the Russian dimension of this drama. A similar threat involving Turkey and Iran was fortunately averted with Aliev's accession to power, and as a result of the changes in the Turkish political scene since 1990. Although he was labeled as Moscow's man in many quarters, Aliev has been seeking international support to keep Russian soldiers out of Azerbaijan as would-be peacekeepers. While Turkey does not necessarily need to participate in a UN peace-keeping mission in the region, it will support Aliev in all international fora.

While the connection of these problems with European security may seem tenuous, the linkage is in fact two-fold: the smooth transportation of Caucasian and Central Asian oil and natural gas flow to Europe through Turkey and/or the Russian Federation, depends on peaceful local conditions; this, in turn, obliges international institutions, especially the CSCE, through its 'Minsk Conference', to pursue more active diplomacy with respect to conflict resolution in the region.

In February 1994 Russian Defense Minister, Pavel Grachev announced plans for the establishment of 5 military bases in Georgia, Armenia and Azerbaijan with 23,000 soldiers. This followed Russia's request that CFE be amended to allow increased levels of arms in the Caucasus. According to Chernichev, the Russian Ambassador to Ankara, behind this request was made to ensure the prevention of the 'Lebanonization' of the Caucasus. This policy may work in the case of Georgia, but Azerbaijan is a test case of Russian intentions in regard to international organizations.

Though Turkey would also like to ensure that there will not be a Lebanization of the Caucasus, it does not want to see the CFE agreement changed in favor of Russia, and it made its opposition clear in September 1993. Two main reasons may account for this: increased force levels in the Caucasus will give Russia the potential for intervention in the Middle East; the change in the CFE agreement proposed by Russia would result in a remarkable disequillibrium in favor of Russian forces on the Turkish border and the re-establishment of Cold-War conditions.[20]

In light of this resurgent Russian military power on its borders, Turkey acted through the CSCE. At the foreign ministers meeting in Rome in early December 1993, Turkey was active in forestalling Russia's efforts at getting an endorsement from the organization for its unilateral peacekeeping. Moscow had been pushing hard to get CSCE backing for its drive for world authorization and financing of its role as peacekeeper in conflicts in former Soviet Republics from Moldova to Tajikistan.[21]

This attempt by Moscow to have an international organization legitimate its actions is significant, though it appears that it will not succeed either in this case or in its attempts to change CFE force levels. Should Moscow go ahead with its unilateral interventions in its former republics, it will do so without international endorsement. Thus, the psychological impact of the CSCE on a country that seeks acceptance into the international community should not be underestimated, despite its inability to enforce compliance. The choice depends on the challenger; the reward is acceptance within the international society.

In sum, it is up to the international institutions to prevent, mediate, coerce, or deter, depending on the situation. The question is why is the West walking on a tight rope trying to accommodate Russia within the international system in the absence of political burdensharing by that country.

The north-west axis of Turkey is not the only security linkage with Europe. Its south-east axis is also of concern in the international arena. Perhaps the first threat is that of nuclear proliferation. Although Syria and Iran have accepted IAEA safeguards as NPT signatories, they may well follow Iraq's model of covert proliferation.[22] In view of the recent Middle East peace process, this potential threat from Syria may be diminishing, but that from Iran is not likely to decline.

The second threat comes from the ambiguous position of Iraq, with its potential for upsetting the regional balance of power. The second Gulf crisis resulted in the creation of a semi-autonomous Kurdistan in Northern Iraq. Turkey's policy towards the issue is seemingly paradoxical. While it supports the territorial integrity of Iraq, it also hosts the forces of the United Nations Operation Provide Comfort to deter Saddam Hussein from further retaliation against Iraqi Kurds. An independent Kurdish State in Iraq is not in Turkey's interest; this is not because it would serve as a model for its Kurds, but because it would alter the regional balance of power. Such a landlocked Kurdish state would be dependent on Turkey economically. Iran cannot be expected to tolerate a Kurdish state under Turkish influence. An Iranian supported Hezbollah faction clashes with the Iraqi Kurdish factions as well as with the PKK located there. Civil war conditions already exist in the autonomous state and would in all likelihood erupt into a large-scale one if independence is granted. This is another case in which international institutions cannot afford to become captive to the notion of capricious self-determination.

In sum, the evolving system of interlocking institutions in Europe has a formidable dual task: on the one hand, it must ensure security in the continent; on the other it must manage potential challenges from the periphery. It is in this regard that regional balances of power assume importance. By helping maintain such balances interlocking institutions may be the only remedy against the reemergence and consolidation of new and old spheres of influence.

Notes

1. Fuller, Graham E.: 'Turkey's New Eastern Orientation' in Fuller, Graham E. and Ian O. Lesser (Eds.): *Turkey's New Geopolitics*, (Boulder, Colorado: Westview Press, 1993), p.51.

2. 'Birlesmis Milletlere Yeni Bir Karar Mekanizmasi Gerek' (A New Decision-Making Mechanism Is Necessary for the United Nations), *Cumhuriyet*, 4 February 1994.

3. Kilinc, Ugur: *Turkiye-Bati Avrupa Birligi Iliskileri* (Turkey's Relations with the Western European Union), (Ankara: Gazi University, Department of International Relations, Unpublished paper, 1993).

4. Quoted in 'BAB Turkiyesiz Dusunulemez', (Turkey is a Partner of the Western European Union) *Cumhuriyet* 26 November 1993.

5. Quoted in 'Ankara Avrupa Ordusunu Garantiledi,' (Ankara Guaranteed Participation in the Eurocorps) *Cumhuriyet*, 26 November 1993.

6. 'BAB'a Tam Uyelik Gundemde,' (Full Membership in the Western European Union is on the Agenda), *Cumhuriyet*, 21 January 1994.

7. I am indebted to Professors Ali Karaosmanoglu (Bilkent University), Oral Sander (Ankara University), Sukru Gurel (Ankara University), Yuksel Inan (Gazi University) as well as to a number of members of the Turkish Foreign Ministry and Treasury Department for their contributions to the discussion.

8. See 'Türkiye - Avrupa Konseyi İlişkileri', (Turkey's Relations with the Council of Europe), courtesy of the Turkish Ministry of Foreign Affairs, 1993.

9. Lesser, Ian: 'Bridge or Barrier? Turkey and the West after the Cold War.' In Lesser, Ian (Ed.), *op.cit.*, pp.100-132.

10. See 'Makedonya'ya Yeni Engel', *Cumhuriyet*, (A New Obstacle for Macedonia) 8 December 1993.

11. Karaosmanoglu, Ali L.: *Crises in the Balkans* (Geneva: UNIDIR Research Paper No.22, 1993), p.16.

12. Author's discussion with Dr. Hasan Unal, February 1994, Bilkent University.

13. Karaosmanoglu, Ali: *op.cit.*, passim.

14. Ozuye, Oktay: 'Black Sea Economic Cooperation', *Mediterranean Quarterly* (Summer 1992), pp. 48-54.

15.Nihat Gokyigit, 'Economic Relations Between Turkey and the Soviet Union' In Manisalý, Erol (Ed.): *Turkey's Relations with the Soviet Union and East Europe* (Turkish Republic of Northern Cyprus: 1991), pp. 79-84.

16. Sander, Oral: 'Turkey and the Black Sea Economic Cooperation', *International Journal of Turkish Studies*, 1994 (Forthcoming).

17. Lesser, Ian: *Southern Region Perspectives on Security and International Affairs*, a Rand Note (Santa Monica: Rand Corporation, 1990), p.33.

18. Quoted in 'Rusya'dan Parali Hizmet' (Mercenary Service From Russia), *Cumhuriyet*, 8 February 1994.

19. See 'Response to Events in Azerbaijan' *Central Asia and Caucasus Chronicle*, Vol.9, No.1 (March 1990), pp. 8-9; and Altstadt, Audrey L.: 'Baku 1991: One Year After Black January', *Association for the Advancement of Central Asian Research Bulletin*, Vol IV, No.1 (Spring 1991), pp. 8-10.

20. 'Ankara'dan Yeltsin'e 'hayir'' (No to Yeltsin from Ankara) *Cumhuriyet*, 27 September 1993; Elekdag, Sukru: 'Çiller'in ABD'de Ele Almasi Gerekli Konu', (A Subject that Çiller Should Take Up in the USA), *Milliyet*, 10 October 1993; Akyol, Taha: 'Kafkasya Dosyasý', (The Caucasian Dossier), *Milliyet*, 13 October 1993.

21. 'Turkey Stalls Russia's CSCE Bid for Caucasus', *Turkish Daily News*, 4 December 1993.

22. Snyder, Jed C.: 'Proliferation Threats to NATO's Southern Region', *The Mediterranean Quarterly*, No. 4 (Winter 1993).

12 International Institutions and European Security: The Italian Debate

Marta Dassù and Marco De Andreis

Introduction

Reporting on the Italian foreign and security policy debate has never been easy—after all, a real debate never took place, since international issues were carefully kept outside the sphere of domestic politics throughout the postwar period. Italy has been more a security consumer than a security provider. Even today, in spite of the dramatic turn of international events that took place in 1989, the Italian foreign and security policy debate is barely audible. Why? The foremost reason is the current domestic political crisis. In politics, crisis is an abused word, especially in Italy where, it has been mentioned any time the cabinet was reshuffled—more than once a year on average since World War II.

This time around, however, the term crisis seems to be perfectly appropriate: in municipal elections held in November 1993, four of the government coalition parties of the last fifteen years shrank to almost zero, while the fifth (the Christian Democratic Party, which has held the relative majority ever since 1948) lost about half of its electoral support. The big winners were, as expected, the Northern League in the North (a political formation that was almost non-existent only a few years ago), the Democratic Party of the Left (Partito Democratico della Sinistra, PDS, the former Communists) throughout the country; and, unexpectedly, the Italian Social Movement (Movimento Sociale Italiano, MSI, the neo-fascists) in Rome and in the South. The general political elections held in March 1994 confirmed the collapse of the old center of the Italian political system: the Christian Democrats, recently renamed the Italian Popular Party (Partito Popolare

Italiano, PPI) were ousted from power for the first time since the end of the Second World War.

Thanks also to the new electoral law, the political spectrum coalesced around two poles: on the one hand, a center-right coalition holding together the National Alliance (Alleanza Nazionale, a grouping centered around the former MSI), the Northern League and Forza Italia, ('Come on, Italy'), the latter movement founded by the entrepreneur Silvio Berlusconi, which won the elections; on the other hand, the 'progressive' coalition of the left, which was soundly defeated barely four months after its victories in the municipal elections in many large cities. It is Silvio Berlusconi who made the difference with his sudden decision to enter politics. The Radical Party (Partito Radicale), and notably his leader Marco Pannella, further support the winning coalition.

This profound political realignment is only the culmination of a process begun in the spring of 1992 and referred to as *'mani pulite'* (clean hands) or *tangentopoli* ('kickback city'), the result of which has been the prosecution of several prominent politicians, including former prime ministers, as well as defense and foreign affairs ministers. According to a widespread interpretation, those sweeping investigations were made possible by the end of the Cold War, during which, the overriding goal of keeping the Communists out of power had implied the practical invulnerability of the ruling parties, no matter how corrupt.

Finally the electoral law was changed: the shift to a first-past-the-post system (even though one fourth of the parliamentary seats continues to be attributed on a proportional basis) was indeed meant to give further impetus to the process of political realignment (a goal fully met by the first elections), and to make a new edition of the old system of multi-party coalition governments difficult—a target largely missed. Italian policy-making will thus continue to be the result of the interplay of the winning coalition parties, with obvious consequences on the definition of the country's foreign policy.

These events have kept the country's political *élite* focused on the domestic front. But there is also a question of mood. The September 1992 monetary quake, for example, suddenly relegated Rome to the second tier of the European Community (EC). Since much of the prestige and international stature gained by Italy during the eighties stemmed from the dynamism of its economy, this loss of rank undoubtedly contributed to inspiring prudence and a lower profile in the conduct of foreign affairs—besides, of course, calling even more attention to domestic fiscal questions, as mentioned above. Italy's foreign policy thus came to be enveloped in a mood of gloom, at least since Emilio Colombo, in August 1992, was named foreign minister—a mood that, coming on the heels of the euphoria and hyper-activism that had characterized Gianni De Michelis' tenure of *la Farnesina*, was even more evident. To all this it must be added that in 1992-93 attention was also concentrated on domestic affairs elsewhere, for example in Germany, France and the US. Behind the crisis in the European Monetary System (EMS) there was more than Italy's relatively high inflation and burgeoning public deficits.

Thus, Italy, which has had a remarkable postwar record of foreign policy continuity, some change is finally in sight, but it is difficult to predict which form this change will eventually take. Though foreign policy is unlikely to be a priority in the near future, a foreign and security policy debate has been growing among experts and intellectuals—perhaps to fill the void of the official retrenchment. Hopefully, the academic debate may in time involve politicians and parties and eventually help make international relations a concrete issue in Italian politics—which, after all, they have never really been.

The next section of this chapter will focus on the attitudes and positions of policy-makers and intellectuals in the Italian foreign and security policy debate, This will be followed by an examination of the substantive policy issues at stake.

Multilateralism in Italy's Foreign and Security Policy-Making

Official ideas on the role played by multilateral institutions in Italy's foreign and security policy are unambiguous. According to outgoing Minister of Foreign Affairs Beniamino Andreatta, 'the end of the Cold War has not caused a revision of the basic choices: Italy's membership to the European Community and the Atlantic Alliance. It has, however, resulted in the end of rents [from NATO bases] and free-riding. Membership is no longer enough in the new international conditions: one has to qualify oneself through presence and hard work.'[1] From the government point of view, then, the collapse of the bipolar system forces Rome to take a more active role within existing international institutions. Since this approach combines the traditional, postwar emphasis on multilateralism with a new call for assertiveness in Italy's foreign policy, we might call it 'new multilateralism'.

According to its proponents, a successful management of the domestic political and economic transition is clearly a precondition to carry out this strategy. It would indeed be difficult for any country to have a high external profile without internal stability. Another precondition is the continuing vitality of the international institutions themselves, since a generalized drive to the so-called renationalization of policies would immediately hurt Italy, a country that has never been a great power and that is going through a critical domestic transition.

From Rome's point of view, there is no shortage of reasons to be apprehensive about its role in the major multilateral fora: the country no longer belongs to the core group of EU countries; it is a sort of 'adjunct' member of the G-7 (formerly G-5); as a NATO ally, it is much less crucial than it used to be; and it sees the growing importance of the UN Security Council with the clear fear of being left out of its eventual enlargement to new members.

Belonging to the club of nations that really count is a long-standing goal of Italy's foreign policy. What is new here is the perception that to achieve this goal the country can no longer rely on the rent that, during the bloc-to-bloc confrontation, used to accrue just from being in the Western camp. There are few doubts that this perception will continue to prevail, even though it is difficult to see at the moment how it will be manifested in diplomatic terms.

Outside the government majority, there is no serious opposition to multilateralism. In fact, its natural counterweight—unilateralism—may make some sense for a country with the strategic reach and the power of the United States, but few believe it might work for Italy. It goes without saying that another approach that has some currency and historical precedent in the US (i.e. isolationism) is, for any European power, a contradiction in terms. This means that there are no clear-cut cleavages between political forces or schools of thought as regard multilateralism in the country's international relations. Rather, there is a continuum along which the extreme rigth represents (predictably) various forms of nationalism, and the extreme left represents (no less predictably) utopian visions of lasting global peace.

This picture is confirmed by even a cursory comparison of the major parties' platforms: if one excludes both the extreme right (MSI) and the extreme left (Rifondazione Comunista), with their paradoxical convergencies, for example in opposing the Maastricht Treaty, there is still a strong consensus on the main foreign policy issues and approaches.[2] The traditional political forces, and in particular the PPI, are those with the best multilateralist credentials. After all, the former DC is the party that since the days of Alcide De Gasperi, in the aftermath of World War II, has presided over the process of Italy's integration in a complex web of international bodies: the UN, the Bretton Woods institutions, the General Agreement on Tariff and Trade (GATT), the North Atlantic Treaty Organization (NATO), the European Community (EC), and the Western European Union (WEU). Given the cultural background of the DC, one element of which is certainly their ecumenical vision of the world, there is no reason to expect any fundamental change in attitude. Now forced to go into opposition, the Christian Democrats will not have a direct influence on foreign policy-making for the first time in their history.

Although the former Communists were relatively late-comers in their acceptance of Italy's membership to the EC (in the mid-sixties) and NATO (in the mid-seventies), the PDS is no doubt a staunch supporter of Italy's multilateral commitments. When it comes to security, the PDS leadership seems well aware that if it is to make any use of force acceptable to its supporters some form of multilateral blessing—especially from the UN—is necessary. The party's opposition to Italy's participation in the 1991 Gulf war may have been the last of its genre—at least if the PDS support to the ongoing mission in Somalia is any indication. A potential role for NATO in peace operations in Europe with the UN or CSCE blessing would be easily accepted by this party. This became clear when the party supported the first NATO air-strike on Sarajevo in early 1994. This support was given in the course of the first official visit of a PDS official delegation (February 1994) to NATO headquarters in Brussels. Such support can not be taken for granted, however, should the Alliance be involved in North-South crisis management.

Firmly pro-EU, the PDS also favors the creation of a strong

European pillar within the Atlantic Alliance. The party agrees with the former government on the risks of isolating Moscow (though it is critical of the strong official support for President Boris Yeltsin because of his alleged authoritarian domestic rule) should NATO enlarge to the Visegrad countries. For purposes of support to Central and Eastern European security concerns, the PDS's emphasis, perhaps overly optimistic, is on the CSCE as a pan-European security framework, to be used particularly for potential peace-keeping operations in Europe. In this case as well there is a peculiar cultural dimension which favors a multilateralist approach to foreign affairs: a mix of the heritage of the Communist internationalism and Catholic universalism that critics used to call, pejoratively, (*catto-comunismo*).

The above description, though, does not fit all of the leftist parties. *Rifondazione Comunista*, a PDS splinter group of Communists diehards, has a strong anti-NATO and pro-UN rhetoric, even though it is highly critical of the use of Italian troops abroad, including the current UNOSOM experience. A minority within the opposition, this formation will challenge the government from a pacifist, anti-Western stance in foreign policy.

In sum, taking into account their own distinctive backgrounds, both the Christian Democrats and the PDS represent the forces of continuity in Italy's foreign and security policy. And both are now in the opposition.

The same cannot be said of two groups of the new government coalition: the National Alliance and the Northern League. Although the former, once in power, would hardly suggest withdrawing Italy from any major multilateral body, there is no doubt that it does harbor a number of serious second thoughts and resentments. As mentioned above, the party voted against Italy's ratification of the Maastricht Treaty on European Union. Also, the MSI campaign for the mayoral elections in Trieste openly called for a revision of the borders with Slovenia and Croatia. Furthermore, the end of the Cold War has removed from the Atlantic Alliance the very feature the MSI wholeheartedly appreciated anti-communism—thus laying bare a US hegemony that the self-proclaimed heirs of fascism inevitably resent.

In the National Alliance's electoral program, building up 'European nationalism to face off the United States and Russia' is one of the main foreign policy goals. Thus, this party is located on the right, at the nationalist extreme of the Italian political spectrum. It may be more moderate than either the *Republikaner* in Germany or the *Front National* in France, but it is nonetheless the party that positions itself the farthest away from the multilateralist tenets of this postwar era.

Having several decades of political activity behind them, the Christian Democratic Party, the PDS, and the MSI all have a more or less discernible foreign policy platform. This definitely is not true of the Northern League, which leaves the observer with an extremely fragmented record of statements and remarks made by its leaders only when the circumstances force them to. The crucial question indeed is: has the League any interest, let alone expertise, in foreign policy? And the answer, quite possibly, is no. Two or three very broad inferences can nevertheless be made. First, while advocating the transformation of Italy into a federation of three states (respectively in the North, Center, and South of the Peninsula), the League emphasizes the European vocation of the Northern Italian 'state' it seeks to rule. More than a clear, pro-EU stance (though European Federalism is a stated goal of the League's foreign policy), this is the symptom of a strong attraction for what is sometimes called Mitteleuropa.

Second, this attraction is probably stronger than the attention paid to trans-Atlantic ties. In other words, one would guess that in the opinion of the League's leaders Germany comes before the US and—but this is little more than a guess—the WEU comes before NATO: the League supports the creation of a European army. Third, within this 'Mitteleuropean' framework, the League shows its own brand of isolationism: it is the idea that the rich North should not be dragged into the poor South's problems. Here, the terms North and South refer to the hemispheres, rather than to regions of Italy. But evidently the philosophy is the same, whether it applies to economic subsidies for *il Mezzogiorno* (the Italian South), to African immigrants in Italian cities, or to Italy's participation in the United Nations Operation in Somalia (UNOSOM)—which the League opposed since its inception.

The underlying problem is how these different approaches will be combined in the foreign policy of the new government coalition headed by Silvio Berlusconi's Forza Italia. On paper, at least, the foreign policy program of this movement seems intentioned to combine a more active pursuit of national interests (chiefly meaning the country's economic growth) with a high profile participation in Europe's integration process.

The parties mentioned so far do not represent all the currents and undercurrents of the Italian political life. For example, Italy is also the cradle of the 'transnational' Radical Party, a group that, for want of a better term, one is tempted to call 'multilateralist fundamentalist'. This party simply claims that the national level is no longer appropriate for politics, and focuses its efforts on building up a network of members and sympathizers throughout the world for the pursuit of global goals such as the abolition of the death penalty, the legalization of drugs, and the creation of a permanent international criminal court.

Summing up, with end of the First Republic, foreign policy will no longer be the traditional cohesive element of governing coalitions. It was not a crucial element in the electoral campaign: both coalitions easily lived with sharp internal divisions on international affairs. Furthermore, the winners include forces which never took part in the making of Italy's postwar diplomacy. The only party with some foreign policy background—the National Alliance—is in favor of a neo-nationalist break with the past, an approach forcefully rejected by the Northern League. With this background, it seems unlikely that Italy's Second Republic will have a more effective and coherent foreign policy than that of its predecessor.

On a more abstract level, the foreign policy debate looks more lively than it used to be. Openly inspired by the French geopolitical school, a group of intellectuals is advocating that Italy's foreign and security policy be based on a firm definition of the country's national interests.[3] The proponents of this approach are persuaded that a generalized renationalization of security policies in the post-Cold War era is more than a mere possibility: Italy should therefore be quick to renationalize its own, on the basis of its geopolitical goals. Hence they mention special Italian interests in the Balkans—interests that are distinct from the goals of peace, prosperity, and stability shared by the international community. Hence also the calls for reopening the discussions with Slovenia and Croatia on some of the provisions of the 1975 Osimo Treaty, which settled, among other things, the issue of the border between Italy and the former Yugoslavia.

An alternative to this approach has been advocated by Roberto

Aliboni, who wrote that Italy's foreign policy should not be defined according to the defense of national interests, but rather in terms of its ability 'to contribute to a more cooperative world in which Italian interests could normally be reconciled with those of others.'[4] Whatever one may think of their respective merits, the existence of competing theses is doubtlessly the sign of a renewed attention to the country's international relations.

The geopolitical approach, seems to have made some inroads beyond the level of intellectual speculation. One example comes from the experience of UNOSOM I and II. Right from the beginning, in December 1992, the Italian contingent has attempted to carve out a special role for itself. Quarrels with other contingents (and especially with the US) about the operation's command structure, about the wisdom of disarming one particular Somali faction, and about some of the tactics employed led the UN Secretary General, in July 1993, to ask Rome to recall the army general who headed the Italian troops—a diplomatic incident later patched up.

Though further developments vindicated the substance of the Italian approach, the fact remains that this search for a high national profile has to do with the idea that Italy has its own sphere of influence to defend and promote in the Horn of Africa. Curiously enough, what seems to have suggested the pursuit of a high profile (Rome's colonial past in Somalia and, more recently, its support for the dictatorship of Siad Barre) would once have inspired the opposite course of action, i.e. a cautious approach. The fact that the government was so concentrated on the domestic crisis as to let the military largely run the operation may also explain this new Italian assertiveness.[5]

This is not to say that the Italian military are the spokesmen of the country's new nationalism. On the contrary, more than four decades of multilateral experience in NATO have molded the majority of the Italian soldiers. Similar considerations may be made with regard to Italy's diplomatic corps. In both cases, though, and despite some differences in emphasis, one can detect an acute attention for the opportunities opened by the end of the Cold War to play a national role—within as well as outside a multilateral context. A rationale often heard among foreign policy bureaucrats runs more or less as follows: 'If others play nationally and cultivate their own spheres of influence, we should do the same.' But quite apart from the problem of whether Rome has the means to pursue a similar course, the inherent risk is that misperceptions may fuel other misperceptions, and that worst case assumptions may turn into self-fulfilling prophecies.

The Policy Issues

Official, post-1989 security perceptions depict Italy as more vulnerable than before, given the tensions coming from both the Balkans and the Mediterranean. On the other hand, concrete risks have yet to materialize: Serbian threats of missile strikes against the Italian territory were rightly shrugged off as duds; the flow of refugees from the former Yugoslavia has been contained through a restrictive immigration policy; in the Mediterranean NATO has never enjoyed a clearer superiority, the Israeli-Palestinian accord—even if fragile—should lower the general level of tensions, whereas Islamic fundamentalism, despite being on the rise on the North-African coast, is still perceived in Rome as a rather remote threat.

If this is true, then Italy's main security problems were associated with facilitating the democratic transition in Central and Eastern Europe, and curbing the spread of the Balkan conflict. The role of the international institutions to which Italy belongs is crucial on both counts. Hence Rome's interest in the institutional architecture—an interest shared by both former Foreign Ministers De Michelis and Andreatta. In this respect, a problem acutely felt in Italy is how to avoid being in the slower tier of a two-speed Europe. Marginalization from Economic and Monetary Union is feared not only for reasons of status: the fact is that the European dimension has always been the crucial vehicle of Italy's international integration. Rome's fears of being excluded from the EU informal directorate are also compounded by the northward and eastward shift in the Union's center of gravity which is likely to follow from the accession of several countries of the European Free Trade Association (EFTA).

Against this difficult background, former Foreign Minister Andreatta put forward his own variation on the theme of a two-speed Europe, calling it a 'wedding cake' concept. Accordingly, Italy would be a member of the EU hard core of founding countries which, together with Spain, should negotiate a federal treaty providing for, among other things, a European currency and a European army. Pushed out of the core group of EU countries for economic reasons, Rome would thus try to re-enter through political will, i.e. by floating the idea of a federal Europe that would be smaller than the current Union, excluding countries which, like Britain and Denmark, have no intention of integrating beyond the Maastricht treaty's first phase.

Rome's version of a 'variable geometry' Europe can also be read as an attempt to solve the old dilemma of Europe's 'deepening versus widening'. If the founders of the former Community committed themselves to a new federal treaty, the EU could open the door to North and Central Europe by establishing a confederal form of relationship with them. In the eyes of its proponents, this solution would serve the crucial security objective of fostering the democratic transition in the Visegrad countries.

But the main goal of Italian diplomacy is to balance Europe's next round of enlargement toward the North and the East with a stronger federalism of key EU countries. If the former, in fact, potentially goes to Italy's detriment by moving the EU center of gravity away, Rome is convinced that the answer lies in the collective management rather than in the renationalization of European foreign policies. According to this thesis, Italian security interests are better served in a multilateral framework of European security than through competition—a thesis criticized by the neo-nationalist intellectuals, who simply do not believe in the chances of the federalist approach. The solution also allows Rome to occupy a middle ground—if not to play a mediating role, which is the recurrent ambition of Italian foreign policy—between London's preference for a great free trade area in the European continent and Bonn's official penchant for balancing this with a further impulse toward a federal Europe.

Beyond the EU, the CSCE is seen as the larger framework of the European security architecture—a framework that, while having the clear virtue of keeping both the US and Russia linked to the old continent, needs to be strengthened to be able to represent the ultimate guarantee of a pan-European order. Italy is not the only country that often pays lip service to the security potentials of the CSCE. So far, though, ideas such as using NATO and Russian troops in peacekeeping operations in Europe under a CSCE mandate, have not been pursued in depth. In principle, Rome is also committed to making the CSCE a regional organization under the UN charter, as well as to trying to relaunch De Michelis' proposal of a Conference on Security and Cooperation in the Mediterranean (CSCM).

The Central European Initiative, a regional cooperation forum championed by De Michelis in 1989 with the aim of both avoiding the EC enlargement and balancing the German influence in the region, has seen its relevance decrease rapidly, due to the Yugoslav civil war on the one hand, and to Italy's inability to provide adequate financial incentives on the other.[6]

The government approach to the EU enlargement and, more generally, the main lines of its vision of Europe's institutional architecture have, on balance, a high degree of domestic consensus. On the former issue, however, the PDS supports a faster political integration of the Visegrad countries, while the League advocates a 'Europe of regions' that bears little resemblance to the institutions of the real world.

Italy continues to see NATO as the hallmark of international stability; though, it agrees that NATO should be adapted to the new international environment, its short-term enlargement toward the East is not considered favorably because of concerns about Russia, a reluctance to extend concrete defense commitments, and the Italian preference for the EU and the CSCE as vehicles for political and economic cooperation. Therefore, it should not come as a surprise that Italian diplomacy found the 'Partnership for Peace' agreed upon at the Brussels Summit of January 1994 a good compromise solution to the thorny problem of NATO's relations with its eastern neighbors.

Interestingly enough, Andreatta (a professor of economics when not involved in politics), has also proposed a new Atlantic Charter 'to spell out the rules of law for the resolution of economic conflicts.'[7] At 1993 round-table discussion, he said that 'Italy is interested in participating in the collective actions of the international community: since there is a lesser need for defense at national level, Italy has a great interest in NATO taking up out-of-area missions.'[8] But for NATO to be involved in crisis management, both inside and outside Europe, a clear UN endorsement is considered a necessary condition. The Yugoslav crisis highlighted the inherent difficulties of Andreatta's approach to pursuing a high national profile in the context of multilateral diplomacy. Being a country just across the border from the conflict, the UN has kept Italy from participating in the peacekeeping operations—though Rome has since proposed, unsuccessfully, to change these rules. At the same time, however, Italy has provided the main logistic base for NATO peace-enforcing.

After the Somali experience, Italy has also insisted on the necessity of giving the countries that contribute peacekeeping troops both a role in the field operations' command structure, and a voice in the UN Security Council decision-making. This concern is reflected in the more encompassing proposal for the reform of the Security Council, whereby 20 'semi-permanent' members (chosen according to economic, demographic, cultural, and peace-keeping contribution criteria) would rotate in 7-8 seats. The total number of seats in the body would thus reach 22-23. The scheme represents a departure from De Michelis' idea of creating a European permanent seat by merging the French and the British ones—an idea still supported by the PDS. More generally, the forces belonging to the new government coalition have all mentioned the need of a UN reform.

When it comes to the prospects of European defense integration, the Italian official attitude has always been characterized by considerable skepticism. The reason is relatively straightforward: from Rome's point of view, a European defense built around the Bonn-Paris axis would automatically mean a second rank status, whereas the trans-Atlantic link serves more as an equalizer of European ambitions. In other words, Italy has always feared that an integrated European defense, especially if coupled with a reduction of the US presence in the Mediterranean, would add a strategic dimension to a two-speed Europe.[9]

Consistent with this approach, for example, was the October 1991 joint British-Italian position paper on European security, whereby the development of a European defense identity through the WEU was presented as strengthening NATO. By the same token, the creation of a WEU rapid reaction force was presented as capable of providing NATO with more flexibility for out-of-area contingencies.[10] This Italian view was to have acted as Europe's (and NATO's) broker, by bringing Britain (and through Britain the US as well) to accept the prospect of a common European defense policy before the Maastricht summit. Once again, Italy's long-time ambition to play the role of an international mediator became evident.

But that ambition was rapidly frustrated by the Franco-German position paper on European defense.[11] Its main concrete result was the announced creation of the Eurocorps, as an alternative to the British-Italian initiative. Needless to say, neither Britain nor Italy has shown much short-term interest in the Eurocorps. The same aversion to a Euro-directorate probably contributes to explaining Rome's dislike for a European nuclear deterrent based on the British and French arsenals. Two years later, however, the clearest limit of the British-Italian document (and, incidentally, of the latest government blueprint on Italy's defense) lies in the emphasis attributed to a potential WEU role for operations in NATO out-of-area regions—a solution now overtaken by the *de facto* cancellation of NATO geographical boundaries implied by the June and December 1992 decisions to offer troops to, respectively, the CSCE and the UN for peace operations.

Within the WEU, Rome has recently shown a certain propensity to take the lead. For example, an Italian general is heading the WEU planning cell. The aeromaritime cooperation concept was promoted by Rome, Paris, and Madrid before being adopted by the Union in September 1992. Italy is currently advocating the creation of a pre-planned, on-call European Multinational Force—a proposal so far supported by France and Spain. On European defense, it seems rather likely that a more favorable stance will be taken, given the consensus uniting on this issue the government (including National Alliance) and the PDS.

At the level of the political debate, a division between the pro-German, who privilege continental Europe, and the pro-American, who favor the Mediterranean, is still possible. The latter attitude was typical of the military through the seventies and the eighties, but it has been somewhat damaged by quarrels in Somalia. Should the situation deteriorate further and extend to the next generation of political leadership, then the future of the American bases in Italy may become less bright than it would now appear.

Summing up, if Italy's central foreign and security policy goal is to remain in the club of Western nations that really count—and to raise the country's profile within it—then the question of whether Rome has adequate means to achieve this goal becomes crucial. In this regard, the first problem to be solved is the country's defense posture. The debate on it is so stale now as to make a mockery of the term used to indicate it: the *new defense model*. While the military struggle to keep the maximum level of forces allowed by a shrinking defense budget—an attitude which is understandable but not terribly effective—the few innovations have come from two parties, namely the League and the PDS, which have at least put forward their ideas on the resources and force levels they would assign to the country's defense. It is interesting to note a good degree of convergence in these two proposals, for example insofar as the recourse to professional soldiers is concerned.

Neo-nationalist intellectuals are persuaded that, since quasi-automatic US security guarantees are definitely over, Italy's foreign policy must count on a strong defense.[12] In the present phase they are thus on the side of the chiefs of staff, calling for a sharp increase of defense expenditures—an increase that evidently clashes with the overriding objective of reducing the public budget deficit. A similar stance is taken in Forza Italia's program, even though there is no explicit reference to raising military outlays.

The problem here is not lack of discussion; rather, it is too much of it. There is, however, a continued absence of decisions on missions, structure, and composition of the armed forces. Obviously, as long as this is the case, the military have reasons to lament a state of perennial uncertainty that cannot but damage the conduct of foreign affairs.

A second prominent foreign policy tool for a country with Italy's ambition is the availability of financial resources. Here the current budgetary austerity is more critical than in the case of defense. A law approved in 1992, for example, foresaw the allocation of 900 bn Lire over the first three years to support the transition in Central and Eastern Europe. For 1994-1996, the government proposed to allocate 344 bn Lire, including some funds appropriated in 1992 and 1993 but not yet spent. Italy's Official Development Aid planned at 1,200 bn Lire in 1994, will be able to count on 200 bn Lire and 2,500 bn Lire less than 1993 and 1992, respectively. Thus, a country that only a couple of years ago was the third development agency donor in the EU (after France and Germany) has now fallen well behind Britain, the Netherlands, Sweden, and, in absolute terms, to the level of countries, such Norway and Denmark, which have a far smaller economy.[13] There is little doubt that, from the point of view of the potential recipients in the East and South, the present cuts will entail a sharp reduction of Italy's influence and prestige—i.e. the very features so dear to those neo-nationalists who are advocating an increase in military spending.

Conclusions

If Italy is to play a more active role within the international institutions according to the last government's 'New Multilateralism'; or to try to combine national interests and European integration—according to Forza Italia—at least two preconditions have to be met. First, the domestic political crisis has to be overcome, so as to restore the internal component of the international credibility enjoyed, at least partially, in the eighties. Second, the debt crisis has to be overcome, both to strengthen the image and prestige of the country, and to make available the economic resources needed to support the key foreign policy choices. Within a framework of more financial certitude, the question of finding the most appropriate defense posture can also be solved.

The competition between multilateralists and nationalists will be more acute than ever before, but more at the intellectual than at the political level. Not since 1948 has it been as difficult to make meaningful predictions on how foreign policy will be managed, as the new government coalition has no tradition, and sharp internal divisions.

Forza Italia will attempt to mediate between the national Alliance and the Northern League. It is likely that the openings to the neo-nationalists will not go beyond the rhetorical policy of better defending the Italian minorities in Slovenia and Croatia. The economic performance of the new government will nevertheless be crucial, even for foreign policy. If it is successful in this area, Italy will try to re-enter the first tier of the EU, the rest of the country's international relations being subordinated to this strategic option, in line with the diplomatic tradition. At least during the initial phase, however, the government will concentrate on domestic priorities, i.e. the creation of the institutional basis of the Second Republic. It is thus most likely that foreign policy will be based on a businesslike approach. Chances are that multilateralism will continue to prevail over nationalism, in part because of the continuity embodied by the foreign ministry staff.

Less likely in the immediate term, but not impossible over the longer term, is a more negative scenario in which the government's mismanagement of the economy would end up increasing Italy's divergence vis-à-vis the fiscal and monetary targets set forth in the Maastricht Treaty. Rome's marginalization could thus fuel a revanchist approach based on the renationalization of its foreign policy. Such an approach, being able to count neither on a sufficient level of domestic consensus, nor on adequate foreign policy tools, would certainly be highly detrimental to Italy's long term interests.

Notes

1. Andreatta, Beniamino: 'Una politica estera per l'Italia' (A Foreign Policy for Italy), *Il Mulino*, November-December, 1993.

2. A comparison of major parties' programs, by the daily *Il Sole-24 Ore* (15 March 1994) confirms a strong consensus on foreign policy and the relatively little attention devoted to this issue. PDS and the National Alliance are partial exceptions to this rule.

3. For a few examples of this school of thought, see various chapters in Santoro, Carlo M. (Ed.): *L'elmo di Scipio* (Bologna: Il Mulino, 1993).

4. Istituto Affari Internazionali, L'Italia nella politica internazionale, edizione 1993 (Roma: Editore SIPI, 1993).

5. As the Italian contingent returned home, not much remained of Italy's special role. The same could be said of the long-term results of the much vaunted *Operazione Pellicano* in Albania.

6. The forum was set up in 1989 by Austria, Hungary, Italy, and Yugoslavia. It later became known as the *Pentagonale* and *Esagonale*. After the disintegration of Yugoslavia and the break-up of Czechoslovakia, it now comprises ten countries.

7. 'Una politica estera per l'Italia,' *op.cit.*

8. See the round table on 'Progetti per un continente' (Projects for a Continent) in *Limes*, No. 4, 1993.

9. Jean, Carlo: 'Difesa Comune? Teniamoci la NATO,' ([European] Common Defense? Let's Stick to NATO), in *Limes*, No. 4, 1993.

10. For the text of the joint paper see British Embassy in Rome, 'Note di Documentazione,' No. 17, October 10, 1991.

11. The text is in *Nouvelles Atlantiques*, October 18, 1991.

12. See Panebianco, Angelo: 'Il paese disarmato' (The Unarmed Country), *Il Mulino*, No. 5, 1993.

13. See Rhi-Sausi, José Luis (Ed.): *Rapporto CeSPI sulla Cooperazione allo Sviluppo dell'Italia 1992-1993* (Report on Italy's Development Cooperation Programs), (Roma: Edizioni Associate, forthcoming).

Index